A Gestalt Institute
of Cleveland Publication

Healing Tasks

James I. Kepner

Healing Tasks

Psychotherapy
with Adult Survivors
of Childhood Abuse

Jossey-Bass Publishers • San Francisco

A Gestalt Institute of Cleveland publication.

Substantial discounts on bulk quantities of Jossey-Bass books are available to corporations, professional associations, and other organizations. For details and discount information, contact the special sales department at Jossey-Bass Inc., Publishers. (415) 433-1740; Fax (415) 433-0499.

 Manufactured in the United States of America on Lyons Falls Pathfinder Tradebook. This paper is acid-free and 100 percent totally chlorine-free.

Figures 9.2 through 9.9 by Judy Marz.

Produced by *Publishing Professionals*, Eugene, Oregon

Library of Congress Cataloging-in-Publication Data

Kepner, James I.
    Healing tasks : psychotherapy with adult survivors of child abuse / James I. Kepner. — 1st ed.
       p. cm. — (The Jossey-Bass social and behavioral science series)
    Includes bibliographical references and index.
    ISBN 0-7879-0155-5 (alk. paper)
    1. Adult child abuse victims. 2. Gestalt therapy. I. Title II. Series
RC569.5.C55K47 1995
616. 85' 83690651—dc20
                                   95-22349
                                     CIP

HB Printing   10 9 8 7 6 5 4 3 2 1   FIRST EDITION

The Jossey-Bass

Social and Behavioral Science Series

I gratefully dedicate this book to my family.

Contents

"Comes a time, often at forty or so, that something within releases the lock on memory. But the memory doesn't say 'abuse,' certainly not at first, not until you label it. The memory is just itself; it stuns in a way nothing ever has. When it hits it's like putting an ax through a beehive in your mind: You're filled with a maddened buzzing, the beating of so many tiny wings, the pain of so many stingers, the smell of fresh honey. Things shatter—marriages, friendships, jobs, ideas, or whatever happens to be around. Or, rather, the falseness in things shatters, and anything made of too much falseness shatters for keeps. Still, even falseness is a hard thing to lose, it gives protection. And it's such a shock to find that all this time your mother, uncle, or whoever it was lives inside you in the form of a sticky, stinging, too-sweet, terribly purposeful thing buzzing at the quick of your sexuality."
—Michael Ventura
New Age Journal (March/April 1995, p. 56)

From the book *Letters at 3* A.M.: *Reports on Endarkenment* (Spring Publications), as seen in *New Age Journal*.

Preface

The work of recovery from the impact of childhood trauma, from emotional, sexual, and physical abuse, and from severely dysfunctional families of origin has finally taken focus in psychotherapy. We have shed the classical psychoanalytic denial of the reality of such trauma in shaping adult experience; now we are free to create new models for understanding human process, and these can help us direct our efforts to heal.

I began working with the emerging stories of abuse that clients were discovering in the early 1980s and was then faced with uncovering my own memories of sexual assault as a child. There were no significant models to guide treatment and recovery. The existing literature consisted of some of the early works of Miller (1983a, 1983b, 1984), Rush (1980), and Forward and Buck (1978), which described the problem but not its resolution, as well as a few discussions of treatment often focused in then obscure areas, such as Multiple Personality Disorder (Braun, 1986). There was also a developing literature on Posttraumatic Stress Disorder, which was starting to apply the lessons learned from treating Vietnam-era veterans and survivors of other traumas. Nevertheless, the few models that these works presented often seemed rooted in psychoanalytic understanding. To my mind, they continued to pathologize the client, misunderstanding and labeling much creatively adaptive behavior as resistance or defenses. Other models, with an emphasis on abreaction as the main treatment technique, seemed to produce as many symptoms and as much distress as they intended to alleviate. I repeatedly saw clients who were being treated within abreactive models deteriorate over the course of therapy, becoming more overwhelmed, anxious, and even suicidal, despite the therapist's healing intent.

By contrast, my own training as a therapist, as well as what I had learned to assume about healing, seemed to modulate the therapy process in a way that minimized some of these iatrogenic difficulties. This impression was borne out both in my own practice as a therapist and in my own personal work in therapy. The road of healing was certainly not easy or pleasant, but neither was there the kind of unnecessary, exaggerated distress, produced by the treatment itself, which I had witnessed in other forms of therapy for abuse.

For me, there was a link to Gestalt therapy training that informed my practice through its principles and theory. As I began to try to articulate the principles from which I was intuitively working, a model began to emerge. It was rooted in good Gestalt therapy practice, as I had experienced it in my own therapy and in my training at the Gestalt Institute of Cleveland. It included an understanding of behavior as creative adjustment, a nonpejorative appreciation of "resistance," careful work with the contacting process in the here-and-now, help with developing skills and support for contacting, and especially the willingness to accept the validity and truth of another person's experience.

For readers unfamiliar with Gestalt therapy, or who have seen only the 1960s stereotypes of Gestalt work in confrontation and the empty-chair "hot seat" technique, this statement may be surprising. But Gestalt therapy has a rich base of theory rooted in existentialism, holism, and phenomenology, as well as in psychoanalysis. The synthesis of the Cleveland school, where I received most of my training, was richly influenced by Laura Perls, with her emphasis on support for contacting, by Isadore From, with his theoretical rigor and interest in the inherent creativity of the contacting process, and by systems and field theory, with their emphasis on the contextual basis of behavior. The Gestalt model of health is not focused on adjusting the client to society. Based on the existential and phenomenological method, it emphasizes the discovery of one's subjective truth. This emphasis has allowed many of us to support our clients' initial reports of abuse, even against our own culture-laden tendency to deny or minimize them. This philosophy has also allowed us to respect and nurture our clients' particular journeys and choices in healing directions, since we value the self-regulatory capacity of people when they are in good contact with themselves and with their environments.

I also sensed intuitively that there was some kind of order inherent in the healing process. What would help me understand when it was time to do one kind of work with a survivor, and when another? What would help us understand why abreaction seemed so damaging in one phase of the work and so helpful in another? The answer was that childhood abuse, and its context, are a *developmental* problem for the child. Therefore, the healing would be guided if we could reestablish the sequence of the developmental process that had been disrupted by the abuse.

The model presented here has evolved gradually since I first developed its basic framework, in 1987. Since that time, I have taught the Healing Tasks Model in numerous workshops and used it to inform my own work with clients in private practice and groups. I have also received feedback on it from professionals and teachers working in the field of abuse and in Gestalt therapy. The present volume began as an outline for a workshop and was then developed over the years, so that workshop participants would have a guide to take with them as they went back to their practices and tried out what had been taught. It was then expanded into a paper published by the Gestalt Institute of Cleveland Press. The Healing Tasks Model has been refined and changed over the years, to incorporate the feedback I have received and embody a more useful and understandable outline of the healing process.

Since then, other treatment guides have appeared: Curtois's essential book on the treatment of incest (1988), Lew's guide to working with male survivors of sexual abuse (1988), and the popular guide by Bass and Davis (1988), as well as books by Briere (1989, 1992), Gil (1988), and others. All of these, and the others that are still emerging, offer us great assistance in this difficult and essential healing process. I do not see the present volume as containing a stand-alone model of treatment; rather, it provides an organizing framework for applying the many techniques and understandings that have evolved in this field. I hope that the Healing Tasks Model will be a useful addition to the literature on the process of healing from childhood abuse.

Overview of the Contents

Chapter One introduces the developmental and growth orientation to healing, which underlies the whole Healing Tasks approach. The essential idea presented in Chapter One is that the problems of adults who have suffered childhood abuse result not so much from illness or wounds, as a medical model might have it, as from compromises of the normal pathway of growth and development. These compromises are understood here as *creative adjustments* by the child to the realities of the context and are seen as products of the fundamentally adaptive and interactive nature of human functioning. Healing, then, is described as fundamentally a process of *growth*. These creative adjustments to the abusive context of childhood can be discovered, explored, and experimented with in the safe environment of the therapeutic relationship. In this way, new creative adjustments can be formulated, leaving the person more flexible, more capable, and more whole than the adjustments keyed to abuse had allowed. This developmental process is one of working through the healing tasks. The interactive and holographic nature of these tasks is discussed and charted in Chapter One. One task may define a particular phase of healing, since that task is the predominant concern at that point, but each task is involved in every phase of healing and is revisited as healing progresses. Understanding the healing *tasks* being accomplished and the *phase* of healing that the client is in allows the clinician to determine the appropriate level of developmental work, minimizing retraumatization and iatrogenesis.

Chapter Two details the healing task of *developing support*. The adult survivor frequently lacks what is needed to face life's difficulties, let alone the challenge of healing from the hurts of childhood. One of the missing elements is the personal, interpersonal, and systemic support that backs us up in the face of stresses and challenges. Survivors, often isolated and alone, may find it difficult to reach out and trust others, which means that they have more to do than an individual can do alone. This situation reflects the realities of the abusive context, rather than the innate character of the survivor. Survivors have shaped themselves to survive with the minimal support that matches the limits of what was safely available in the childhood environment, but this adaptation is insufficient for the task of healing. Chapter Two describes the basic therapeutic work of developing support and discusses the theme of shame for survivors.

Chapter Three describes the healing task of *developing the self-functions* and the self-functions phase of healing. Self functions are the means by which we manage our moment-to-moment experience and our interactions in the world. Survivors have notable difficulty managing feelings, personal and interpersonal boundaries, and the intensity and pace of experience. The abusive context frequently militates against the development of the self. Dissociation, numbing, and emotional extremes, while appropriate to the abusive context, are too limited and narrow for fuller functioning in life—the goal of healing. Healing requires the survivor to acquire these capacities. Without them, the challenges of daily living and dealing with traumatic memories are excessively chaotic and difficult.

Chapter Four describes the task of *undoing, redoing,* and *mourning*, as well as the phase of healing where this task is foreground. Here we see how the survivor, having developed adequate support and the necessary self functions, now has the capacity to face undoing the deeper effects of the traumatic past, manifested in horrific memories, somatic symptoms, interpersonal problems, and the deeply held core of shame and self-doubt. Healing requires the therapeutic "return to the environment" of whatever the survivor had to contain as a child. The deep reality of loss can then be fully mourned, and some peace can be made with the effects of childhood abuse.

Chapter Five gives a view of the *reconsolidation* task, which embodies the final phase of the healing process. It consists of assimilating and integrating the reality of the abuse into the larger context of oneself and one's life. Like the other tasks, the reconsolidation task has been going on throughout the healing process, although it becomes more marked toward the latter part of healing. Intrinsic to this process is the formulation of some kind of transcendent context, often a spiritual one, within which the experience of being abused and surviving acquires a meaning that goes beyond the individual self. Only by placing the horrible events into a transcendent context of meaning does the survivor have something large enough to hold the reality of what has happened to him or her, and to others in the world as well; the self alone is not large enough.

Chapter Six completes the presentation of the healing tasks proper. It condenses the principles and indicators given in the first five chapters into a form that can be used to estimate and appraise the client's phase of healing and the healing tasks and resources available to the client.

In Chapter Seven, the question of traumatic memories is discussed from the perspective of the healing tasks. This is a complex issue, and clinicians need guidelines for dealing reasonably with it. The Healing Tasks approach has its own contribution to guiding the therapist in negotiating this issue.

Chapter Eight presents one approach to formulating present experience and symptoms in ways that allow the client to experiment with their meaning against a different context. This process, which I call *recontextualization*, is presented in Chapter Eight to show how the reorganization of figure and ground (in Gestalt terms) is essential to the healing process for survivors. Otherwise confusing current experience can be explored and compared to a different context by means of a *phenomenological* method, rather than an interpretive one (which could risk greater contamination and influence from the therapist).

Chapter Nine, on *body process* in healing, enlarges the understanding of the healing process in the direction of the bodily nature of trauma. Chapter Nine explains the holistic viewpoint, which sees bodily experience as intrinsic to the self. Trauma is fundamentally the abuse of the bodily self, and survivors often have had to sever themselves from their bodily nature and experience. The delicate process of healing the breach between the body (where the trauma was experienced and encapsulated) and the rest of the self is described, and a detailed case example of body-oriented psychotherapy with a survivor is given.

July 1995   James I. Kepner
                                                  Shaker Heights, Ohio

Acknowledgments

This book would not have been possible without the encouragement, support, help, and love that many people have graced me with through the years of its development. I am deeply thankful to them all.

Over the years, as I refined versions of the model between rising to the demands of a young family and immersing myself in brief periods of writing, my friends and colleagues kept telling me about the value of my early ideas and encouraging me to continue developing them. Katherine Styles, Mark McConville, Mitchel Wax, Lynne Jacobs, Elaine Kepner, Alan Kepner, Rene Fantz, Marrie Creelman, Sonia Nevis, Ed Nevis, Joe Melnick, Jean Marie Robine, Jean Berrgren, Tom Cutolo, Frances Baker, and Michael Clemmens are among those I wish especially to thank. I also wish to thank the many students in my Healing Tasks workshops, who gave the model the test of fire in a wide variety of clinical settings and allowed me to experiment with new ideas along the way. My appreciation goes also to Joyce Levine-MacCombie, who graciously offered to edit the assessment questionnaire discussed in Chapter Six, and whose comments and suggestions were a major contribution. The Gestalt Writers' Conference group has also had a significant part in keeping me going through years when I thought I might never finish this work, by offering suggestions, comments, and a forum within which to express my ideas.

My special thanks go to Gordon Wheeler for his cogent editing, his abiding friendship and love, and his help in getting me through the dumps and slumps of the final push to produce a manuscript.

My friend Carol DeSanto has been instrumental in my growth and development over these many years. Along with my dear teacher Rosalyn Bruyere, Carol has supported and encouraged me in developing such inklings of spiritual wisdom as I possess. I thank them both for their perseverance.

I also wish to extend my deep appreciation to Joseph Zinker, who mentored me for many years, and whose deep commitment to phenomenology and the wisdom of inner experience has formed the core of much of this work. Without him, I would not have known that healing was possible. Another mentor to whom I owe a debt of gratitude is James Schuerger, who welcomed me into the world of psychology, supervised me with respect and encouragement in my first field placement, and stood by me during my doctoral research. Until now, I have never properly thanked him or acknowledged his great help.

Finally, and most especially, I thank my wife, Mary Ann Kraus, who supported and encouraged me in my writing and tested the model in her work, and my children, who had to tolerate a father who was often preoccupied. My life with them all continues to heal me. They ground me in what is most real and most human—my connection with those I love.

J.I.K.

The Author

James I. Kepner is a psychologist in private practice in Cleveland, Ohio, where he is also on the professional staff of the Gestalt Institute of Cleveland (GIC). He is the chairperson of the GIC training program, *Working with Physical Process*, and he is an associate editor of the Gestalt Institute of Cleveland Press. He received his B.A. degree (1976) magna cum laude in psychology from Cleveland State University, where he also received his M.A. degree (1978) in clinical community psychology. He received his Ph.D. degree (1982) in counseling psychology from Kent State University.

Kepner's professional interests include teaching Gestalt therapy, training psychotherapists in body-oriented methods, and treating abuse survivors with the Healing Tasks approach. His special interests are the treatment of adult survivors of childhood abuse, body-oriented psychotherapy, and the integration of healing methods and psychotherapy in the treatment of chronic disease states. He conducts training workshops internationally in these areas.

Kepner is the father of two children.

Chapter One

Healing Tasks
for Survivors of Abuse

The Healing Tasks Model for survivors of abusive trauma is based on principles and concepts derived from Gestalt therapy. The model is oriented to the framing of the tasks for client and therapist. In the journey of healing from difficult life experiences, these tasks influence the choices made about the timing and the nature of therapeutic work. There are no easy answers and, in my experience, there is no magic that can make the healing process quicker or simpler. Even those who do "brief therapy" acknowledge that these issues are not amenable to quick solutions, that survivors often need an ongoing relational context for healing, and that treatment can be only "as brief as possible" (Dolan, 1991).

But there is some sense to the process of healing, and there are understandings that can help to prevent it from being more difficult and painful than it needs to be. The Healing Tasks Model is a guide to making sense of this process. Healing cannot be pain-free, but we certainly should aim to minimize, as much as possible, the traumatizing effects of the treatment itself.

Healing as Cure Versus Healing as Growth

I have focused on the tasks involved in the healing process because I believe that healing is fundamentally about growth. In our culture, we are biased in our understanding of what healing means because of the pervasive metaphor of scientific medicine: one goes through specific stages of healing from a "disease" toward an eventual

static state, from wound to sepsis to control of infection to scar-
ring; or from infection to mobilization of the immune system to
control of infection to recovery. The medical model sees disease
as a foreign condition against which one's body mobilizes to cope;
with proper aid, the body will fight disease off in stepwise fashion,
with a resulting end state of health if treatment is successful. This
metaphor of healing has had great utility in the mastering of
certain conditions. But with the advent of psychoneuroimmu-
nology, even modern medicine is finding it to be limited in
significant ways.

The model presented here looks at healing somewhat differently. Broadly speaking, the survivor of traumatic situations is not
dealing so much with a "disease" as with compromises of the natural course of growth that were made in the service of survival and
self-integrity. As a result of the abusive trauma and the coexisting
problematic environment, the natural processes of attachment
(Bowlby, 1969; Winnicott, 1960, 1988), learning, accomplishment, assimilation, and differentiation (Piaget, 1962) have been
reshaped in relation to many critical developmental functions.
Healing, then, is really the process of reestablishing the natural
cycle of growth and development in relation to those developmental issues that have been most affected (distorted, truncated,
redirected, rigidified, or fixated) by the abusive situation. *Healing
from the impact of childhood abuse and trauma is fundamentally a process of growth.*

In healing as *growth*, as opposed to a linear progression toward
cure, we address and readdress certain issues in ever more accomplished and more differentiated ways, in much the same way as we
learn any complex task—speaking, reading, or writing, for example. We do not achieve one stage and move on to the next, leaving
the previous stage behind. Rather, the healing process is more like
the creation of an oil painting: the background is painted in, and
then details are added, and then washes and tone are overlaid on
the whole. But the painting is not yet done, for the background
still has to be refined in light of the emerging details, and then

more details will be added and shifted, and as these elements take on new weight and interactions, the tone and the cast of the canvas will be shifted and refined by the artist. Each part of the painting supports and refines the previous part and is supported and refined in turn.

To put this idea another way, growth proceeds in a spiral fashion. We visit and revisit complex issues and tasks with increasing mastery, breadth, and capacity. We approach previously intolerable risks at each new level of the spiral. At each round, at each pass, a new reorganization of the whole field, the whole *gestalt*, occurs as new capacities are integrated and assimilated, old traumas are undone, and a new self emerges in engagement with the world. The growth tasks that I see as most central to healing from such childhood trauma are described in the section that follows.

Developing Support

Support is the relational ground of the environment that provides the context for all growth and development. It is the essential framework of attachment and relationship to caring and responsive others, by whose actions we learn to affirm our own existence, basic trust, and to care for ourselves. Most survivors, by virtue of the distinct lack of support they received developmentally, and of their current need for support, given the overwhelming quality of their symptoms and their life experience, find this task crucial to the creation of an adequate systemic frame for life and growth.

In human development, support is the fundamental interpersonal base on which all other developments must rest. The infant or child is embedded in an interpersonal field of caretakers, family, and community (Stern, 1985; Winnicott, 1960, 1988; Bowlby, 1969). The disturbance of support that is so common—indeed, virtually definitional—in the abusive context means that survivors often remember abuse without useful or adequate support in the present because they adapted themselves to living without it in the past. And without support, little else can be usefully addressed.

Development of the Self Functions

Self functions embody the capacity to manage and integrate experience, interactions with the environment, and interactions with oneself. Self functions, the means by which we manage our experience and interactions, are learned in relation to the developmental context in which we are growing. If our developmental context provides a place where we can experiment, then our self functions will be flexible. If our developmental context responds to our feelings, then we will learn to have a differentiated variety of modulated feelings. If we can engage with the environment in a way that allows us to experience and test our interpersonal boundaries, and if the environment both supports our differentiation and places appropriate limits on our use of aggression toward others, then we will develop a clear sense of both self and other, of how to connect as well as separate.

Survivors typically have had only a few choices and have only a narrow range of skills for managing their experience. The abusive context skewed the development of self functions either in the direction of dealing with the overwhelming, the violating, and the uncaring or in the direction of compliance, withdrawal, and disconnection from bodily boundaries. A context that recognizes no ownership of personal boundaries skews the development of boundary functions. A context that floods a child with overwhelming feelings and sensations skews the development of feeling functions toward numbing, dissociation, lack of differentiation, or explosive expression. An environment that does not respond to or help modulate the intensity of stimulation does not support the development of the self functions by which the child could regulate and pace his or her own experience of stimulation.

Without adequate self functions, the abreaction of traumatic memories is itself often experienced as traumatic because nothing *new* is brought into the survivor's relationship to the archaic situation so as to make contact with it in the present experientially *different* from contact in the past. Here is the greatest flaw in the abreactive method of dealing with trauma.

Undoing, Redoing, and Mourning

Because the survivor was a child when the abuse occurred and had little power or capacity to maintain his or her boundaries with integrity, much of the abusive context has become internalized and is experienced as information about himself or herself, rather than about experience in relation to another. If we are not allowed or able to act on our own behalf—to run away, to push away, and to stop what is occurring—then we must turn such impulses, which are directed at the environment, in some other direction. Usually they are turned back on the self (*retroflected*), so that we become frozen, self-punishing, full of self-restraint and caution, and they are internalized (*introjected*, or swallowed whole), so that we become full of beliefs, statements about ourselves, and so on, which are actually foreign material and inappropriate to our needs. If the environment shames and humiliates us, then we may come to feel that we are shameful or worthless. If secrecy is demanded of us, then we may become self-contained, silent, and full of secrets that even we do not know.

What is essentially contextual—an engagement between the child and a particular environment—will be perceived as personal *when it is removed from its context.* By virtue of the limits placed on the child's ability to engage fruitfully with the environment, and because the child has to act on himself or herself in order to manage and adapt, the adaptations come to be experienced as if they had to do only with the child's side of the engagement. Instead of being able to respond to shaming by saying, "Stop making me feel bad," the child comes to feel that he or she *is* bad. If to avoid unpredictable punishment the child has to constrain his or her behavior so as not to be noticed, he or she develops tense muscles and a withdrawn posture.

Thus, in current behavior, "personality style," interpersonal relations, and current symptoms, we see much that is actually reenactment of the abusive context, much that is actually internalization of or adaptation to the traumatic context, much that is actually derived from the environment or learned in relation to it. Undoing involves restoring the proper relationship of organism to environment through expressive work, therapeutic reenactment, and dialogue, as well as through real-life actions. Such intense work is appropriately done only when adequate support and self functions exist for the survivor, to allow dealing with this task in a way that is not itself traumatic. And, as the realities of the survivor's history are fully confronted, the survivor must also mourn and come to terms with the losses suffered through abuse: the loss of childhood, the struggle just to live, the loss of an idealized image of the parent, and so on.

Reconsolidation

Learning comes in many forms, and all learning results in growth of some kind. A lot of learning appears to be incremental; we steadily build our pool of understanding, knowledge, skills, and capacities. Other learning requires more than adding a new layer of bricks to an existing structure. This learning restructures the existing edifice and completely reorganizes it—broadening, encompassing, and integrating all its parts into a new whole, a new *gestalt*. This process is akin to the paradigm shift described by Kuhn (1970) and to the process of accommodation described by Piaget (1962). The reorganization is not just of one's "internal" process; it is a reorganization of one's perceptions, one's behavior toward others and the way one makes meaning of oneself and the world. Thus, it is a reorganization of the whole *field*, by which we mean the person or organism *and* the environment.[1] Our sense of self is not formed in isolation; it includes our whole environment, our whole being (known and unknown), and our life context—past, present, and future.

I use the term *reconsolidation* to refer to this reorganization of the field because it is a repetitive process by which we solidify and reorganize our experience. It results in growth. Reconsolidation is the perceptual and experiential reorganization of the current field so that it can become larger, more complex in its organization, and more differentiated as a whole. It then allows for richer and more satisfying meaning and living.

For the survivor, reconsolidation initially may involve a reconstituting of his definition of life and of his person to include previously unremembered abuse as part of the past and as part of the definition of himself (his "I"). Continuing in the course of growth and development, he must find an increasingly inclusive, more differentiated and complex context of meaning in place of the traumatic experiences in his life. The survivor does not simply add new memories; the new memories often force him to redefine who he knows himself to be. The survivor does not merely learn new skills and capacities; he becomes a *different person*. The survivor does not simply change himself; his relationships, family life, and interactions with others are also changed.

Healing Tasks and the Phases of Healing

Healing from abuse—or healing in general, for that matter—seems not to be a linear process. We can stretch ourselves only so far in one direction before we discover that we must attend to our support. We find ourselves having to go back over what seems to be old ground, reworking and redoing at a more integral and refined level, before we can move ahead into uncharted territory. Our cultural belief in the linearity of progress blinds us to the recursive nature of most human growth and learning. But growth is not circular. With each pass, we are different beings, and the task we revisit contains a deeper complexity and challenge.

But there does seem to be some kind of coherence in the process of healing and growth. It has a kind of order, which helps us assess where we are in the process and helps us understand what we need in order to move forward. To recognize these two perspectives—the spiral shape of healing, on the one hand, and the reality of sequencing, on the other—I have utilized a holographic model.[2] Its components are the *healing tasks*, which define the healing process regardless of where we are in it, and the *phases of the healing process*, which have to do with the particular tasks that are most important and most vividly in our awareness at different times. In Figure 1.1, the four *phases of healing* are arrayed across the top of the diagram, and the four *healing tasks* are arrayed in the columns. Shaded boxes represent tasks that are more in the background during a particular phase. Clear boxes represent tasks that are more in the foreground and thus tend to organize and define the field of therapy at a particular time. (Of course, *all* the tasks are *always* present and being worked with in some fashion.)

When we begin to define the phases of healing, we must be careful not to become so obsessed with the model that we miss an obvious fact: no two people follow the same course of healing.

Figure 1.1. Healing Tasks Hologram.

Support Phase	Self-Functions Phase	Undoing, Redoing, and Mourning Phase	Reconsolidation Phase
Developing support	Developing support	Developing support	Developing support
Developing self functions	Developing self functions	Developing self functions	Developing self functions
Undoing, redoing, and mourning	Undoing, redoing, and mourning	Undoing, redoing, and mourning	Undoing, redoing, and mourning
Reconsolidation	Reconsolidation	Reconsolidation	Reconsolidation

Early	Middle	Late

Course of Therapy

Nevertheless, there is some consistency and commonality in the process of healing, which allows us to make certain generalizations.

Some tasks are more *figural*—more the *focus* of therapy—at different times during the healing process. In the early part of therapy for effects of childhood abuse, the task of developing support is most central. Development of self functions becomes more figural toward the middle of therapy. The task of *undoing, redoing, and mourning* moves into prominence toward the later part of therapy, and *reconsolidation* is more predominant toward the end of the therapy process. Thus, considering the predominant or figural task at each point along the healing process, I will be referring to the *support phase*, the *self-functions phase*, the *undoing, redoing, and mourning phase*, and the *reconsolidation phase*.

Again, even when one task is more figural, work on aspects of other tasks is always going on. For example, the essential task of developing self functions (learning to manage boundaries with the therapist, or learning how to manage stimulation and be grounded in the present) is also going on during the support phase. As therapists, we do not ignore unexplained sadness and mourning in the early part of therapy just because it is supposed to wait for the third phase. Rather, we ask ourselves and our client how much support and what degree of self functions exist at *this* time that would allow us to take on a *portion* of the emerging mourning. We also can see that in the support phase our focus will be on validating the mourning, even if the client does not know why she is mourning, while in the self-functions phase our focus will be on working with the same client to tolerate and manage a fuller and deeper sadness, without dissociating. Then, in the third phase, we will be more concerned with having the survivor, using the support and self functions developed in the two earlier phases, confront the abuse and the specific losses that have resulted from it, claim from the past what she needs to claim for her wholeness, and more fully mourn her losses.

Each phase also contains its own particular elements of the

four healing tasks. The complexity of therapeutic process derives in part from its holographic nature. When we get stuck in diagnosis or intervention, we can always look to some other part of the hologram to understand what elements might be missing or inadequately addressed. For example, when a client seems to be "resistant" to facing a difficult memory, we can ask ourselves what support or self functions might allow her to face this challenge reasonably. When a supervisee reports that his client "can't remember," we can ask what support might be required so that the client could *afford* to remember.

Issues that, superficially, seem the same across tasks may actually be engaged differently at different phases of the healing process. For example, work on the emotion of anger may have entirely different qualities at different points. In the support phase, such work is likely to be focused more on issues of support than on the expression of anger itself. The focus might be on having the therapist validate that anger is permissible and legitimate, or on the client learning to use breathing and grounding methods to ride out the wave of anger without panicking or becoming overwhelmed. In the self-functions phase, the work on anger becomes more direct. The client now has a context and support for feeling anger. Here, the focus might be on tolerating the experience of anger, or on learning to modulate it within reasonable limits, or on learning when anger is appropriate to the present and when it is an overdetermined reaction to the past, or on experiencing the therapist's getting angry with the abuser in a way the client could not or the parents did not. As we move toward the later part of the healing process, the work on anger may focus on direct expression in connection with abusive incidents, or on experiencing the sense of power that anger with the abuser affords, or on raging at the abuser in therapeutic reenactments or empty-chair work.

Understanding the figural phase where the client is working helps guide the therapist's efforts. It allows therapist and client to pace and grade experiments, and to understand the requisite skills and capacities that must be developed to support one's increasing wholeness. What heals at one phase may be off the point or actively harmful at another. Much misdirected, unsuccessful, or damaging treatment results from the failure to appreciate this crucial point. Table 1.1 shows four typical issues that often concern us in working with survivors of abuse. The table illustrates how they would be seen in different phases of the healing process.

Table 1.1. Therapeutic Issues Across Phases.

Focus with Feelings	
Support Phase	• Managing their intensity through support and grounding • Validating and legitimizing them in relation to the seriousness of the abuse • Validating that it's okay to have feelings without knowing why
Self-Functions Phase	• Tolerating increased intensity and variety of feelings • Sorting feelings about the past from those about the present • Finding appropriate levels of feelings for current situations
Undoing, Redoing, and Mourning Phase	• Expression of feelings • Directing them toward appropriate persons in the past • Allowing feelings their full cycle
Reconsolidation Phase	• Broad range of feelings now available for experience and assimilation • Sorting what is left that is due to factors other than abuse

Focus with Memories	
Support Phase	• Tolerating them • Validating that something might have happened • "Just experiencing" them, rather than going for full abreaction • Using present contact with the therapist as support for experiencing memories

	Focus with Memories (cont'd.)
Self-Functions Phase	• Recovering the self functions truncated or left behind • Identifying self functions to be worked on and developed in the present context
Undoing, Redoing, and Mourning Phase	• Working through unfinished mourning • Bringing new self functions to bear on facing trauma memories • Confronting the abuser (symbolically or actually) from an adult standpoint • Claiming for the present what one needs from the past • Mourning losses as they are now remembered
Reconsolidation Phase	• Trauma memories now experienced as in the past • Remembering less disturbing memories; sense of absorbing them into a larger, more cohesive self • "Lived life" as the context for memories to be assimilated • Present and future as the context for living and remembering
	Focus with the Therapist's Use of Self
Support Phase	• Active holding environment • Validation of emerging reality • Setting safe boundaries • Helping client actively check out issues of trust
Self-Functions Phase	• Active teaching of skills • Creation of experiments and exercises to develop skills • Modeling of healthy boundaries • Use of self as a contact object for practice • Modeling of grading and pacing
Undoing, Redoing, and Mourning Phase	• Active support for remembering • Avoidance of contact with memories and fostering of choice • Coaching of higher-intensity expression and working through • More active confronting of distortions and projections

	Focus with the Therapist's Use of Self (cont'd.)
Reconsolidation Phase	• Fostering independence • Bringing perspective • Recognize and affirm development of transcendent wisdom in client

	Focus with Psychotropic Medications
Support Phase	• Reducing flooding and intensity affect • Control of flashbacks • Part of holding the environment
Self-Functions Phase	• Modulation of intensity of affect • Mood elevation • Aid to grounding
Undoing, Redoing, and Mourning Phase	• Backdrop that allows higher-intensity undoing and working through
Reconsolidation Phase	• Tapering off as appropriate

Chapter Two

Developing Support

The task of developing support[3] is most figural in the first part of therapy, although it will continue to emerge as an issue as new phases of healing are approached. Developing support has to do with creating the interpersonal and systemic field that supplies the necessary conditions for other tasks of healing to take place, as it restores the link to other people that is often severed by abuse.

There has been a tendency for therapists to see such concerns as establishing rapport, setting the therapeutic frame, developing interpersonal contact, and so on, as the necessary drudgery of therapy, so that they can get on to the "real" work of digging through symbols and symptoms, abreacting trauma, and making sense of it all. What is missed in this tendency is that the development of support is in and of itself an essential healing process; and for survivors in particular, it is major therapeutic work. It builds the ground conditions on which everything else in human functioning must rest. It generates the internalization of a healthy and functional interpersonal field from which other self structures can grow and be tested.

Without a sense of being fully and empathically supported by the therapist and by others, the survivor will never really engage in the healing process, and there will be no foundation for the later difficult work of mourning, redoing, and undoing. Without supportive connections to others, the survivor remains within the isolation that was part of the victimization and will become dependent on the therapist as his or her only source of human connection and support. Moreover, many survivors have had precious little opportunity to develop a sophisticated and mature variety of self functions with which to manage their ongoing experience. As emotionally charged and intense memories and feelings emerge, these may be faced with no more coping resources than existed when the original abuse occurred, and so these survivors must resort to the basic modes of dissociation, numbing, desensitization, denial, and so on. In this early phase of treatment, many survivors will be relying predominantly on the therapist's support for help with difficult or overwhelming experience until, through therapy, they can develop systemic support, as well as a greater capacity to be self-supporting. This chapter describes the foundational tasks of healing in this phase.

Phenomenology of the Abusive Context

Abuse, whether physical, emotional, or sexual, and like any other event in a child's development, occurs within an interpersonal context. Indeed, in many cases abuse is the predominant frame for the interpersonal world in which the child is embedded. In other cases, abuse is a figural event that stands out against the particular interpersonal and systemic ground of the family. It is this figure-ground relationship, of event to context or of event *as* context, that will largely influence the kind of impact that the abuse has on the developing child. For example, when a child is traumatized outside the family but returns to a family context where his distress is noticed, concern is expressed, he is believed and validated for reporting it, and there are legal and therapeutic resources, this child will probably have a very different experience from the child whose story is minimized or denied, or whose parents are too wrapped up in their own distress to particularly notice the child's. When the primary abuser and the primary caretaker are the same person, the ground of betrayal and confusion presents another kind of challenge and another kind of difficulty to surmount.

To understand the nature of the distress that survivors experience, and which brings them into therapy, and to understand how survivors' adaptations to their developmental contexts have shaped their responses to their current fields, we must appreciate how the abuse fits in with the rest of the childhood context. Focusing on the traumatic event itself is too narrow an approach to inform us adequately.

We can look to at least three different aspects of the traumatic occurrence: the environment in which it took place, and the degree of support within it; the particular child and his or her phase of development, as well as his or her internal and external resources and style of adaptation; and the trauma itself (whether it was a single event or repeated, the degree of threat or violence, and so on). Our interest for now is in the nature of the support for the child within the family context and in how it will influence the therapeutic stance and the needs of the first phase of therapy.

If anything can be said to be characteristic of the interpersonal world of the abusive family, certainly there is tremendous denial of and lack of support for the abused child's reality, and for the developing self. Denial is often part of a pattern of family alcoholic or drug-abuse codependency, where violence, chaos, and ill will are considered normal and natural to family functioning. In families where sexual abuse is occurring, its evidence is usually vociferously denied by the abuser and often by the nonperpetrating spouse, and in some families the sexual abuse of a child is actively encouraged by the nonperpetrating spouse, and the child is sacrificed to the maintenance of the marital system.

When abuse has occurred outside the home, threats may have forced the child to remain silent and repress what happened, or the family context may not have supported the child to reveal the trauma because it would have been denied, minimized, or disbelieved. The family's emotional resources may have been very limited, and little attention was available to distressed members. Such responses do not have the sticky, collusive, enmeshed, psychotic quality of denial that intrafamilial abuse seems to carry with it, but they do force a kind of schism and disconnection within the child, and this mimics the dislocation between trauma and context that occurs in these situations.

Abuse, particularly sexual abuse, often entails issues of secrecy, repression of memory, and so on, brought about by threats, denial, minimization, neglect, inattention to a child's distress, or the child's own shame about having had such a thing happen. This is why survivors of sexual abuse so often display the symptoms of silence, lack of memory, and shame whenever they get close to remembering. They have a sense of harboring a deep and un-known "badness" inside them.

Physical and emotional abuse often but not always takes place in public or semipublic space (public within the family, but not when "outsiders" are there). When this has occurred, the diffi-culty is not that the abuse was secret but that it was known and not rendered meaningful in a caring context. There was and is much pretending that it did not exist, that the events that oc-curred did not happen or at least "weren't important," or that such events were really discipline or legitimate punishment, justifiable on religious or other "reasonable" grounds. Survivors of physical and emotional abuse often carry this context in such symptoms as numbness, lack of empathy with others' pain, inability to know when something is hurtful to themselves or others, acting out in their current lives, and so on. Violence and emotional abuse can also take place in secret, of course, as is often the case in sibling abuse, religious cults, childcare when the parents are away, and situations where one parent loses control while the other parent is away and then denies the abusive actions later. Survivors of these situations show the effects of this secrecy in their sympto-matic patterns.

The phenomenological world of abused children is one where they are essentially without support and validation from others for their own experience. A survivor may have acquiesced in the fam-ily's denial of the abuse by repressing all memory of it. She may have come to take a hostile and defensive stance toward others.

She may have come to believe that there is no possibility of being supported in her own right without giving "favors" of a sexual or narcissistic kind. She may experience tremendous self-doubt, not having been believed as a child when she tried to tell what was being done to her, or having been denied the possibility of telling because of threats from the abuser. And, she may be expecting others to deny or rationalize her reports of abuse, as some therapists have done by automatically interpreting such reports as "fantasy" or, more recently, as "false memory syndrome." [4]

If an individual is just beginning to recover memories of abuse that were previously unavailable, he will be undergoing a tremendous destructuring of his definition of himself and his world. He will be in a state of doubt and disbelief, looking to others for confirmation or denial of what is often only vaguely and tenuously emerging. He may present only vague or fragmentary impressions (flashbacks, "snapshot" images, "knowing," symbolic, or kinesthetic representations). He will probably feel shaken and disorganized. The emerging memories and feelings may also have precipitated intense anxiety, depression, and dissociative or even psychotic reactions. Courtois (1988) has called this the "intrusion phase" because of the way in which memories and feelings seem to impinge on the experience of the survivor in a way that feels foreign, as if they were outside the self.

Thus adult survivors face the interpersonal world of the therapist (and the interpersonal world in general) with the issue of support uppermost in their experience, although not necessarily in their awareness as a question: Will I be believed? Will you support me in believing in myself? Will you accept me? Will you be there for me if I'm not supplying you with goodies (kudos, admiration, sex)? Will you tolerate my challenges and my hostility or withdrawal? Will you be able to deal with the strong feelings that I myself have avoided and pushed away? Will you blame me, as my family did in making me out to be the sick one?

These questions are often not in a survivor's awareness because the whole notion of acting in the world to *obtain support* for oneself, as opposed to acting in the world to *defend* or *protect* oneself, may be foreign and even frightening. The survivor has generally had to operate in a retroflective mode, doing everything for herself, because support (nurturance, help, validation) was either unavailable or dangerous in that it made her vulnerable to further abuse or invalidation. Survivors often become like those self-sealing tires that take care of their own punctures. Yet each time the tire self-seals, it loses more air.

The fundamental reality of human functioning is that we cannot be closed systems without running down. Our life and growth depend on our being open, relational beings, with independence and interdependence *both* as our birthright. Competent adulthood involves not doing everything for oneself alone, but also knowing when one needs help and being able to obtain it. Wholeness, and thus healing, will involve the capacity for moving along the polarity of independence and dependence, which at higher levels of functioning is resolved as *interdependence*. The survivor, having had little in the way of support from the environment, has often become rigidly self-supportive, unable to seek help or support because that is felt as "weakness" or exposes him to what is still felt as dangerous (even though the real danger is in the past).

As is more common in my own practice, survivors may be characteristically shaky, weak, unsupported, and virtually unable to obtain or seek support from the environment. As a result, they are thrown by even the most minor stresses. Whether rigidly self-supportive or characteristically unsupported, the survivor is ultimately in a fragile position. The rigid survivor is empty and brittle, unable to get support when she needs it because she cannot let go of her self-protective mode long enough to experience the possibility of support from the environment. The shaky survivor lacks an adequate internal structure but also cannot take support in from the environment. The developmental reality is that true independence grows from a ground of adequate support from early caretakers, which allows us to internalize the range of choices necessary for mature contact.

Many survivors also need to disconfirm their emerging memories or knowledge. By disconfirming their own experience and perceptions, they may be enacting on themselves the disconfirmation of others. They may be trying to cope with the huge disparity between family history as it was told and the unspoken truths that are now emerging. They may be hoping to hold on to the sense of security that comes with the known lie versus the unknown truth.

These issues are most focal in the initial period of therapy but are also returned to again and again as new memories emerge, as positive and negative transference develops, as new levels of risk are approached, and as the survivor becomes more differentiated in his or her interpersonal behavior. Put another way, the questions are these: Will therapy replicate the abusive environment that I am expecting, am used to, and know how to deal with? Or will therapy present me with a *different* reality, which will both support and challenge me to learn new ways of organizing myself and my contacting?

Establishing the Therapeutic Environment as Support

Given the phenomenology, characteristics, and effects of the abusive context, the first issue in therapy is to establish the therapeutic environment as a safe and supportive one. Survivors enter therapy from a variety of starting points. Some come in the rush of first memories and are in crisis. Others have a sense or belief that they suffered some childhood trauma, but they have no other confirming data and wish to explore this possibility. Others have no particular awareness of or curiosity about abuse in their backgrounds but are coming to therapy for attention to symptoms or other concerns.

The therapy environment is a cocreation that involves work by both the therapist and the client. From a life context of danger, betrayal, distrust, and invalidation—the tacit or acknowledged base of experience for the survivor—an environment of safety, trust, certainty, and validation has to be created. This constellation of attributes generates the "holding environment" (Winnicott, 1960, 1988), the container wherein growth and healing can take place.

The holding by this environment needs to be an active holding, not a passive one. The therapist has to validate the process of the client actively, framing and normalizing the disruptiveness of that process (depathologizing), helping the person actively determine safe boundaries and articulate concerns about the therapy process. In this phase of therapy, the therapist must provide an environment of empathy, trust, and acceptance while creating a treatment frame of healthy professional boundaries (ethics, clarity about financial issues, time management) and behavioral limits. With some clients, the responsibility in this early phase of therapy is primarily on the therapist, since the client cannot reasonably be expected to manage what he does not have skills for and in fact is in therapy to learn about. In this phase of therapy and of healing, the aim is to build confidence in the therapeutic context as a place where the client can trust, be safe, be believed (even when he is doubting himself), and be supported in the often difficult and rocky process of growth, remembering, and healing—or at least be safe enough to conduct small, controlled experiments that progressively test and thus build a safe therapeutic context. The following sections explore some of the key issues in establishing the therapeutic environment.

Trust

This issue involves the client's discovering that the therapist is not dangerous or abusive, is willing to believe the client without disparagement, and can tolerate and work with the client's flooding affect without being overwhelmed. When therapists are too questioning of emerging memories or fragments, or are too intrusive, problem-oriented, or pushy, or indicate that the client's strong affect is not acceptable or is frightening to them, therapy will stop before it starts.

To some extent, trust can be developed only over time, with repeated experience of the therapist's consistency, support, presence, willingness to engage honestly with difficulties, and healthy interpersonal boundaries. Survivors develop a number of indirect strategies for dealing with the thorny question of trust. Some have developed "tests" of trust, which may range from outrageous or obnoxious behavior to the expression of needs that are so subtle that it would take a therapist of unusual and exquisite sensitivity to notice them. Other clients take a passive "wait and see" stance; it is safe but it does not give them the opportunity to engage with the environment on their own behalf. Still others may take a naïve, "trust everyone" stance, which repeatedly results in boundary violations by others and replications of the original abuse. All of these indirect strategies with respect to trust can create great confusion in interpersonal relationships, including the relationship between client and therapist, because these strategies are open to such great misinterpretation. Therefore, some of the work of therapy at this phase is to try to make such indirect, covert tests of trust more explicit, so that their meaning can be made clear. Our aim is gradually and gently to make the issue of trust one that we can *engage* the client in, so that it becomes available as a self function rather than as a passive response.

There are active experiments that help teach the survivor that the trust-mistrust continuum can be actively explored, rather than only subjected to indirect tests or passively watched. I might work with a passive, naïvely trusting client to figure out what questions he would need to ask me about myself, my attitudes toward survivors' issues, and so on. I might also encourage him to articulate and explore all the legitimate reasons why he should *not* trust me or should reserve his full trust for now. I would talk with him about how such caution helps him gather adequate data about people, so that his trust of them is earned over time. I might ask him, "What do you trust me for at *this* time, and what remains to be explored and discovered?" This kind of exploration has crucial significance for survivors who seem to engage repeatedly in abusive relationships, or who make poor choices in friends or partners, because trust for them has been an all-or-nothing proposition, rather than a process of testing and observation. For indirect or covert tests, such as late or missed sessions, subtle nonverbal indications of the need for attention, and so on, I might work with the survivor to make these indirect messages explicit and explore how their indirectness creates problems for me in knowing how to respond.

If we view trust not as a unipolar event, as it is often viewed in psychotherapy, but as a bipolar event that includes both trust *and* mistrust, then we free up considerable therapeutic space to explore the trust-mistrust continuum with the client instead of becoming engaged in efforts to "create trust," which inevitably create "resistance" in the client-therapist dyad because the survivor naturally comes to therapy both with a genuine wish to find someone she can trust enough to help her and with ample experience of having been hurt or betrayed by her trust. Survivors organize themselves to deal with this polarity by organizing the interpersonal field around the expectation of betrayal. Some lead with their mistrust and keep the therapist at a safe distance for considerable periods of time before they become willing to explore the "trust" side of the polarity.

The therapist must be in a position to hold both the client's trust *and* his or her mistrust as important aspects of self functioning and not invalidate any side of the polarity. It is often our tendency as therapists to emphasize only one side of a polarity: we want to develop trust and avoid distrust; we want to help the client change, and so we undervalue the part of the client that wants to avoid risk; we want to promote connection, and so we may not recognize the benefits of keeping one's distance. Thus we may unwittingly engender much "resistance" as the client holds on to his or her sense of integrity by swinging to the underrepresented or underacknowledged polarity. For healing to occur, space must be made for *all* of the client.

Trust is not won when we challenge mistrust but when we explore and validate the importance of cautiousness and place such caution into its original abusive context. I attend carefully to the signs of mistrust shown by survivors, and I try to bring these out in explicit ways, so that the question of mistrust can be tested actively instead of left to exist as a structural given of how the client organizes his or her relationship with me. I am interested in the client's choice to avoid certain areas of discussion—how she seems to shut down if I become too personable, how she holds herself in a guarded or stiff manner, her sense of distance and aloofness, how she is poised to leave the room—because I want to confirm the importance of her remaining guarded (after all, she doesn't really know me yet) and explore how she will be able to know when she is safe. This way, we can make the whole issue of trust one that we can talk about and check on from session to session. Because of the polar nature of human personality, we all find it more possible to open up to our more hidden and less known polarity (in this case, trust) when the one that we lead with is supported and validated.

Other survivors organize themselves in relation to trust by pretending, even to themselves, that they trust others. Thus their signals of mistrust and distancing tend to be entirely outside their awareness. If therapist and survivor assume that the surface presentation is the whole reality, then they will not understand how the covert distancing strategies are creating dilemmas in the therapy, and they will miss an opportunity to validate the mistrusting side of the client and make his mistrust part of his self function,[5] so that he can test the therapist legitimately. Many survivors, instead of being able to express distrust by distancing from the therapist in posture, stance, or intentional silence, become dissociative, spaced out, or emotionally numb. They experience these feelings as "coming over them," and they usually do not connect these experiences to the environmental context, such as what the therapist just did, or to thoughts or feelings that have occurred to them.

When we attend to these events as they occur in the here-and-now of therapy, we can begin to experiment with clients expressing their mistrust in more explicit and more useful ways. For example, in one early session with a survivor, I suddenly became aware that I was still talking but nobody seemed to be home on the receiving end. My client's eyes looked glazed. She was barely breathing and seemed disconnected from her body, although she was nodding her head as if she understood what I was saying. I paused and asked her what she was experiencing as we talked. She reported that she was not really understanding what I was saying, and that I seemed "farther away" from her, but that she felt nothing else. I began to tell her how she looked to me. As she attended to her minimal breathing, spacey expression, and physical stiffness, she began to feel somewhat anxious. I explored with her whether this was a response to me or to something she had felt or imagined, by experimenting with whether her anxiety increased when she attended to herself, as opposed to me. I had her alternate or "shuttle" her focus from herself to me and compare the resulting internal sensations. As we experimented, it became clear that I was the stimulus of her anxiety. She would feel a pull to become more spaced out and "move away" from me when she attended to me. As we articulated this process of her moving away from me, I offered some sentences she could say, to see if any captured what was being left unsaid in this nonverbal adaptive process: "I want you to get away from me, but I can't ask you to, so I'll move away by spacing out." "You are getting too close to me, so I have to get away." "What you have been saying to me brings me too close to remembering, so I have to go numb and space out."[6] As she tried these statements, she could begin to identify some elements that seemed to fit her experience. She eventually reformulated these statements herself: "You are presuming too much, and I feel like you are boring in too intrusively with what you are saying about my history, so I have to back away from you. I can't trust you right now to be delicate enough with me." Being able to make this statement aloud was enormously relieving to her (although it felt risky at first to try), and it opened the door for us to talk about my "boring in" and her need to go more slowly. I was able to acknowledge and own that I do get ambitious at times and push toward more emotion-laden material than may be appropriate. Examining the roots of my "ambition," I had to grapple with my own unwillingness to let her be spaced out, my aggressive need to have an impact on her, and my anxious feeling that she was disconnected from me and that I could not reach her. I told her this as I became aware of it, judging that her self functions were sufficient to hear these statements as being about me, rather than as being a shaming commentary on her.[7] She was able to recognize how she modified *herself* instead of engaging with *the environment* when she was uncomfortable. We then could experiment with her telling me to back off, expressing her mistrust of me out loud, and claiming the right to intervene when she felt I was going too fast or getting too close to her or to material that she was not ready to share with me. We can note here that the context for this process—her inability to get her abuser to back off, his "boring in" on her when she was a defenseless child—was the deeper ground for her transferential experience with me.

I may or may not choose to extend and explore my present work with a client into this original context; that depends on the client. We must be careful of unwittingly reenacting the abusive context through prematurely deep therapeutic work. We must take care not to operate from some therapeutic dictum about the "correct" thing to do. We need to respect the client's engagement with us. Many survivors in the support phase are just trying to *tolerate* their experience. If a survivor can manage her experience *in the present*, then she will be in a better position to manage her current life, and this experience will form the crucial support and basis of the self functions necessary to dealing with the deeper ground of traumatic memory in the phase of undoing, redoing, and mourning.

The Healing Tasks Model serves as a guide for making therapeutic judgments about what level and intensity of experiment we might wish to offer at any given phase. It is worth noting here, however, that although most of what the model helps us do is grade down experiments and abreactive work in the support phase, it is the client who ultimately must guide us, not some theoretical model. For example, I was working with a support-phase client who was remembering an intense incident of rape and abuse by a relative. As she remembered, she appeared to me to become disconnected from my presence as a support, dislocated from the present context, and ungrounded. Like a good therapist, I periodically encouraged her to pause, feel her feet on the ground, look around the room, breathe, and then go back to the memory. After a cycle or two of this, she looked at me with exasperation and said, "Will you just let me stay with this memory? If you keep interrupting me, I'm going to lose hold of it, and it's important!" I sheepishly backed off, dealt with my own anxiety, which was motivating my urgency in keeping her grounded, and let her remember as she needed to do.

Safety, Containment Boundaries, and the Treatment Frame

The survivor is faced with a curious dilemma at the beginning of therapy. On the one hand, he needs to feel safe in order to pursue the healing process. On the other hand, safety is often experienced as something outside his control; it is a "given," which is either there or not, rather than something cocreated with another person. Safety is often looked on as a feeling, rather than as an interpersonal *process* that involves activity on the survivor's part. Survivors have often been revictimized, sometimes by therapists, because they have not had an opportunity to discover how trust and safety are *created*, and because they have not had the opportunity to develop useful interpersonal boundaries.

Survivors need to know that there is a consistent set of expectations for the therapeutic relationship. These include the times of sessions, procedures for cancellation, availability of the thera-pist by phone, and so on. Because survivors often want the thera-pist to have the boundless concern that their abusive parents lacked, and because they feel a great deal of distress and are look-ing for relief, the therapist often overlooks the fact that survivors have survived without the therapist. Establishing a frame for heal-ing means acknowledging the real limitations of the therapist as a real person. The fantasy of the enfolding, always available womb of therapy is grist for the mill of exploration. A lot of mourning for what was not available in childhood is contained within it and can be looked at during the appropriate phase of healing. But per-petual availability is not a requirement that therapists must or can fulfill.

Beginning therapists who have survivors as clients often have difficulty empathically supporting their clients and establishing the limits of the treatment frame at the same time. Common er-rors are either to become overinvolved and boundlessly empathic with a client's distress, or to overemphasize boundary setting from fear of the internal chaos and affect that the client is undergoing. The therapist's overinvolvement gives clients no sense that he or she will provide limits where, in their distress, they have had none. Overemphasis on boundaries leads clients to feel invali-dated and pathologized. In the initial work, there is a testing phase: the client is testing the therapist, and therapy is testing the client. The therapist must provide a firm boundary *and* act sup-portively and empathically.

Discovering and Articulating the Truth Behind One's Symptoms

This process is about validating and organizing the initial story of abuse.[8] One of the markers of having passed through the first phase of healing is that one has accepted that one was abused. This does not mean that a clear memory of an abusive episode has to exist; often there will be only fragments, or even just a sense of "knowing." To achieve this marker requires breaking some of the bonds of secrecy and denial that surround the recognition of the abuse.

Secrecy is almost invariably part and parcel of the abusive environment and thus of the coping style of the survivor. Even when secrecy was not held within the family where the abuse occurred, it was usually held against "outsiders." One of the first barriers that the survivor faces in utilizing the support offered by therapy is the taboo of secrecy about the abuse. This taboo is felt in the very fiber of the survivor's being and is rarely articulated as an obvious rule. It simply *is*. These things are "just not talked about." As we have seen, the silence of some survivors has been won by the perpetrators with threats of harm. For these survivors to tell anything about what happened to them (even if they do not consciously know yet what happened to them) brings about fear, anxiety, terror, or even suicidal ideation.[9]

Secrecy is often enacted in speechlessness, reluctance, or awkwardness about talking about oneself, speaking only about superficial topics, and avoiding certain topics, or it is indicated by blank spots and amnesia for certain periods of childhood history. We often see a kind of layered effect as well; some memories are more easily accessible, whereas others seem guarded by intense denial, avoidance, or shame. Almost invariably, in my experience, the amount of secrecy or avoidance is related to the intensity of the trauma itself, to the degree of coercion, fear, or violence directed at the victim by the perpetrator in order to ensure silence, or to postabuse denial by significant others, which invalidated the child's reality. Thus difficulty in divulging, revealing, or even remembering trauma has a contextual basis.

Because the initial stages of recollecting trauma are, by their very nature, often disturbing, confusing, and filled with self-doubt and the wish to deny, outside support for the emerging truth is essential. The survivor faces the emergence of traumatic memory not only with her own defenses (denial, self-doubt, dissociation, and so on) but also with whatever she has introjected from her environment. If the therapist starts out with a mistrustful or questioning stance, it may replicate the family's or outsider's denial of the abuse and collude with the client's repression, denial, or dissociation. As a result, the material may be repressed again, or the therapy process may be blocked. The therapist must be willing to support the reality or the possibility of the abuse and its effects. At the same time, the therapist has to be open to the many forms of memory through which the initial and later history of the abuse unfolds. These include visual memories, auditory memories, kinesthetic memories, and a variety of enactments through symptoms and behavior. To appreciate the importance of the therapist's support during this early phase of recalling and presenting traumatic memories, it is helpful to understand how the Healing Tasks Model sees the process by which these memories were forgotten and how they are recalled.

Forgetting as a Field Phenomenon

Traumatic material is "forgotten," not because of some mechanical fault in memory, but because of the dynamics of the field conditions. By the term *field* I am referring here to Lewin's concept (1951) that we must always consider *both* the organism (O), or person, *and* the environment (E) in which that person is embedded, in order to understand any problem of human functioning. Nowhere is it more apparent that organism and environment are a unitary gestalt, an interdependent whole, than in the forgetting and recollection of trauma.

If we consider the field of the abusive situation, we have a child who has whatever internal resources and capacities he has been able to develop up to that point, given the available support; an assaultive perpetrator, who is controlling and coercing the choices available to the child; and, often, caretakers who participate in the suppression of the truth, either directly, in alliance with the abuser, or indirectly, through denial or neglect. The dynamic mix of these particulars—the *child* and the *context*—

determines whether an event will be included as part of the continuous narrative description of the child's life or split off from it, and the balance of this total mix of organism and environment (O/E) determines what is possible. The elements of the mix are, again, the child and his resources and developmental capacities, the degree of threat or coercion and control by the perpetrator, the degree of violence in the abusive assault itself, the number of perpetrators involved, and the possibility that other adults could acknowledge what happened and respond in a supportive and meaningful way. This total mix is different for every survivor, and it is even different for different traumatic events, some of which may be remembered and some of which may not.

For many survivors, the problem is not that they had to split off the memory of the event itself; it may be quite clearly recalled, remembered as part of the life narrative, and even freely spoken of within the family. It was not the event and its factual details that were split off, but the survivor's own *feelings* and organization of the *meaning* of the event. Not infrequently, therapists hear clients recount quite traumatic events in neutral or distant tones, without much feeling or sense of their impact, and with an organization of meaning that is unconvincing or seems to have been introjected from others: "These things just happen sometimes." "That was a long time ago. It doesn't affect me now." "One shouldn't dwell on those things." This kind of resolution is essentially the same as forgetting, and both kinds of adjustment require an atmosphere of support in order for new meanings to be organized.

Remembering as a Field Phenomenon

If events are severed from narrative continuity and recede into the background of our awareness because of the field conditions around them, then they are brought back into the foreground of our awareness (remembered) and reconnected to our life narrative if our current field conditions are *different* enough from the original conditions. The issue of support for remembering has to do with creating the necessary environmental conditions for traumatic memories to be held as they come into the foreground, so that the person can determine their validity and truth and decide whether they should be part of the life narrative. The field conditions of the present must outweigh those of the past before disconnected memories can emerge from the background and be held in the foreground long enough to be considered and explored. Several field conditions in the present are *minimally* required in order to support the validation process.[10]

First, the environment must be receptive and must not deny or minimize. A purely neutral or detached stance on the part of the therapist is not appropriate, in my view. It leaves the client too much on her own, without adequate support in the face of difficult, anxiety- or terror-provoking recollections. Minimization and denial in the face of emerging impressions often mimic reactions from others at the time of the original abuse and are common ways in which survivors keep their memories at a distance. Therefore, a neutral stance does not allow anyone in the room to take the emerging impressions seriously *enough*.

Second, the environment must be able to hold and look at any possibilities. I have heard it suggested that "fantastic" or "outlandish" memories, such as those of ritual abuse, are not believable and should be automatically discounted by therapists. But the first reports of the Holocaust were also considered too outlandish to be believed by many people (and are still denied by some, despite film footage and eyewitness reports). Reports about the prevalence of incest were also doubted and denied as survivors began to come forth. It is not the therapist's job to sit in judgment of the truth. Survivors bringing forth memories of incest, molestation, beatings, neglect, and mistreatment are often doubting themselves. For the survivor to be met with doubts or questioning at this phase proves to him that this O/E field is not different enough from the original field, and the emerging impressions will be pushed back into unawareness.

Third, the environment must not be coercive or exert pressure for a particular view or version of the truth. Coercion to interpret or view impressions in any particular light, either as abuse or as fantasy, is inappropriate. The pressure to question or doubt a memory recreates the original pressure to deny or minimize the abuse. At any rate, it leaves survivors who are in a delicate, vulnerable place without the support to begin to trust their experience. It is just as true that the pressure to interpret impressions as abuse is inappropriate. A colleague told me that, during a workshop, a woman reported a traumatic impression of people with masks crowding around her. A number of participants in the workshop were convinced that this was an impression of ritual abuse. As she was supported to stay with the impression and let her *own* perceptions develop, it actually turned out to be the memory of a childhood surgery—indeed a traumatic memory for this person, but not a memory of ritual abuse.

Fourth, the environment must be able to support the client to hold fragmentary, conflicting, or unclear impressions over time, without doubting them and without prematurely assigning meanings to them, until a pattern of truth and meaning can be discerned by the client. Impressions must speak for themselves as they form enough of a pattern to be comprehensible. Since memories often emerge in fragmentary, impressionistic ways, staying with these impressions requires encouragement and support from the therapist. There is truth even in distorted, misremembered, or symbolic impressions, and only time and experience will allow their meanings to be discerned. The client needs to be supported in trusting this process.

Beyond the Minimal Conditions for Support

I believe that it is legitimate for the therapist to take the following stance: unless there is a specific reason for doubting the validity of what is being reported, there is no reason *not* to believe the client. This is not to say that we must believe that all the details are being reported with perfect factual accuracy. We do not necessarily assume this when someone reports *any* kind of memory, even what he or she had for breakfast. But we can legitimately believe the report unless there are reasons to doubt it. Our approach here is fundamentally a phenomenological one, concerned with the client's *experience,* and so it is probably wise to stay close to what the client asks us when he or she is asking for our support. Here are some questions and some possible responses that are affirming but not coercive or suggestive. They stick to what the client is asking in the moment:

"Could this have happened?"	"It's possible." "Does it feel real to you?" "It's possible for such things to happen to people."
"Do you believe this is true?"	"I don't hear anything that would make me doubt you." "I can't tell you that it's true, but it sounds consistent with what I know about you." "I don't know if there is any way to determine what's true or not right now. But I trust that if we can help you sit with it and hold it over time, you'll come to know what's true for yourself."
"Do such things actually happen to people?"	"I believe they do." "Some people doubt that this happens, but I have come to believe that such things do happen. What the full story is for you, we'll have to see over time."

"Do you believe me?"   "Yes."
                             "I don't know if all the de-
                             tails are exact, but I believe
                             that this is essentially what
                             happened to you."

"Is this a joke?"   "I take seriously what you are
                             telling me."

The experience of being "held" by a trusted other is what allows the survivor to experiment with believing himself or herself.
The trust of another in the survivor's emerging experience is what
plants the seeds of the survivor's learning to trust himself or herself. Through the interpersonal manifestation of trust in and support for the survivor, the assurance that his or her experience has
meaning and validity, the survivor begins to solidify some core
experiences, which become supportive in the healing process.

Shame as a Barrier to Affirmation

As a survivor begins to recall, speak of, or try to affirm the reality
of abuse and its significance, the most common accompaniment
is a powerful feeling of shame. Shame can be described as the feeling of self-diminishment. We observe the way in which the feeling
of shame literally makes a person shrink: the eyes drop, the head
hangs, the chest collapses, the shoulders curve forward. It is not
just the emotion that is the problem in shame; it is also the meanings that shame has in our interpersonal world. The affect or sensation of shame, like other difficult feelings that the survivor is
learning to tolerate and manage at this phase of healing, can be
worked with through grounding and support, but the work is un-
dermined or limited by the interpersonal nature of shame's meaning. Shame is the feeling that accompanies the meaning "You are
unworthy of belonging, of having comfort or goodness, of being
part of the human family." How does one receive support for man-

aging the experience of shame when shame, by its very nature, means that one is unworthy of contact with others?

At this point in healing, the feeling of shame can be so powerful for the survivor, coming as it does at the phase when the bonds of support are still tenuous and thus easily threatened by all the implications shame carries, that the survivor becomes blocked in accomplishing the task of developing support and affirming the reality of abuse. For the therapist, the degree to which shame becomes a major obstacle to progress in the support phase (or in any other phase of healing, for that matter) can generate significant countertransference-based responses. I have made what in retrospect seem to be some of my dumbest responses to "resistance" in my attempts to deal with my frustration at not being able to "get through" to clients who were immersed in shame. I have reassured them that they were not what they thought of themselves (thus shaming them for thinking "wrongly"). I have tried to talk them out of their shame-based beliefs (likewise shaming them). I have tried to batter down the walls of shame they have raised (thus invalidating the creative adjustment that shame is part of in the adaptation to a particular field problem). As therapists, we have particular neurotic concerns that drive our countertransference responses. (My own neurotic avoidance of feeling my own shame has taken the form of combating my encroaching feelings of being "ineffective" as a therapist.) We also need a full enough appreciation of the phenomenon of shame to understand what it is and what work is appropriate to a particular phase of development and healing.

Figure 2.1 represents some of the components of shame that survivors often feel. The experience of shame (central oval) is surrounded by elements of experience and process that have become connected to the shame response and need to be sorted out and worked through over the course of therapy.

As a primary affect, shame seems to develop out of precursor reactions that infants respond with as moderators of excitement in the presence of uncertainty or overstimulation (Tomkins,

Figure 2.1. Aspects of Shame.

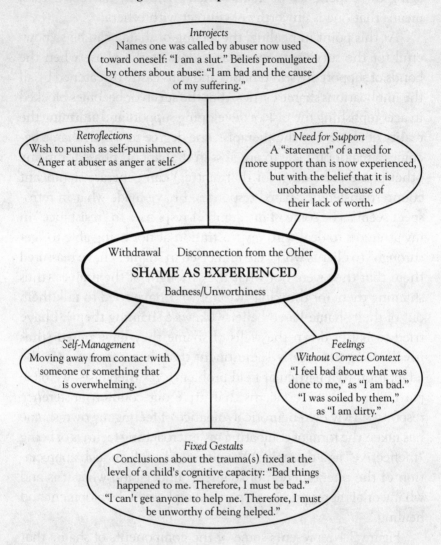

Introjects
Names one was called by abuser now used toward oneself: "I am a slut." Beliefs promulgated by others about abuse: "I am bad and the cause of my suffering."

Retroflections
Wish to punish as self-punishment. Anger at abuser as anger at self.

Need for Support
A "statement" of a need for more support than is now experienced, but with the belief that it is unobtainable because of their lack of worth.

Withdrawal   Disconnection from the Other
SHAME AS EXPERIENCED
Badness/Unworthiness

Self-Management
Moving away from contact with someone or something that is overwhelming.

Feelings
Without Correct Context
"I feel bad about what was done to me," as "I am bad." "I was soiled by them," as "I am dirty."

Fixed Gestalts
Conclusions about the trauma(s) fixed at the level of a child's cognitive capacity: "Bad things happened to me. Therefore, I must be bad." "I can't get anyone to help me. Therefore, I must be unworthy of being helped."

1962, 1987). Tomkins observes how infants drop their eyes and heads and hunch their shoulders (the facial and postural signs of shame) in response to a number of situations in which excitement must be modulated and toned down. These include both inter-personal and object-oriented stimulus events. In field terms, these responses are part of the innate self functions by which we regulate situations of excitement and interest in the environment that involve simultaneous uncertainty or danger. Another way to say this is that the shame response is how we regulate our organismic impulses in an environment that presents uncertainty as to how our impulses will be received. As human development proceeds, this affect becomes more specifically linked to interactions with others in which embarrassment, disapproval, and rejection are the primary stimuli for the feeling. Shame is an affect that by its very nature interrupts, manages, and reduces excitement or stimulation and interpersonal contact.

We see this aspect of the shame response frequently as survivors face the task of recalling and speaking of abuse. Shame emerges and floods the awareness before the memory of abuse can grow clear. The feeling of shame is so strong that the story cannot be told without the risk of rejection, humiliation, and loss of support. Thus shame comes to have a place in the psychic economy of many survivors (see the oval "Self-Management" in Figure 2.1) because it serves to move them *away from* potentially overwhelming experiences and *away from* potentially overwhelming interpersonal interactions. Therefore, they may be deflected into shame when they come too close to remembering some trauma or are about to have some other feeling that is inadmissible for some reason or when there is a real possibility of being positively received by another (a possibility that increases vulnerability to further hurt or disappointment).

As Kaufman (1992) has pointed out, shame, more than any other affect that we feel, represents the loss of connection between ourselves and others. Shame creates a gap that separates us from the world of belonging to others, separates us from parents, family, tribe, or community. Thus shame is about the loss of fundamental support and the perceived impossibility of ever obtaining it again in adequate form.

Shame is not simply an affect, particularly for a child, whose sense of being is inextricably bound to others. It is an experience of the field. What does it mean to be severed from the interpersonal ground on which one's very existence depends? How can one who is so horrible, so unacceptable, so sullied and dirty, possibly expect support and validation? Phenomenologically, shame is experienced by the child as a kind of "psychic death."[11] An infant or young child does not experience herself to be a separate self in the way that we come to imagine ourselves as adults (Stern, 1985). The child's developing sense of self is necessarily dependent on an engagement with her caretakers.[12] Of course, this is also true for adults, although our cultural myth obscures our interdependence with others.

To be held up as an object, without the interpersonal world as a supportive background, can be unbearable to a child, whose self functions are still unformed. It is like being dangled over an abyss. The spontaneous way of managing this unmanageable gap at the boundary between self and other is to break contact with the other by dropping one's eyes, pulling oneself in. We lessen the pain of ridicule by choosing to sever our connections to others: "I must pull away." "I am unworthy." "I am isolated and cannot expect comfort."

Shame also comes about as a result of the conclusions we reach in our attempts to make sense of traumatic events (see the oval "Fixed Gestalts" in Figure 2.1). In childhood trauma, we can make sense of things only from the perspective of the child-level concrete reasoning capacity that is available to us ("I must have been bad for such bad things to have happened to me."). These conclusions can become rigidly held beliefs that remain unexamined and thus unassimilated into our current experience of self.

Shame may also come about (see the oval "Introjects") as a result of the introjection, or swallowing whole, of things said by abusers or by others either before or after the abuse. ("Children can't be trusted." "You deserved it." "If you tell, everyone will know it was your fault."). These phrases may come to exist independently of the voices of others and may become the voice of oneself: self-criticisms, names one calls oneself, the litany of self-shaming, and so on.

Shame may also contain aspects of retroflection. Since so many feelings and responses to the abusive situation had to be withheld and left unexpressed, shame was useful for turning their expression away from the environment, where it was too dangerous, and referring it back to the self. The impossible expression of power is kept in check by diminishing oneself through self-shaming: "I am nothing." "I am inadequate." "I don't deserve to stand up for myself." Reaching out for help may be similarly restrained: "I am an idiot." "No one would want me."

Shame can also result from feelings that have become severed from their original environmental context and are therefore misperceived as being about *oneself* rather than about a *situation* (see the oval "Feelings Without Correct Context"). "I feel bad about the bad things that were done to me" can become "I *am* bad" when the bad feelings are referenced to the ground of oneself rather than to the ground of the abusive situation. Similarly, "I still feel wounded by what they did to me" can become "I am a flawed human being."

Clearly, there is no way in which the therapist can magically know what elements form the ground for any particular shame response that a client demonstrates in the moment. It is not up to the therapist to interpret the meaning of shame for the client, but rather to collaborate on an exploration through which the possibilities in the client's shame can be experimented with, discovered, and thereby worked through. What needs to be addressed first? In the support phase of healing, where even recognizing or exposing the existence of feelings of shame can be a great risk for the survivor, I start in the center of the complex, with the experience of shame itself. Often, simply identifying that the feeling being experienced *is* shame can be a significant intervention for survivors, because it is so much a part of their ongoing experience that it has never been identified as something in particular. Identifying a feeling as shame can give survivors a moment of stepping back, can give the message "This is a feeling you are having" rather than the message that this is who they *are.*

Another aim in therapy at this point with respect to shame is to build what Kaufman (1992, p. 141) calls "the interpersonal bridge": "Shame feelings need to be actively approached and openly validated by the therapist. When this occurs, exposure fears become reduced, thereby enabling the client's awareness of his internal shame processes to deepen even further. In effect, the client learns an important interpersonal lesson, namely, that expression of shame will not be shamed again. Therapist approach and validation need to follow each time the client dips into shame. Otherwise, the client will feel abandoned, shamed again, or experience his shame as too threatening for the therapist." Since the figural task of the support phase is to generate the interpersonal field basic to development and essential to the creation of the context in which other forms of healing work can be "held" adequately, Kaufman's suggestions are highly appropriate to our present concerns. As trust and support increase over the course of this phase, or with particular survivors who may have enough preexisting self functions, shame can be explored a bit more—say, through experimenting with recontextualization and rephrasing (see Chapter Eight).

Although there may not yet be enough of a basis for working these issues through in the support phase, they must at least be noticed and articulated so that they become part of the spoken context rather than the unspeakable ground. This way, opportunities can be found for reassurance, externalization, normalization ("This is something shared by many survivors"), and perhaps the linking of feelings of shame or unworthiness to the emerging background of the unknown history. The therapist cannot magically make a survivor feel better about herself, no matter how much the therapist compliments or reassures her. The therapist can only demonstrate trust, show interest, be curious and genuine, and help the survivor explore and contextualize her own experience.

Managing Levels of Stimulation and Arousal: Essential Self Functions for the Support Phase

The tendency for survivors to swing between extremes of overstimulation and numbing or withdrawal, and to seek out extremes of both positive and negative experience, is considered virtually classic in Posttraumatic Stress Disorder. At this stage of healing, survivors commonly tend to be hypersensitive to situations that have even vague similarities to any features of the original abuse. For example, one client who had been abused by her older sister as a child, had panic attacks in the presence of taller, aggressive women.

The survivor often demonstrates a low threshold for becoming flooded by any stimulus of a sexual or violent nature. Watching the news on television is experienced as traumatic. A co-worker who becomes upset with a survivor is called an abuser. Negative feedback is experienced as if it were a violation. Survivors at this phase may have poor tolerance for intense interpersonal contact, and even normal interpersonal contact can be experienced as overwhelming.

A general problem associated with this phase is that the client quickly becomes flooded with affect and feels overwhelmed. Therapy itself may come to be experienced as retraumatizing. The survivor retraumatized by therapy can be pushed beyond numbing, dissociating, and repression, into even more primitive suicidal, paranoid, or psychotic states. There is mounting evidence that trauma conditions the nervous system to a poor capacity for dealing with stimulation (Kolb, 1987; van der Kolk, 1987).

To begin to sort out the past from the present and make the therapy experience manageable, the client needs to develop certain fundamental skills for managing stimulation. These skills are actually a basic subset of the self functions that will become more figural in a later phase of healing, but they are fundamental process skills essential to the support phase of healing.

Grounding Skills

Grounding has to do with the ability to be oriented to and in contact with the present, in contact with one's bodily experience, aware of one's body in space, and able to use this contact to ride out difficult or intense experiences such as feelings. Survivors, particularly in the early phases of healing, are typically ungrounded. They become flooded with internal sensations or memories and quickly lose contact with the present. They dissociate under stress and lose contact with their bodily presence and with the concrete reality of the room or with the therapist. They become disoriented in time and place during flashbacks. They often report feeling insubstantial and disconnected, and they may appear this way to others. Those who have not experienced such a condition need to understand that it does not feel good. To unground and disconnect from traumatic reality was a useful childhood adaptation, but it does not leave one with any resources to face difficult or intense experience in the here-and-now. It merely replicates the field of the original trauma. The survivor must learn that there are ways to remain present and face the difficulty with new resources. I attend carefully to opportunities for teaching clients how to ground themselves when they become overwhelmed, flooded, or dissociated during therapy sessions.

Sensory Contact. As I observe a client beginning to space out or become ungrounded, I may call this to her attention and ask her to pause, notice the chair under her, feel her feet on the floor, look around the room, and otherwise make specific contact with the environment she is in. I wish to consciously and willfully *distract* her from whatever she is being flooded with and make her present contact with the environment more figural. Remember, this is not an abreactive model, which might push for full reliving of her traumatic experience. Our aim in the Healing Tasks Model is to work with what is *phase-appropriate*. This kind of environmental contact initially takes persistent coaching from the therapist. The client will gradually learn it over time as a skill that she can choose to apply for herself.

Awareness of the Therapist's Presence. The therapist's presence can help the client stay in contact with something in the present environment that will allow him to manage the intensity of his internal experience, but awareness of this kind depends on a base of support and rapport with the therapist. A client will often stare into the distance or drop his gaze to the floor as he becomes overwhelmed, essentially cutting himself off from contact with the present, and particularly with the therapist, thus losing the therapist's presence as support. When this happens, I may gently insist that the client look at me, blink his eyes as he does so, and be aware that I am in the room with him. I may take the client's hand and ask him to squeeze and feel my hand as he looks at me, or focus him on the sensation of my hand holding his if looking itself is too difficult (usually because it is experienced as shaming).

General Bodily Awareness. Contact with one's legs as support, the feeling of one's body in the chair, movement and stretching to facilitate contact with one's body—all of these counter derealization and depersonalization. In derealization, the person feels the environment as somehow unreal, or she feels distant or disconnected from it. In depersonalization, she feels herself floating, disembodied, or disconnected from herself. Both of these are forms of dissociation, ways of managing difficult experience by disconnecting from bodily experience (the dimension of self where the problematic sensation exists). If we investigate these phenomena with the client, we will quickly find that she has lost contact with her bodily experience and is numb or unfeeling.

I may ask the client to move and stretch, press her feet into the floor or her hands into the arms of the chair, stand up and walk around the office, move the muscles of her face and eyes, and do things that generally restore bodily sensation at the *periphery* of the body, where we make contact with the environment, rather than at the bodily *core* (torso, gut, pelvis), where traumatic feelings are often experienced. I will usually ease the client's self-consciousness by doing these things with her; after all, it is not a bad idea, by any means, for the therapist to be in good contact with his or her own body as well.

Modulation of Stimulation. I teach clients active ways to manage stimulation through general work with breathing, relaxation, and simple meditation techniques. Our most accessible and continual process of grounding and relaxation is our breathing. As a body-oriented therapist, I find breathing to be a readily available tool in the course of therapeutic work, as well as a readily available tool for the client in daily life. Dissociation, which I see as disconnection from the bodily ground, typically involves virtually stopping one's breathing, or making breathing minimal in order to dampen or desensitize a potentially overwhelming sensation by "leaving the scene." On the other side of the equation, panic or fear will typically bring about rapid breathing, which tends, paradoxically, to further unground one by actually creating *more* stimulation (increased body sensation) if one does not have the opportunity to translate the increased oxygenation into motor-activity.[13]

In both cases, proper use and modulation of breathing can assist in grounding and reorienting. In the case of someone who is becoming dissociated and spacey, I might remind him, "Let yourself breathe, and as you do, look around the room and feel the chair under you." The combination of breathing (to connect himself to his bodily experience) and contact with the environment (to shift the focus from overwhelming bodily sensations to the bodily self in the present environment) helps ground the survivor. We must keep coaching him until he has ridden out the wave of the difficult experience and reached the other side: "Inhale again. Blink your eyes as you look at me and breathe. Let your breath out gently, and move your feet."

When panic and hyperventilation are the problem, I coach the client to slow his breathing, letting himself pause after he has exhaled (to rebalance the insufficiency of carbon dioxide that occurs with hyperventilation), and help him pace his breathing until he has reconnected with the present: "Slow down your breathing. That's right. Let yourself pause after you exhale. A little longer. Now, just a gentle inhalation. Don't hold it. Let it out.

Now pause. Feel the floor under your feet."

More detailed relaxation processes can be taught and practiced as well. I find audiotapes that use methods for muscular relaxation, rhythmic breathing, imagery, and so on, to be very helpful for survivors. Such methods must be explored and tailored to the individual needs of each client. Similarly, basic meditation practices (breathing, concentration, repeating some neutral or positive word, prayer, and so on) are very helpful in teaching the survivor to create an oasis of calm in the whirl of internal events.

Making a Safe Space

Another classic method of helping someone manage overwhelming stimulation is to help her create a "safe space" through imagery or hypnosis. This method uses a strong, compelling image of a pleasant, safe, relaxing environment, an image that is associated with good feelings, one that the client can go to in times of stress, to "take a break" from an unpleasant stimulus. This method takes advantage of the often natural response of dissociation, by giving the survivor a place to dissociate *to*, instead of just becoming disoriented and vague. It is not grounding in the present environment, but it does serve as an alternative internal environment for grounding when the present cannot be managed. It is also extremely useful in Multiple Personality Disorder (MPD) when one wishes to help one alter personality be safe and protected "elsewhere" (and thus grounded *somewhere*) while helping another alter be grounded in the present.

Using Psychotropic Medications

Psychotropic medication is a legitimate and often essential support for survivors dealing with the impact of overstimulation. At the same time, its use can be considered a self function, in the sense of making a choice to control the intensity and quality of one's experience rather than being subject to it. When medication works, it provides a platform of support that can raise the threshold for panic and flashbacks and make survivors less susceptible to such intrusions. Then, the survivor can gradually build his or her own support and self functions, which eventually will replace the medication. In later phases of healing, the extra support of medication can allow experiments with the developing self functions to start at a higher level than otherwise would be tolerable, and more rapid learning and assimilation of necessary skills will also become possible.

I ask survivors to ask themselves whether there is any reason why they should have to suffer and struggle when some support might be available. Is there any real virtue in struggle and suffering as such, or might there be some value in making the choice to get enough support to feel better and make the tasks of healing tolerable and possible? These questions are part of the process of exploration in considering the possibility of medication as support. Yet it is very common for survivors to express a distinct aversion to taking medication, even when they are suffering quite miserably from anxiety, depression, and flashbacks that make life extremely chaotic. This aversion to psychotropic medication is not just due to fear of side effects, or to the time that must be spent finding the correct medication and dosage. It is also related to therapeutic issues in the support phase of healing.

With some survivors, medication may be perceived as a further intrusion into the bodily state and sense of bodily reality. It is seen as foreign, much as the original trauma was. This phobia about any intrusion means that anything new will automatically be rejected, whether potentially helpful or not. The need to guard against further intrusion supersedes the capacity to consider and make contact with what is being offered at one's boundary. It is a kind of reaction formation that keeps everything threatening out, as well as everything helpful. With regard to medication, this phobia is probably an adaptation that has already appeared in other therapeutic interactions as well; that is, it is a general mode of contact. Part of the therapeutic work is to explore and make it possible to experiment with opening one's boundary in safety and learning how one can know when opening up is safe and when it is not, how one can distinguish an automatic response from a useful response, and so on. This work includes sorting through concerns about using medication as a support to differentiate reactivity to intrusion from other legitimate concerns.

Another fear about using medication is that the survivor's fear will somehow displace and overwhelm his already tenuous and chaotic experience of self. We can see this issue from the survivor's perspective: "I am already shaky. My grip on my internal experience is fragile. I am afraid to add something that may make me feel even more out of control than I already feel." If one's bodily state or moods already feel out of control, fluctuating and foreign, then adding a new variable into the equation seems unbearable. The therapist must be knowledgeable about medication and its side effects, aware of how long it takes for the main effect and side effects to show up, and willing to consult actively and coach the client on what to expect, how to wait out the typical cycles, how to pace the doses, and so on.

The abhorrence of medication that is so common with survivors may be a replication of the "I'll go it alone without help" attitude that had such survival value in childhood. Many a survivor, betrayed by potential helpers, had to become a "fortress of self." Any reaching out for help, from entering therapy to feeling less depressed through medication, feels like breaching a stone wall. This reluctance may also reflect shame (taking medication as a sign of inadequacy). All these issues have to be explored and worked with if medication is to be a useful support to the healing process.

Since I am not a biological psychiatrist, I don't share the belief that psychotropic medication is curative or even always helpful. On many occasions, I have witnessed the overuse of psychotropic medications by zealous psychiatrists who confused biological psychiatry with scientific fact. Despite the claims for medications like Prozac (Kramer, 1993), I have not witnessed any major personality transformations brought about by the use of such drugs. But I have seen survivors move from having *nowhere to stand*, because they were constantly anxious, depressed, hurting inside, and never able to rely on a stable feeling state, to having enough internal stability and sense of solidity to face the tasks before them.

It is not enough for a consulting psychiatrist to have biological knowledge and a medical stance. Healing is a developmental process. A medical consultant needs to be available as a coach, willing to help adjust dosages and medications with attention to the particular demands of the particular phase of healing that the client is working on. He or she must take the client's increasing self-determination seriously as the client's healing progresses.

Systemic Social Support

The development of systemic social support becomes a crucial issue in the later phases of therapy, when intense and affect-laden material is squarely faced. Social support includes the support of friends, family members and intimate others, co-workers, church groups, and personal physicians, as well as therapy groups, twelve-step programs, and so on. One thing that seems to be characteristic of survivors' history and adaptation is the social isolation wrought by secrecy and familial neglect. Survivors commonly have few friendships, tend to isolate themselves and withdraw under stress or distress, and lack any real network of systemic support for their lives. They appear to act as relatively closed systems, without recourse to the help and support of others.

As a supportive connection develops with the therapist, in the early stages of treatment, the therapist is often the "one and only" in the survivor's world—the only one with whom she can talk, complain, reveal her distress, and derive support. This can be a heavy burden for the therapist, and it does not provide a wide enough base of support for the survivor in the difficult work of therapy. The therapist and the client are often anxious when the client leaves the treatment room; it is as if both were being cast into an abyss of uncertainty between sessions.

Much of the countertransference and burnout for therapists who I have supervised, and for myself in my own work as a therapist, has been indicative of just such a lack of systemic social support in the client's life. This creates a double bind for both the therapist and the client: for the therapist, because it is difficult to encourage new risks or confront the client's blind spots when this will invariably be felt as "betrayal"; for the client, because she begins to feel excessively dependent on the therapist in a way that may reenact the dependent relationship she had with the abuser or with colluding others. Therefore, the Healing Tasks Model places a premium on developing a variety of systemic and social support in the first phase of healing, to provide a more cohesive framework for the entire healing process. Paradoxically, however, it takes a certain level of risk to move into the social sphere in order to derive support from it. Survivors often cannot afford to take such a risk in the early phase of healing, even if the support that might be gained is potentially great.

Clients at this phase of healing are often too frightened by the thought of facing a whole group of people (fellow survivors or not) to join a group. Their current significant others and friends may be poor choices for revealing sensitive information to or drawing support from, because they may have been chosen out of reenactments, transference, and codependency, or because they resemble the original abusers and are themselves abusive to various degrees. Moreover, at this stage a single "failure" to obtain support can be difficult to tolerate and may be blown out of proportion. This can make the *normal* process of trial and error in developing social support difficult to tolerate and see through.

Still, starting small and finding *one* place in the survivor's life, other than therapy, where he can speak the truth and feel supported in his being a survivor, can assist the healing process immeasurably. This one place can be gradually widened as the client's tolerance permits and as learning is derived from each interaction. This may mean seeing a friend, or going to a self-help group or twelve-step program and simply listening for a time, or beginning to do some reading about abuse that can help him understand that others experience similar symptoms, so that he can begin to understand that he is not unusual or alone in his struggle. It is crucial to build and expand *gradually* the variety of support and the level of risk involved in finding it.

It is also important for the survivor to learn that broad-based support means not putting all his eggs in one basket. Like anyone else, he can expect certain kinds of support from some people and other kinds of support from others. It is neither possible nor desirable for any *one* individual to provide *all* the kinds of support he might need. Some people can listen to memories of abuse, and others cannot. Some can empathize but cannot tolerate actual descriptions. Some people are good for encouraging him to keep on working, and others are good for encouraging him to take a break. With a variety of available support, the survivor has a number of resources to help him manage the healing process and learn to select what he needs at any given moment. This helps counter the scarcity mentality that many survivors carry over from their early experience in families where there were few emotional resources.

The process of healing cannot be adequately held by one or even two individuals; therapy seems to limp haltingly along in these circumstances. The healing tasks are like a pyramid: the wider the base of support, the higher the pyramid can be. This is why, when progress seems stymied in later phases, we often find that we need to return to support-phase tasks and broaden the base so that we can move on. Healing is not just "the resolving of trauma." It is the transformation of the whole context of the person-environment relationship, of the survivor in the personal and interpersonal field.

It is not unusual the for survivor to develop, over time, a kind of "healing family," a network of therapists, physicians, groups, friends, and so on, who provide a healthy frame of support for growth and development. Developmentally, it is much like the "good enough" family of origin that the survivor lacked in childhood, and which should have provided the framework for healthy growth and development. We must learn to respect the client's need to find in others what we ourselves cannot provide, even when it seems confusing because we are used to a one-to-one relationship with clients, and even if it arouses our resentment because of our grandiose wish to be the exclusive source of support for the client. In the early phase of therapy, the therapist encourages development of systemic social support that is *within the survivor's current capacity to handle*.

Initial Reorganizing of the Sense of Reality and Self

This process involves assimilating initial memories or fragments into one's sense of self and into one's perception of one's childhood. This is the task of *reconsolidation* as it appears in the support phase of the healing process. This task is marked by the survivor's sense of self, the "I," now coming to *include* the abuse experience instead of leaving it outside the phenomenological boundaries of the "I" (see Figure 2.2).

This reorganization often results in a paradoxical combination of feelings. There may well be feelings of grief and anger as the reality of the abuse is now accepted and the survivor better understands its impact on his or her life. At the same time, there may be feelings of settling down, diminished struggle, and perhaps even a hiatus during which the survivor feels less focused on the abuse, wanting to "get on with life."

If the childhood abuse has only now come to light, or if it has been ignored or minimized and kept in the background, the whole sense of self and the world must be reconfigured to include the experience as truly real, important, and valid. If we look at "the self" as the figure of our current experience against the ground of what is known to us about our experience over time, then this is truly the establishment of a "new self" in the sense that the ground for this figure is now richer, different from the way it had been conceived, and completely reorganized.

Frequently, an active remembrance of childhood has been

Figure 2.2. Inclusion of Traumatic Memory.

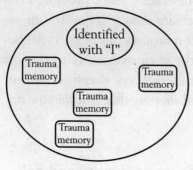

1. Trauma memories are outside the boundary of what is expected as "I" or self.

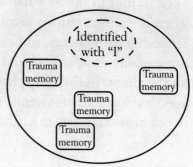

2. The boundary of the "I" becomes more diffuse (hence anxiety and depression) to trauma memory.

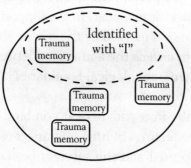

3. Boundary expands to include traumatic memory.

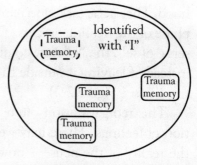

4. "I" boundary firms up as person reconsolidates and adapts to reality or possibility of trauma.

romanticized or idealized, with abuse glossed over, explained away, justified, or completely repressed. Therefore, accepting the reality of the abuse and validating oneself as a helpless child who was the *victim* and not the *cause* of the abuse is not as simple as just "knowing the truth." The whole *structure* of one's beliefs about one's childhood and family, perceptions of others, perceptions and definitions of oneself, and so on, is being reorganized. This process only begins here, and it is returned to again and again throughout the healing process; but it is in this first phase of healing that the initial reconfiguration takes place and is grappled with for the first time.

How do we begin to elicit and formulate the initial picture with respect to the history of abuse? First, we need to understand what this is, and how it may be different for different survivors. For some, it may mean understanding that *something* happened, even if what it was remains unknown, confused, or indefinite. For others, it may mean coming to the acknowledgment and understanding that symptoms have *some* context, even if it is still unknown or unclear, and that the symptoms make sense, or at least have the potential to make sense. For still others, it may mean learning to hold the initial "snapshots," visual or bodily memories, long enough and with enough support to get through the tendencies to deny, distance, and disbelieve. The creative tension of holding the possibility (ground condition) of trauma against the figures of current symptoms, life-style, feelings, and so on, allows for a true reformulation and reconfiguration of the gestalt of oneself. A new meaningfulness emerges, and the self grows.

Although the reconsolidation process can be enormously strengthening to the survivor, it also brings some anxieties. The reality of the abusive history can help bring organization and understanding to previously "irrational" aspects of experience and behavior, but it also brings the existential reality of loss and suffering more fully into awareness. In this way, the assimilation of the abusive reality into the sense of self can precipitate significant depression, especially if the dimension of grief and mourning is not adequately acknowledged by the client and the therapist. The feeling is: "So, now I know what happened to me. How can I bear it?" The interpersonal support and treatment boundaries developed during the first phase of treatment must be drawn on to help the survivor through feelings of mourning for which he may not yet have adequate resources to cope.

Resolution of the Support Phase

As the support phase resolves itself, a number of features begin to stand out. These indicate that some cycle has been completed.

The survivor is now in a very different position from where she started. She has experienced support and validation in the therapeutic relationship. She has learned some basic skills to make her life and her internal experience more manageable. She has, at the very least, a clear sense that *something* happened, that some real events underlie her feelings and symptoms, and that she is not crazy. She has more systemic social support and resources than she has probably ever had in her life. Since her sense of self now *includes* the abuse in some way, we see increased trusting in herself, belief in the validity of her own experience, and we see her supporting the importance and value of getting help for herself and learning to choose support instead of getting by on the bare minimum.

She may now feel more stable (although delicately so) than she has for a while. She is less constantly flooded by flashbacks, and life feels more manageable. She may have reached a plateau. Consequently, she may be very reluctant to dig deeper into her history or deal with anything that could threaten her hard-won and tentative stability. Life is not easy or always pleasant, but it feels "good enough." Some survivors decide at this point to take a break or perhaps terminate therapy. From the perspective of the idealized insistence that we therapists often have to "resolve everything," this backing away from continued work on the trauma could be seen as "resistance," that is, as an avoidance that must be confronted therapeutically so the client can "move on." And certainly, the Healing Tasks Model outlines further stages and progress in therapy beyond the support phase, and so stopping here would not mean that healing was in any way complete. But there are a number of reasons for legitimately supporting a hiatus at the end of the support phase. For one thing, the achievement of all that goes into the support phase and the task of building support is considerable in its own right. It is important to honor this piece of work and not diminish it by insisting that its achievement is insufficient. Insufficient for what? For the therapist's theory? Another reason is that taking a break can be seen within the

Healing Tasks Model as a legitimate self function, which affirms that now it is the *survivor* who has control over the timing and pace of his own stimulation level.

The degree of preexisting self functions and capacities will determine how difficult and how long this reorganization will take. The more resources the survivor has, personally and environmentally, the less difficult and the shorter this reorganization will be. For some, the support phase may take many years; for others, it may be the focus of therapy for only a few weeks or months. For still others, going beyond the support phase may not be possible because of financial or time constraints or factors in the social matrix and milieu: there is enough support to work through the support phase, but not enough to move beyond it.

In general, the more severe the presenting symptoms of the client, and the fewer the personal economic and social resources, the longer the support task will need to remain figural. With more severely dysfunctional or resource-impoverished individuals, those for whom support is mostly absent and difficult to acquire, trust and support may be the predominant concerns for a number of years. The longer time seems directly related to the scarcity of support while they were growing up; they have little fundamental sense of inner or outer security.

With some survivors, the very nature of their adaptation to abuse is what makes the support phase lengthy. In MPD, for example, because the memories of abuse are held by different personalities, and because there are distinct barriers of amnesia between personalities, the whole process of validation and reorganization can be considerably more difficult. The therapist has to contend not just with one person's denial and amnesia but with the denial and amnesia of a whole system of other personalities that are specifically organized to maintain barriers against awareness. Because acceptance of the diagnosis (which implies acceptance of a different version of the "truth" than has been previously held) is crucial to progress in treating MPD (Putnam, 1989) this aspect of the support phase may take some time and effort. Not infrequently, the diagnosis of MPD is not even made until the host personality (the one who is "out" most frequently or who first came for therapy) has achieved, through years of treatment, some measure of support and self functions independent of alters that remain hidden in the background. In this way, the host becomes the ground of support for the alters as they initiate the journey into awareness, by virtue of their own healing (often entirely in-dependent of other alters). It is a bit like having a later-phase survivor in a group of earlier-phase clients: his or her advanced phase of healing provides a model and support for the other mem-bers of the system as they finally venture out to take risks.

These and other conditions make for variations in the length of the support phase from individual to individual. There is no one "right" amount of time, no managed-care allotment of ses-sions for this phase. Adding all the pieces of the clinical picture together, we can make some educated guesses about what will be required for a given individual, as long as we leave room for indi-viduals' creativity, their changing resources and conditions, and the possibility that grace will improve things in ways beyond our control. Tragedy is not the only thing that happens unexpectedly.

Chapter Three

Developing Self Functions

Survivors of abuse may vary quite widely in level of functioning. Some hold demanding jobs, raise families, and deal with the usual stresses of life. Others seem highly intolerant of stress, are easily overwhelmed by feelings, have great difficulty coping with other people, and so on. In other words, survivors vary in the resources with which they can manage their experiences and interactions in the world. In the Healing Tasks Model, these resources and capacities are called self functions. The development of those self functions necessary for a full range of contact is a major part of the middle phase of healing.

Gestalt therapy describes the *self* as that aspect of the organism (person) that organizes, modulates, and experiences the process of contact (contact being interaction at a boundary). In the Gestalt approach, the self is not a structure or an entity as understood in other theories, but rather the *experiencer* and *organizer* of *contact*. To the Gestalt therapist, in this sense, the self is ephemeral and exists *only in contacting*. It has no structural status apart from the here-and-now except as we develop a description of the particular style of contacting over time, this description being called *personality* in Gestalt therapy (Perls, Hefferline, and Goodman, 1951).[14]

The means by which the self organizes, manages, and modulates the process of contact are referred to as the *self functions* (Perls, Hefferline, and Goodman, 1951).[15] The self functions, which will be detailed in this chapter, can be seen as the tools, capacities, abilities, and qualities that we all bring to negotiating our actions and our interactions, managing the intensity of our experiences, and experiencing the sense of self in contact.

An adequate process of child development involves, among many other things, the acquisition of an increasingly various, complex, and sophisticated array of self functions. Given an environment that can organize itself to engage adequately with the child, the child adjusts, experiments, learns, is taught and encouraged, tests, practices, masters, and acquires many different tools and resources with which to meet the environment on behalf of his or her needs and cope with internal experiences (emotions, urges, distress) as they occur. Abusive experiences and traumatic environments, however, can significantly disturb the development or expression of the self functions, so that the child is left without the necessary or sufficient capacities for managing experiences and interactions.

Whether the self functions emerge through the natural genetic unfolding or are learned through contact with the environment, their expression depends on the response of the environmental field. We learn to have personal boundaries if it is permissible to say no, if we can say *stop* when we are being tickled and the tickler stops. We learn that our body is our own being when our bodily privacy and ownership are respected and encouraged. We learn to pace and grade the intensity of our experience when the environment does not flood us with stimulation that we cannot manage, when we are allowed to rest when we need to, and when the environment helps us calm down when we are out of control. We learn to love and care for ourselves and value our person when we are loved and cared for by others, and when loving and caring are demonstrated toward others by our caretakers.

The abusive context is like an infertile, toxic, or untended garden where plants have great difficulty growing properly. Many self functions are not learned, or they are learned incompletely in an infertile environment for learning. Trauma and abuse are frequently part of a larger developmental and familial or community context of neglect. This context may include insufficient material or emotional resources; chronic overstimulation in some areas (sexuality, noise, violence, motor behavior) and understimulation in others (perceptual discrimination, cultural stimulation, soothing); lack of consciousness among adults and others of a developing child's needs for interaction, experiment, and engagement; a narcissistic family system that sees family members as existing only to supply gratification for those in power; and so on.

Children are "learning machines" and will creatively adapt themselves to the demands and exigencies of the environment. In the process, they will develop self functions that match the demands of this kind of environment, and they will not learn those that are not supported. Instead of learning about boundaries, the child may find it more functional and adaptive to disconnect from his body and learn dissociation, endurance, and numbing as self functions. Instead of learning that emotions can be graded events, she learns that emotions are felt and expressed only as extremes. Instead of learning to engage actively and directly with others on behalf of his own needs, he learns to nurture and care for others in the hope (usually vain) that they will reciprocate. Instead of learning that she can make choices about the intensity and pacing of stimuli, she learns to expect overstimulation, to numb out and dissociate rather than decline engagement in overwhelming situations.

It should come as no surprise that the survivor, grown up, will have difficulty negotiating and managing experience in any environment that places new and different demands for contact on him. We all tend to seek environments that match the self functions we have. Why should we expect survivors, whose resources may allow them to engage only with environments that do not respect boundaries, are overstimulating, and are emotionally extreme, to seek out environments and relationships that are different from what they have known? When survivors manage, as they often do, given their innate striving for growth and change, to find environments that do not replicate their childhood environments, they must meet these "brave new worlds" with tools and resources that are not well shaped to the current demands. That is why the therapeutic environment has to be a place of experiment, engagement, and practice, where new self functions can be acquired and added to the repertoire of those that were learned in the context of trauma.

Abuse and abusive experience can also take self functions that are in the process of development and drive them underground, truncating and distorting their development. For example, the development of motor competence can become disjointed at the age of significant trauma if the child who is trying to master motor skills must dissociate from bodily life in order to manage the experience of physical intrusion from rape or beatings. It is not uncommon for survivors to experience themselves as uncoordinated or physically clumsy because of this kind of bodily dissociation.

Similarly, emotions that were accessible at one point, such as anger or hurt, may have become alienated and repressed if their expression would have endangered the child: "I'll give you something to cry about."

These repressed or truncated self functions are like missing steps on a stairway. They are unavailable when they are needed and appropriate in the present. The survivor often experiences them as holes in functioning. A cherished pet dies, but the survivor cannot feel sad or cry. A co-worker acts rudely, but the survivor feels frozen, unable to say anything. Some survivors find themselves numb and unfeeling in such circumstances. Others have a narrow repertoire of permissible feelings: one emotion (say, sadness) may become the outlet for all the others that are repressed; no matter what is fundamentally being felt, tears and sadness are the only outlet, even if the original feeling is anger, shame, frustration, or something else. Feelings may also be expressed only indirectly and passively, since direct expression was experienced as profoundly dangerous. Anger and aggressive feelings, for example, may be seen in passive-aggressive behavior. Hurt and shame may be detected indirectly, in the survivor's avoidance of certain interactions and situations. Love and longing may appear only as gruff sarcastic comments; the need for boundaries, in bodily tension and closed-off postures.

Survivors may also be seen by others as "choppy" or "missing in action" at certain points in relationship and contact. They may start relationships well but back off and withdraw as demands for intimacy increase. They may avoid confrontation or differentiation in relationships. By contrast, they may feel connected only through conflict, finding themselves at a loss for softer, warmer ways of connecting with others.

Survivors themselves make choices of directions they will take and those they will not. Often these choices take the form of vows: "I will never . . . " or "I will always . . . ." These statements outline one pole that will be allowed and the pole that will be disallowed. One incest survivor vowed that no one would ever take advantage of her again, and so she assumed a consistent stance of mistrust and suspicion, no matter what anyone ever actually did. This stance, of course, colored all her relationships, so that otherwise trustworthy and well-meaning acquaintances would eventually give up on her as a friend. She had no idea of what would constitute trust, no idea of how to tolerate the normal risks of forming new relationships, so that the small betrayals and disappointments common to intimate bonds could become survivable and normal. Her building of self functions—tolerating difficulties in relationships, becoming aware of her habitual contact stance, sorting out her projections from actual here-and-now reality, learning to appreciate how the current range of available behavior and affects with acquaintances was different from that of her family of origin—contributed to her being able eventually to undo her vow and begin to make more differentiated responses to others.

Another survivor vowed as an adolescent that he would never mistreat others, since he himself had been so badly mistreated. Consequently, he developed into an exceptionally kind, helpful, serving, and caretaking man who could not bring himself to acknowledge anything critical or negative about anything or anyone.

He became stuck in his healing when his development began to require more aggression (for confronting his memories and differentiating himself from his abuser) than he could allow himself. Likewise, his relationships faltered when they demanded the ability to differentiate himself from his lovers, friends, and bosses and stand up for himself. It was a significant challenge for him to learn that *difference* is not *violence*, that disagreement can actually stimulate a relationship rather than harm it, and that aggression could help him find his own inner strength and power without having to hurt others. This kind of learning was deeply at odds with the ways in which difference, disagreement, and aggression had been used in his family of origin. It was almost inconceivable to him that aggression could be used to support his healing and not also to harm someone else.

All the usual adaptational modes (repression, fantasy, dissociation, desensitization, and retroflection) leave the survivor at a loss as her development and healing proceed. As a child, in the service of psychic and physical survival, she used the resources available to her at her level of development when the abuse occurred (van der Kolk, 1987). These resources were often so powerfully effective at the time that they tended to take precedence over the more sophisticated and differentiated self functions that ordinarily would have developed later in life as she and her world became more complex. That is why these adaptations have such strength of persistence. We cannot expect the survivor to change ways of being that have worked so well for her in desperate conditions unless we have first helped her to develop new resources in the present and a sufficient sense of support. We must validate both her need for survival, from the past, and the realities of the present, which require new and creative solutions.

Adequate self functions allow us to manage our experience of self and other in a way that finds the proper balance between inner and outer. Without sufficiently developed and differentiated self functions, psychotherapeutic work with memories and feelings overwhelms and retraumatizes the survivor, since he faces the task of remembering without any more choices than he had when the abuse originally occurred. The development and refinement of self functions goes hand in hand with the uncovering and working through of traumatic memories. The self functions outlined in this chapter[16] are those that most often require development in the course of healing from childhood abuse.

Boundary Functions

In the course of normal development, children experiment with and come to learn how to manage their contact at the interpersonal boundary with others. With a reasonably supportive and responsive environment, they learn that they have a "yes" and a "no," and the limits of both. They learn how to negotiate interpersonal contact to get what they need, and they learn that they have some measure of self-determination over their physical space and bodily boundaries.

Important work in therapy is to establish control and skill in relation to interpersonal and bodily boundaries. For the most part, this work is best conducted in experimental situations, which develop from what is observed in the here-and-now contact between client and therapist. But it is also done by coaching the survivor through interactions with those who are part of his current life situation. Sometimes it can be done directly with those others, during the therapy hour. At other times, it takes the form of consultation or role playing.

Abusive trauma is, by definition, an assault on the boundaries—physical, emotional, personal—of the self. The abused child is given a number of messages about interpersonal process: about what happens in interaction with powerful others; about the right to control and protect her own bodily boundaries and body functions; about her right to say yes or no to others and be responded to as if her voice mattered. These messages teach her that interpersonal contact is by nature problematic and overwhelming and can be controlled only through indirect means, if at all.

One client, who had been a victim of incest, prostitution, beatings, and other violence from the age of two, had hardly any sense of her boundaries in any domain. She could not say no to her children, and as a result she was overwhelmed by their demands. She was verbally, physically, and sexually assaulted by her husband. She was easily taken advantage of by friends, for whom she would do boundless favors. She had adjusted to her traumatic circumstances by developing multiple personalities. Any aggression within her, which might have supported better boundaries (but which, in childhood, would have brought about retribution) was turned against herself through the mediation of alters modeled after the original perpetrators. This adaptation was her attempt to control her own behavior preemptively and so perhaps avoid the exacerbation of boundary violations. In other words, since she had not been able to control her environment and stop the abuse, she became self-punishing through the medium of these punitive, abusive alter personalities, as if she might be able to control abuse by others by becoming self-controlling enough, careful enough, quiet enough, and so on. This retroflective strategy can even give a child an illusion of control over the abuse, but the control actually rests in the hands of the perpetrators. This client's endless accommodations and turning of aggression against herself left her vulnerable to further abuse, without the skills or aggressive energy to have well-bounded relationships with others in the present.

Boundary Concerns by Phase

Therapeutic work often starts with the adult survivor both seeking help or support and feeling highly vulnerable, self-protective, cautious, and therefore quite reticent. Initial boundary questions in the support phase take these forms: Am I safe here? Will you hurt me? Do I have the right to say yes or no to your interventions? Will the price of therapy be my giving up my bodily boundaries to you? In other words, is the therapeutic environment going to be as assaultive or as little in my control as the original abusive environment was? Sad to say, some survivors have had previous ther-apy that did indeed replicate the abusive trauma, in terms of boundaries. The replication may range from intrusive interpreta-tions to confrontive methods or premature emphasis on abreac-tion to sexual exploitation by the therapist. These particular concerns appear first in the support phase of the healing process, but they are often revisited and reviewed later on as well. In the support phase the survivor is typically anxious about boundaries (or their absence) but must depend on the therapist to have clear boundaries and to help articulate boundary concerns as they ap-pear in the background. In the phase of developing the self func-tions, the survivor is engaged in the process of becoming aware of how he manage his boundaries, and in learning and practicing new skills in this regard. In the phase of undoing, redoing, and mourning, the survivor takes the new capacities and skills he has now acquired and uses them more fully. He reclaims what has been left behind in the past, confronting the full meaning and weight of what was done to him and engaging with the perpetra-tors on behalf of his self-integrity.

The specific boundary issues will differ from person to person but often include developing awareness of boundaries and bound-ary space, learning the ways in which one can be more open or more closed to interactions by noticing behavioral and nonverbal signals, and acquiring the right and ability to say no.

Negotiation of Interpersonal Boundaries

Survivors of abuse, because of the pattern of the boundary assaults that they have experienced at the hands of powerful others, often have had to develop rather polarized ways of managing contact at the interpersonal boundary. These modes of contacting (Wheeler, 1991) often become stereotyped, in the sense of becoming rigidly applied, without regard to the actual environment. They make for problems in interpersonal relationships, as well as unsatisfying con-tact. To be protected in one context may mean being unavailable (and therefore starved) in another. To give over control of one's person, because in one context there was no choice, may mean being perpetually vulnerable to further abuse even when choices are available.

Some survivors have learned to use aggression and anger as an impenetrable wall. Having had their boundaries violated without hindrance, they now let nothing close. They automatically reject attempts at contact, saying no to almost everything even before they know what is being offered. This strategy is particularly common among male survivors, who may use the culturally acceptable norms of male behavior (being insulated, aggressive, distant, unfeeling) to create a protective shield around an otherwise wounded and damaged little boy.[17] But female survivors also use this mode, of course, mobilizing anger and defensiveness to ward off any potentially hurtful contact, just as a male survivor may assume the passive stance and surrender himself to others. The therapist's job is to look for opportunities (and readiness) to generate awareness of the survivor's way of negotiating interpersonal boundaries, and then to develop experiments that help to develop skills and choices along a *continuum*, so that the survivor is not stuck in a limited and polarized mode.

I noticed with one woman, over the course of our work together, that whenever I suggested an alternative to some choice she was making, she automatically put herself down and elevated my suggestion to the status of law: "I don't have very good judgment. Of course you know the best way to proceed." When I tried to point out her way of meeting different opinions (during the support phase), she could only use it as further evidence of her failure, promising to do better next time. In other words, she experienced my observation only within a context of support, as a threat of *withdrawal* of support, and tried to modify herself rather than engage with the environment at the boundary. This was very much the way she had needed to behave as a child, since truly engaging with others on her own behalf was virtually impossible and only called down more abuse on her. No amount of my pointing this out had any impact, not because she was "resistant" to my interventions (although at times I had a difficult time recognizing this) but because of her developmental and our relational level. Until her sense of being supported and accepted by me could provide the holding environment for her to begin affirming and accepting herself, observations and feedback that differentiated or demanded difference could be experienced only as rejection or disapproval. Her self-other boundary was diffuse and dependent on the other's orientation toward her.

As she moved into the phase of self functions, she was finally able to hear my observations as interesting rather than critical. Since she knew that she had "problems with self-esteem," in a general sense, she could begin to appreciate that if she put herself down every time someone in a power relationship differed with her opinion, she could not possibly come away from such interactions feeling good about herself. These instances occurred first with me in therapy, and then (through "homework") in relation to others in her life. We directed her awareness to all the instances in which she tended to diminish herself in relation to others. She began to recognize this pattern as her way of adapting to a powerfully controlling and abusive father, who demanded that his family agree with his "father knows best" opinions, harshly criticizing and shaming anyone in the family who tried to hold a different view. She would not have the resources to confront this "retroflected core" by challenging her father (through therapeutic enactment or otherwise) until she could have the experience of meeting me and others in her *current* world without diminishing herself. Boundaries can be developed in the here-and-now of current life.

As this client became more able to catch herself at the moment of self-diminishment, we began to explore other choices she might wish to make, such as when she held an opinion different from mine. We generated a continuum of responses, ranging from "Your opinion must be better than mine," to "How interesting, let me hear what your opinion has to offer me," to "We have two opinions here, let's discuss them," to "I'd like to hear your view, Jim, but I don't think you've really listened to mine sufficiently yet," and so on, all the way to her father's absolute "Only what I think counts around here."

We might think of this as a rough continuum of statements marking out the polarities of rigidly self-bounded egotism and self-diminishment (see Figure 3.1). Needless to say, actually trying these statements out in interactions with me was more difficult for her than it sounds, since anything other than self-diminishment was a violation of the family taboo. Historically, it had brought about severe punishment and the risk of humiliation and shaming. The safe environment in therapy, and the trust we had developed in the support phase, allowed her to experiment with more of a range. Our marker of progress on this front was the time when, in response to my offering completely unsolicited advice about something or other, she said, "You know, Jim, I don't think I asked for your opinion about that." All I could do was acknowledge her correction. The client's growth requires adjustments from the therapist as well!

Figure 3.1. Continuum of Boundary Statements in an Experiment.

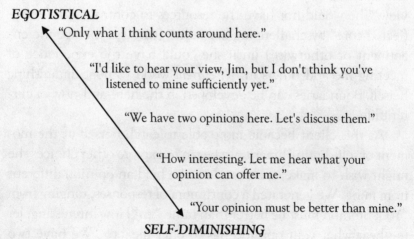

EGOTISTICAL

"Only what I think counts around here."

"I'd like to hear your view, Jim, but I don't think you've listened to mine sufficiently yet."

"We have two opinions here. Let's discuss them."

"How interesting. Let me hear what your opinion can offer me."

"Your opinion must be better than mine."

SELF-DIMINISHING

Bodily Boundaries

In a previous work (Kepner, 1987), I described the importance of bodily space and bodily boundaries. The assault on the bodily self that abuse entails leaves the victim with few options for control and ownership of the physical space around him or of his bodily self. Survivors adapt with a number of approaches. One will virtually leave his body and completely give it up and so feel ungrounded, unsupported, and spacey. Another will give up the surface, the skin and the musculature, and retreat inside, to somewhere deep in the bodily core. Still another will harden the musculature into a seemingly impenetrable shell or encase himself in fat, creating a fixed *structural* boundary in place of more adaptable (but less automatically reliable) *boundary-setting behavior*, such as the kinds of movement and expression that were denied to them in the abusive context.

In keeping with the style of adaptation, I try to work with clients on discovering, experimenting with, and reclaiming their bodily boundaries, just as we experiment with and develop the interpersonal boundaries. With one woman, I was able to observe how she would withdraw and collapse when anyone moved toward her. For example, once when I leaned toward her abruptly, in order to pick up the box of tissues and give it to her when she had been crying, she quite visibly wilted, curling her shoulders over her chest, dropping her head, and bringing her legs slightly up to become concave as she faced me. She was literally retreating from her bodily surface and from her boundary with me.

After exploring this adaptation and validating its context— the way she had needed to retreat from her mother's beatings—we began to experiment with what it would be like for her to maintain her posture in the face of someone's being physically close. Our experimenting led to some insight into a discomfort she had felt about her co-workers' always being "too close." She had been unable to see her postural retreat as a signal that she required more space. Her retreat was the literal giving up of her personal space;

the thought that she might be able to claim her own bodily space was impossible. Because she trusted me enough to know that I would not harm her, we were able to develop gradual and graded experiments with this essential self function.

First, we intentionally set up situations (experiments) in which I would move toward her and "provoke" her postural retreat, but slowly enough so that she could begin to feel and own more fully *what* she did and feel *when* she was doing it. She could begin to feel her fear, which, in the automatic quality of the process, she had not noticed before, and then she was able to coach herself through this moment by noting the difference between the present and the past: "This is Jim. He is not my father. I am not in danger. It's okay." Second, we explored how she could support herself physically so that she did not collapse (which inevitably left her feeling weak and ineffectual) and retreat from her bodily boundary (which left her feeling spacey and disconnected). I was able to help her develop ways of breathing that kept her energy and sense of inner strength up. I taught her about posture, practiced new stances with her, and worked with her to claim and own her proximal bodily space—to establish the basic sense of an "I" rooted in her physical being, which *included* her skin and was expansive in nature. Eventually, this work supported further experiments with her bodily boundaries, so that she could begin to claim the more distal space (Kepner, 1987, p. 169) around her, using posture, stance, breathing, and eye contact to meet the other *before* he or she came too close for comfort. We also generated experiments in which I would walk gradually toward her across the room, and she would stand her ground rather than collapse. At one point, she found that she was now actually able to use her arms and hands, not just to protect herself as she recoiled but to push outward with a truly expansive energy and breath as she confronted my approach. To my surprise, and hers, she pushed me all the way across the room with her vigorous claiming of her space. Having asserted these self functions in the therapy environment, she was amply prepared for the later work of undoing in therapy, where she would take her hard-won skills and use them to sym-bolically confront her abuser on behalf of the victimized child whom she could now defend.

With another survivor, after I commented that he appeared un-comfortable, he was able to admit that he felt I was sitting too close to him. Since his chair was against the wall, he felt he had no choice but to tighten up and brace himself from the "assault" of my prox-imity. That he should attempt to solve his problem through retroflection was not surprising, since he had experienced little abil-ity to influence his environment as a child, and to do so would have brought shaming and punishment from his father. It was an indica-tion of the safety we had established together that he could risk admitting his discomfort to me. We began to experiment with ex-ploring and manipulating the space of the room and his distance from me to suit his level of comfort. I suggested that he try sitting in different parts of the room—near the door, at the far end of the room from me, across from my desk, and so on. I tried to start with what was natural to him: to affect himself first. Then he was able to experiment with returning to his chair and telling *me* where to sit, how far to move my chair, and so on. Over time, this work was generalized into other environments where he tended to take what had been given to him in terms of personal space rather than shape the environment to support his own comfort.

The kinds of experiments generated in the here-and-now of the therapy room, in carefully graded ways, must also be extended to "homework" situations, so that the client can experiment with using these self functions where they count: in personal and work relationships. With the first client, we developed a process for her to observe how her co-workers used body language and posture to regulate their interpersonal space. As she developed a bodily "vo-cabulary" of interpersonal boundary setting, she began to try these stances and gestures herself and experiment with them. This was not always easy, since she often felt that she was doing something wrong and bad by establishing any kind of boundary with others. It was only from a position of strength, from her having developed some boundaries in the belief that this was a good direction for her, that she was able to appreciate how she had been deprived of this sort of growing up and could begin to marshal some genuine anger to strengthen her claim to her bodily self.

The second client began to pay attention to those times when he felt himself collapsing in on himself. He looked at how he could reshape the environment to get more physical space: rearranging his seat, using his books and magazines at library tables to claim his share of space, and so on. Eventually, his capacity to claim space for himself put him into a position where he felt he could afford to explore how to deal with his own response of collapsing. Now we could truly direct ourselves toward his claiming his bodily space as his own, since he had a place to exist within the physical environment. This was a challenging task, since he had to begin confronting his abuser (in symbolic terms), who held title of ownership over his body. In other words, to avoid retreating from his own bodily boundaries meant claiming his body back from the abuser to whom he had given over control of its surface. We see how development of one self function leads to the need and ability to develop the next and more complex level.

With those who present an overbounded stance (rigid and tense musculature, or thick layers of body fat or muscular armor), the work that will allow them to afford some softening and safe human contact will also involve graded experiments. Many such survivors are in fact underbounded. They use such physical structures in place of behavioral skills. Others do have the skills to establish bodily and interpersonal boundaries, but they do not know how or when to let them open. For these clients, the ability to discern clearly when someone is safe must be developed before they can learn to lower the shields that are always up as a matter of policy.

One such woman, who had been persistently tortured and sexually abused over many years as a child, finally was able to stop the abuse only by becoming "big enough" through physical maturation and obesity. In a rage, she assaulted the family member who was abusing her and ended the abuse. Needless to say, the success of this strategy became a major mode of adaptation for her (not that she learned to physically assault others, although some survivors do adopt this mode, and their survivorship is seen only through their interactions with the criminal justice system). Nevertheless, she had learned that mobilizing her anger and keeping a thick bodily boundary kept others at a safe distance. Her mode of operation was to challenge authorities, vigorously establish her presence in any group in which she found herself, and maintain a thick and well-protected bodily boundary through fat and thick, slablike, heavy musculature, making it difficult for others to get close to her. Over the long course of her work in therapy, her chaotic and confused life began to settle down through the development of support and the gradual working through of memories. We began to discover dissociated personalities who both harbored memories of abuse and maintained her anger and rage, so that it could be available for her survival. As these personalities were gradually able to accept support from me, they were eventually able to experiment with learning the difference between safe people and unsafe people and redirect their anger at the abusers of the past, rather than projecting it onto difficult or unpleasant people in the present. The client explored body-oriented work to learn to soften her musculature and find different modes of physical being. Her work in therapy, along with spiritual pursuits that valued acceptance of others and an open heart, developing friendships, and a love relationship, encouraged her to learn how to soften her body, let down her physical shielding, and learn to tolerate bodily sensations of softness and vulnerability. She has not lost her ability to be angry and bounded when she needs to be, but she no longer uses this mode as her central or exclusive way of operating. She now deeply values operating from a more loving and open stance.

Boundary Functions and the Perpetrator

As survivors begin to improve their boundaries with others, the question of confronting the perpetrators of their abuse may arise.

The literature on survivors (for example, Bass & Davis, 1988) has sometimes left the impression that confronting one's abuser is a necessary step in healing, and that it should be done relatively early in the process. Some survivors may indeed feel a strong urge to confront their abusers as if to test their newly acquired boundaries with the primary object of their concern. My orientation to this question, however, is that it is certainly *not* necessary to everyone's healing, although particular survivors may determine that it is important to their own. I use a key criterion in exploring the question of confrontation with survivors who bring it up: *their feeling of the confrontation's importance to them must not depend on any expectation of a response from the abuser.* The act of confronting the abuser must have value to their healing regardless of the particular response they may get from the abuser.

I hold to this criterion because we cannot predict the kind of response we might get from such a confrontation. In my own experience with clients, only siblings have admitted to perpetrating sexual abuse. Fathers and mothers confronted with sexual abuse have never admitted it, or have justified it, or have blamed the victim. Often, physical abuse has been flatly denied, despite witnesses. In other words, if a survivor is confronting an abuser from some wish to be validated, or in the hope of receiving an apology, then he is setting himself up for deep disappointment. Such a decision should not be based on wishes like these but on mature consideration.

This is also not a decision that should be pushed by the therapist. The client must make up his or her own mind. The question of whether the abuser should or must be confronted has been and remains highly politicized. I have known of therapists who believed that unless an abuser were confronted, the survivor would still be subjecting herself to male dominance and would be unable to "find her power." Survivors have been pushed, on political grounds, to make this decision before they were able to make the decision fully on personal grounds. My belief is that this is an individual choice, not a mandate. What is healing for one may be self-abusive for another.

When this question comes up, it is part of the therapeutic process to examine it carefully. What would be gained by such a confrontation? What are the risks to the survivor? Does she have the support to deal with the possible outcomes? Is she doing it for herself? because of pressure from others? from introjected and thus unassimilated beliefs? Is the decision based on wishful fantasy or on realistic appraisal of the situation?

Most survivors cannot even consider this question until they are in the phase of undoing, redoing, and mourning and have the resources to do expressive work. For some, however, who have adequate support and self functions at this point, the choice to confront an abuser by mail or in person has been important. For one woman, who was working on healing from her mother's physical and emotional abuse, acknowledging the abuse in a letter felt like a crucial act in that she felt that her "let's pretend" relationship with her mother was a constant betrayal of herself. She expected denial from her parents about the cruelty of her mother's actions toward her as a child, but she felt that what was important to her was that *she herself* was no longer going to betray herself by pretending.

Another survivor experienced her family of origin as constantly assaulting her as an adult: they tormented her with frequent phone calls, constant criticism, expectations of caretaking, and shaming comments. She felt that she was continuing to serve as the "doormat" that she had always been in her family. We explored a variety of options, which included distancing from her family, working on confronting instances of shaming, learning to say no to demands, and so on. For her, the thought of engaging in constant warfare in order to reclaim her integrity from the family felt not worth the benefits; it would be too draining. Confrontation also felt like more than she had resources to cope with at this time. Instead, she chose to disengage gradually and distance herself from her family, so that over time the interactions became less frequent and shorter. This gave her the space in which to heal and focus on herself for a change. The question of confronting her abuser could be left until she had the wherewithal to consider it properly.

Experiencing Functions

The abused child is often at an age when the nervous system is not able to cope with high levels of stimulation. Therapy itself, despite its healing intent, can become a source of overstimulation and recreation of the intensity and flooding of experience inherent in the original trauma.

Survivors characteristically have little sense of stimulation along a *continuum* (a little, some more, a lot, too much). Instead, stimulation may feel like a binary phenomenon: off/on, overwhelmed/numb, pleasure/pain, hyperkinetic/asleep. This makes it difficult to have middle-range experience and therefore a normal, *average* life. It is crucial for survivors to learn to manage and determine the pacing and intensity of their stimulation and experience, and it is essential for therapists to pay attention to pacing in the process of therapy.

We see indications of the need to develop the experiencing functions when a survivor cannot tolerate groups or crowds without feeling overstimulated or overwhelmed, or when she constantly seeks out experiences that leave her flooded and uncomfortable, or when she overloads herself with survivor literature until it feels as if all her experience is focused on abuse, or when she holds three jobs and never has time for rest and recuperation. We also see these indications in poor tolerance of stress and in the constant need for withdrawal. In therapy, we see these indications when the survivor (or the therapist, for that matter) constantly pushes to remember and abreact, even when all the other indications are that she is deteriorating or becoming less functional, or when work on abuse displaces other necessary directions in therapy (such as, for example, the strengthening of *present* relationships), or when the client becomes fearful and avoidant of coming to sessions because the work is too grueling.

Pacing and grading involve the self functions available to the individual survivor and the way in which the therapist-client dyad makes choices about how much to do in any given period: how fast to work, the level of intensity at which to work, when to take breaks, what kind of material to work on. From the perspective of the Healing Tasks Model, it is considered crucial for the survivor to learn that experience can be *managed*, that choices can be made about the pace of experience, that taking a break is a legitimate *choice*, not just "avoidance," and that the process of therapy, unlike the abuse, is *his* to determine.

There is no question that, for the full process of healing, memories must be recovered and worked through. But recovering and working through will take place in the larger context of becoming a functional person; they will not become the predominant focus of treatment. Memory work *must* take place in the context of the person, not the other way around. The survivor must be able to be "bigger than" the memory, so that the memory is recovered and assimilated to herself; otherwise, she experiences herself as smaller than the memory. She feels as if she is being absorbed into it, overwhelmed by it. Self functions that allow the survivor to choose and manage experience help make truly healing memory work possible.

Grading of experience has to do with choices about what *level of difficulty or intensity* (Zinker, 1977) one is ready and supported to experiment with at any given time. *Pacing* has to do with the *rhythm and frequency of work* on an issue. Zinker has described grading in terms of choices about the level of intensity of a given experiment, but it is not so much a feature of experiment as it is the human capacity to manage the quality of experience at the boundary, particularly with regard to anything novel. Since an experiment is by nature novel, a "safe emergency" (Perls, Hefferline, and Goodman, 1951) that allows growth and change, grading and pacing are both essential to the experimental process, as Zinker points out. They are what make the "emergency" of the experiment safe enough to take a risk with. In Healing Tasks work with survivors, grading and pacing as relevant growth issues are themselves the figure for experiment, not just background structures that support the development of experiments.

Grading is about making choices that influence the *intensity* of an experience: how stimulating it is, what is too much, what is too little, and what supports are needed to increase the gradation of stimulation without feeling overwhelmed. These are often difficult choices in therapy about the balance between avoiding things that seem too difficult and frightening or flooding oneself with too many intense and difficult things (e.g., memories).

Survivors of abuse often have not learned reasonable norms for grading their experience. They may have come from environments where family interactions alternated between high-stimulation abuse and violence, on the one hand, and uncaring isolation, on the other. The nature of abuse means that the survivor was personally flooded with overwhelming experience when her own bodily and emotional boundaries were violated. Survivors frequently learn to seek highly stimulating experiences as an adaptive mode, to keep from feeling what they are carrying inside. Overwork, drug and alcohol use, promiscuous sex, and danger-seeking activities are examples. Some survivors also feel distressed enough to jump into deep, intense work on troubling memories or symptoms, in the hope that by doing so they will "get it over with." But what they actually do is replicate the flooded, overstimulated environment that they are trying to recover from. Survivors must learn to make choices about what, at any given time, they have the internal and environmental support to address without retraumatizing themselves. This is a self function that must be developed before abreactive work can become manageable and assimilable.

In the support phase of healing, I teach survivors how to manage intense experiences through breathing, relaxation, and grounding skills. My concern is that they learn to have control over stimulation, whether from memories, difficult affects, noise, or confusion, without having to resort so much to dissociation, numbing, or repression. As we move into the middle or self-function phase, I try to work with survivors to move beyond moment-to-moment management of stimuli, helping them determine how they have shaped their adaptive patterns in general to being overwhelmed and overstimulated. At any rate, survivors often seek out overwhelming experiences, and they do not see this behavior as a *choice*. But what is truly healing is not doing more, faster. *What is truly healing is to treat oneself better than one's abuser did*, by doing what is just right for one's own organism.

As for pacing, teaching survivors how to perceive and respect their natural rhythms of experience, instead of making choices from fear or other-directed motivations, is one of the essential healing tasks. Apart from the often unpredictable course of major traumas themselves, the family environment may have been chaotic and unpredictable as well, leaving the survivor without the capacity to regulate experience other than through dissociation or desensitization.

The therapist needs to be attuned to the incipient signs that the client is "full," and the focus of the work needs to be shifted to other areas while a particular unit of work is absorbed. Clients coming in "resistant" to an ongoing piece of work, or beginning to blunt their affect about a theme that has been affect-laden, are often giving signs that they are "stuffed to the gills" and need to move away from the topic for a period. As a supervisor of therapists working with survivors, I have frequently seen therapists become polarized and pushy on this issue, labeling such hesitation in the client as "resistance" and not recognizing it as a signal that pacing needs to be attended to. These signals occur indirectly because for the survivor they have never been linked before to an available choice: to take a break, do something different, say no, slow down and digest. Initially, the therapist is the only reference point for the client about what is "normal" grading and pacing. Therefore, it is crucial that the therapist attend to the relevant countertransference issues that need to be managed. The therapist who needs the client to feel better quickly, or who needs to be "successful," may push the client to increase the pace and intensity of the work when this would not be healthy.

Attention to grading and pacing gives us a wide range of choices in therapy about how to approach work on abuse and other issues. One survivor described her abuse memories metaphorically, as "an unexploded bomb in the middle of a field." From her perspective, we needed to move in and work with these memories in order to "defuse" them. But every time we approached the memories, she would become extremely anxious and dissociative, and this would affect her detrimentally between our sessions. Finally getting the picture, I told her that the bomb squad would never approach an unexploded bomb directly. Rather, the squad would walk around the perimeter of the field and view the bomb from all sides, through binoculars, only gradually moving in on it, until there was enough knowledge to move more directly and confidently.

This became the guiding metaphor for our work. We paid a lot of attention to signs and signals that we had approached too closely or too directly: overwhelming anxiety, dissociation, numbing of feelings, and so on. Reading these signals, we would back off, change the topic for a bit, find less direct ways to talk about the subject, and so on, until she settled down enough to make an approach again. This way of working appears to take more time than a direct abreactive approach, but it taught her some essential skills. She learned to see her "symptoms" as signals of her self-regulation needs. She learned that she could *determine* her own actions, and the subsequent intensity of her feeling states, and she began to discern the difference between passive avoidance of difficult material and active management of working with it. When we eventually got to the center of the field and entered into the core memories, our caution and care were validated. These turned out to be truly horrific memories of being used for child prostitution. It was clear that without the skills and self functions she had learned along the way as we "circled the field," she would not have been able to face and hold such devastating memories.

Self-Support Functions

These involve the necessary skills and attitudes involved in self-esteem, self-care, self-concern, self-consideration, and so on. In normal development, by virtue of the care and support of the adults around us, we learn to care for ourselves, feel good about ourselves, and have a sense of self-worth and importance. Developmentally, this is learned later than obtaining support from another. Out of this come the behavioral manifestations of self-support: standing up for oneself, resting when tired, eating when hungry, being able to self-soothe and self-comfort when others are not available, being nice to oneself, and so on.

Quite typically, survivors of abuse have great difficulty giving themselves support in even the simplest ways. The abusive environment often offered no models of caring or conveyed the clear message that the survivor's needs were unimportant compared with the needs of others. Often, only compulsive means of self-soothing are available: overeating, drug and alcohol use, overspending, and so on. In the healing process, self-care is learned through relationship (introjection and assimilation of the therapist's support) and through the undoing of the abusive pattern enacted on oneself.

Self-support requires the capacity to experience the bodily sensations that signal the need for self-care and self-support and allow those sensations to become figural. For example, one client did not notice any signals of hunger (although he was by no means anorexic) until they were extreme and he had been cranky and irritable for some time. At the end of our sessions, I would have to suggest that he pay attention to his hunger and follow up by going to a restaurant. Over time, he learned to attend to and understand his internal signals of needing food, as well as attention and comfort.

Self-support also requires the valuing of one's needs highly enough to act on them. When survivors have been traumatically shamed and diminished, particularly as very young children and infants, they may experience themselves as insignificant and not worth attending to. Here, the gentle process of experiencing the therapist's caring and concern over long periods of time eventually forms the basis for returning to the environment the shame and humiliation that were introjected and mistaken for oneself.

Feeling Functions

The ability to experience a range of affect is an essential self function. Working with affects in the support phase, we emphasized tolerating and managing feelings by using available support and developing some basic self functions. The emphasis in the self-functions phase of therapy is on *experiencing* feelings rather than expressing them (which is more the issue in the undoing, redoing, and mourning phase). Until feelings can be experienced without overwhelming the survivor and reenacting the original trauma that created the need to dissociate or blunt the feelings, strong expression of feelings is damaging rather than healing.

To cope with the original trauma, the survivor often had to give up (retroflect, repress, numb, dissociate, deny) certain feelings, such as pleasure, discomfort, anger, sadness, and fear, or feelings were experienced only in the extreme range. For example, the fear and terror of awaiting the inevitable nighttime visits by an incestuous elder sibling may have been coped with by numbing. Similarly, erotic pleasure, which is not infrequently stimulated physiologically in a young child by an act of rape or other sexual abuse, creates a horrible conflict, which must be dealt with in some form: What does it mean that I feel pleasure when I'm being violated and hurt? This conflict is often coped with by numbing or dissociating from erotic sensations and the pelvis in general, or by becoming fixated on such sensations by identifying with the pleasure and denying the reality of the violation.[18]

In other situations, such as in a chronically chaotic or alcoholic home, emotions came only in extremes: rage, wrenching grief, hysterical laughter, cruelty, spite. Such experiences leave the survivor fearful of his own feeling states, with no experience of the middle range of the continuum: peevishness, sadness, mirth, crankiness. Or the highly charged feeling states brought about by group frenzy in ritual abuse may have been so flooding and disorganizing that the victim disconnected, dissociating into a fugue state or an alter personality.

The reactions were essential to survival, either bodily survival or the survival of the sense of self-integrity, but it also meant losing parts of the self. The dilemma now is that the person cannot function well in his or her current reality with these essential parts of the self unavailable or missing. When sad things happen, the survivor may be blank, unfeeling, and unable to mourn. When a co-worker exhibits mild anger, the survivor may become dissociated. The excitement and energy of the crowd in a baseball stadium may overwhelm the survivor of ritual abuse. The normal tensions of marriage and life in general may feel intolerable, and so relationships and other involvements in life are avoided.

Where therapy is concerned, it is difficult to recover from the trauma of abuse if one cannot tolerate remembering the trauma. When feelings that emerge as memories are retrieved, they are experienced as if they were still just as dangerous as they were in the original trauma. To have a range and continuum of feelings available and included within the "I" allows flexible adaptation and the possibility of both passionate and measured living. In the support phase, our focus with feelings was to teach grounding skills and the use of interpersonal support to help the survivor develop alternatives to dissociating, numbing, or becoming overwhelmed. Now, in the self-functions phase, we are interested in going beyond tolerance and "getting through" feelings. Here, we want to help the survivor *manage* feelings and *assimilate* them, making them *part of the self*. This is a complex task, accomplished only through repeated experiments and working through of the various facets. Besides helping the survivor learn to manage a greater *intensity* of feeling, we want to expand her *range* of available and tolerable feelings, and help her develop more capacity for a *continuum* of feeling intensity that includes the middle range.

The task is one of helping the person ride out the discomfort of the first wave of feeling, differentiate the present from the past as the feeling is experienced, and undo the relevant introjects that maintain the repression. We also experiment with supporting the experience of otherwise avoided feelings when they occur spontaneously.

Feeling as a Wave Phenomenon

One of the essential learnings for survivors is that a feeling, when it is not stopped or impeded, almost always comes in a wave. It has a rise, a crest, a diminishment, and a trough. (See Figure 3.2.) Feeling is a *movement* rather than a state. Abuse-induced feelings, from the child's perspective, seem to go on forever, and the anticipation of a difficult feeling to come leaves the child stuck in a constant feeling state. Therefore, the survivor faces many feelings as if they were constant states, rather than moving and changing phenomena, and when a survivor experiences an emerging feeling that typically overwhelmed him in the abusive situation, he characteristically tries to block and suppress it, usually by holding or modulating his breath, tightening his musculature, and dissociating or distracting himself. The result is paradoxical: the intention is to stop the feeling, but the rising "charge" of the feeling is blocked precisely where its tension is highest. Therefore, the feeling does not peak in the crest, where the tension can be released

Figure 3.2. The Wave of Feeling.

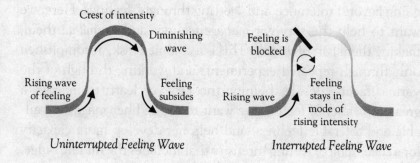

Crest of intensity

Diminishing wave

Feeling is blocked

Rising wave of feeling

Feeling subsides

Rising wave

Feeling stays in mode of rising intensity

Uninterrupted Feeling Wave

Interrupted Feeling Wave

so that the impetus naturally dies off. Feelings that are stopped in this way seem as if they will go on forever, if one lets them occur, because they are only experienced in the mobilizing and energizing part of the cycle rather than the release phase, and their energy seems to build as a pressure. This pressure reinforces the belief that the feeling must be avoided and suppressed, since the survivor has only the experience of difficulty without letup, and not of the full cycle of feeling. (In terms of Gestalt perceptual psychology, we would say that this is an unfinished figure, which carries tension because the survivor naturally wishes to complete it.)

Of course, there is a good reason why the survivor cannot complete this figure and ride out the wave: he lacks the support and the self functions to do so. Useful therapeutic work can be done to help the survivor experiment with using the self functions, developed in the course of the Healing Tasks approach, in the context of riding out the feeling waves. The support of the therapist as coach can help him have faith that the waves can be withstood.

As ocean swimmers know, there are two basic skills in dealing with waves. The first is being able to stand firmly in the sand, letting the wave wash past one while one stays firmly anchored until it has passed, neither trying to push past it nor backing away. The second is being able to ride the swells as the water gets deeper, rather than fighting them tensely—letting them carry one up until one is deposited back down on the sand. Once we have confidence that the survivor can use grounding skills with some facility, we can coach her through moderate experiences of difficult feelings as they occur in the course of therapy: helping her let the wave wash by, while she works to stay grounded, anchored in her body rather than dissociated, learning that she can stay present while the feeling occurs, until it crests and diminishes.

As confidence grows that this work is possible at moderate levels, and as the basic principle of feelings as waves is experienced, we can approach more intense or more traumatically associated feelings. At moderate feeling levels, the bodily sensations of grounding tend to compete with the bodily sensations of the feeling. (This is something like the competitive response relied on in systematic desensitization procedures, but the competing response is grounding and body awareness rather than relaxation.) At more intense levels of feeling, the sensations of the affect are much stronger than the sensations of bodily awareness: the bodily sensations that one is most aware of are those *of* the affect. The grounding work at this point is not to stay anchored while the feeling occurs but rather to stay aware of oneself as a definite presence throughout the experience: to be grounded in the *self* (one's body and personal boundaries remain figural) rather than in one's connection to the environment. The feeling may flood the field of awareness, but the field *includes the self* through bodily awareness, so that there is a thread of continuity, as opposed to the discontinuity of dissociation, numbing, and bodily disconnection.

One client, Dora, had been physically tortured and sexually abused as a child by her mother. Since many of her symptoms took the form of somatic pain and sensations, Dora was very interested in body-oriented work. For quite a long period, we found it extremely helpful. It allowed her gradually to recover more of her bodily experience from the pain of the abuse, to recover and work through her memories of the abuse, and to ease her symptoms. As we continued, however, and particularly as we began to contact bodily areas associated with some of the worst of the torture and abuse, Dora's pattern of improvement began to change. In the course of our work, strong feelings and bodily sensations would flood back, and Dora became dissociative, seeming to enter into her memories of the events and falling out of contact with me and what we were doing. She had little memory of this dissociation at the end of the session. She would leave very spaced out and disconnected, and over a number of weeks she became less and less functional at home and at work.

Clearly, something was not right in the way we were approaching this work, and she brought this up in one session: "Is this supposed to be helpful?" We discussed it, and together we came up with our guess that her dissociation during the work was simply replicating the abuse, not changing it. I suggested that we needed to keep her grounded better during the whole process, so that she could experience being present and feelings and experience could complete themselves while she maintained continuity through them. She was far enough along in the self-functions phase to be capable of this attempt.

As we worked, strong feelings, sensations, and memories began to emerge. We rigorously kept her in contact with her body, in contact with me, and aware of her contact with the ground and the chair or table under her. She was now experiencing stronger feelings, painful bodily sensations, and more intense memories than she had in the past. But she could now sustain her continuity of experience long enough for the wave of feeling and sensation to crest, diminish, and recede. At the end of a session she would be shaken by the memory and strength of the pain she had experienced and filled with sadness at what she had been put through by her mother, but she was not spacey, dissociated, or anxious. Her functioning improved between sessions, and we could continue on the path of reclaiming her body and self from the abuse. With coaching, she was learning to *use* the tools and skills that she was developing in pacing, grounding, and self-support to manage the intensity of her feelings.

Differentiating Present from Past

In the support phase, many survivors experience flashbacks and memories as if they were current events, and they overreact to current situations and stimuli as if they were unconnected to the past abuse. One of the markers that a client has moved midway or farther through the self-functions phase is his having become well enough anchored in his own body and capacity to ground himself in the present that more cognitive work to differentiate past from present can now be useful.

One very helpful Gestalt method is to develop *with the client* a set of "I" statements to use as he experiences a previously intolerable or avoided feeling wave: "When I was a child, my sadness was intolerable because no one was interested. Now, as I feel my sadness, I can see you [the therapist] looking at me with concern, and I can begin to tolerate the sadness." "When I used to feel angry, I had to hurt myself because otherwise I would have been punished. Now I know that I don't have to hurt myself to be safe feeling my anger." "Before, if I had allowed myself to feel my grief, I would have felt hopeless. But now I can allow myself to grieve because I know that I am healing."

Sometimes more exploration will be needed to develop well-grounded statements. The client does not need to have specific memories or full content before experimental statements can be formulated, since our interest is in what fits experientially. The exploration might go something like this:

Therapist: As you talked about that, you seemed to space out a bit. What happened?

Client: I began to feel some anger happening, and then I distracted myself.

T: What was so hard about letting yourself feel anger?

C: It feels impossible.

T: What's impossible about it?

C: If I let myself feel it, I'm afraid I'll feel horribly embarrassed about it.

T: Try "If I was angry growing up, I was embarrassed and shamed about it."

C: I think it's more like "humiliated" than embarrassed or shamed.

T: Try the sentence that way.

C: "If I was angry growing up, I was humiliated." Yes, that's right. It feels right on the money.

T: So, do you have to humiliate yourself now if you feel anger? Would I humiliate you?

C: No, and I know you well enough to know you'd be pleased for me to be able to feel my anger. We've been working on it long enough!

T: So try "When I was angry growing up, I was humiliated, but now as I feel my anger . . . "

C: " . . . I know I'm appreciated, and I can encourage myself. Let me try the whole thing. 'When I was angry growing up, I was humiliated, but now as I feel my anger, I know I'm appreciated and I can encourage myself.'"

T: Breathe more fully now, and let yourself feel whatever anger is still with you.

Of course, not all explorations go so clearly. Sometimes a piece of work develops that takes us away from the initial focus on feelings, to work through some projections or introjects that are part of the dilemma of allowing the feeling to occur:

T: So, do you have to humiliate yourself now if you feel anger? Would I humiliate you?

C: No, but I'm afraid you might think less of me, even though I trust you and I know that's silly.

T: Maybe it's not me you are worried about. Anyone sitting over my shoulder?

Here, we might develop the work more in the direction of undoing the projection of the humiliating parents onto the therapist. Sometimes, just identifying the fact that the client is projecting his parents onto the therapist is enough to free the client to move back toward the feeling experiment. Or we might wish to make a separate place for the parents in the room—say, an empty chair—so that the client can confront the parents' humiliation of him as a child. If this is too direct, the therapist could encourage the client to make some statements about how he feels about his parents' humiliating him, and about whether he is willing to let his parents intimidate him now.

As the parental ghost is brought out of the shadows and identified, we open the possibility of the client's moving back toward the feeling of anger as he confronts his parents through dialogue work, staying with the wave of previously impossible feeling. Although this is technically a piece of "undoing" work, our focus in the latter part of the self-functions phase will be to use the dialogue and the undoing of the projection more as a means of allowing the feeling. We are less concerned here with the amount or fullness of expression or confrontation than with creating room for feeling to emerge, to be tolerated, and to be experienced through the full wave. This is what builds the client's capacity to use the strength of feeling for self-affirmation in the later undoing work, rather than for self-fragmentation, as happens in abreaction-oriented approaches.

Undoing Introjects and Beliefs

As work develops with feelings, significant introjects (fixed beliefs) often need to be worked through and assimilated. Survivors frequently report that if they were to let themselves feel a particular emotion, they would die, hurt people, or go crazy. There is often a core of truth based on the structure of the abuse itself. A survivor of ritual abuse may have been frightened into compliance by seeing others sacrificed if they showed resistance. The survivor may never have experienced anyone around her becoming angry without also seeing someone else physically or emotionally hurt. An affect state may have been so overwhelming as to verge on psychosis in childhood. Or beliefs about feelings may be social introjects (boys don't cry, good girls don't feel pleasure), which can be just as problematic. Perhaps the most prevalent introjects among survivors involve beliefs that one is dirty, worthless, flawed, damaged, fundamentally unacceptable, and so on. There is often a complex of experiences, which may include things said to the child by the abuser while the child was in a state of trauma (trance): You are a slut, you made me do this, you're filthy. The complex may also include feelings related to the abuse (this makes me feel dirty, therefore I am dirty) and child-logic conclusions about the abuse (if I was treated so badly, I must *be* bad). Careful exploration of the nature and origin of such beliefs, and here-and-now work to develop a differentiating experience that can help the survivor destructure the beliefs, will allow for an expanded range of acceptable feeling.

The tools of grading and pacing are essential here as well. Through their application to the dilemma of feelings, the survivor learns that she can *choose* how much and how often to dip into feelings that she had no choice about experiencing during the original abuse. All of this work adds an element of mastery results in expansion of the range of tolerable and survivable feelings. It helps build a larger repertoire or palette of feelings.

Reality-Perception Functions

It is not uncommon for others to experience survivors as overreactive, touchy, and tending to blow things out of proportion. Survivors themselves often note that they respond to current situations in ways that are out of proportion to actual events. They may have strong feelings about someone they hardly know, may find themselves polarizing with others in consistent ways (for example, others frequently are experienced as victimizers, and they themselves are defenders of the weak), or may have an "attitude" that predisposes them to act in certain ways (suspicious, too trusting, angry) toward others. At times, survivors may present significantly distorted perceptions of their interactions with others or with the therapist that cast events in some particularly biased light (hopeless, victimizing, abusive, impossible, overwhelming, and so on).

Broadly speaking, we would generally formulate this problem as projection, but the nature of the dilemma actually goes beyond simple disowning of some aspect of oneself. There are a number of challenges to the survivor's clear perception of current situations, and these must be understood for the sake of relevant interventions.

Right Figure, Wrong Ground

Repression of traumatic memories can be described, in Gestalt terms, as *loss of ground*: what organizes experience (the content of the trauma episode) is given up, but not necessarily its accompaniments (affects, sensations, meanings). If we imagine the memory of abuse to be a three-color mosaic, where blue is the content (visual memory, words said, sequence of events), red is the emotion, and brown is the bodily (kinesthetic) experience, and if we remove the blue, then all we have left is a brown-and-red chaos: emotions and bodily experience, without a content to give organization to it. There is no clear picture, just impressions. Like any unfinished figure, it seeks some completion, some organization that will allow it to be finished, even if the red and brown must form themselves around a current situation, which has only a few smatterings of color resembling the original blue. Much of the survivor's reaction and experience will be both theoretically and experientially groundless. He will experience unexplainable feelings, have strange habits or bodily sensations, overreact to seemingly innocuous stimuli, experience small slights as deep wounds, label the slighter "abusive," and so on.

During the early and middle parts of the self-functions phase, we often see survivors who were once passive, compliant, and lacking in interpersonal boundaries take an equally extreme stance on the bounded side of the continuum. Vowing never again to be abused, they become hypervigilant and reactive toward virtually any firm meeting with another person. Having once been in denial of their mistreatment by friends, family members, and spouses, they now project hurtful intentions or "negative energy" onto others when they experience internal discomfort in an interaction. Having retroflectively blamed themselves for every harm that was done to them, they now swear not to take responsibility for anything that is not theirs, and so they have difficulty looking at their own contributions to problematic interactions. They may blame others when they experience unpleasant reactions to them.

At this phase of healing, there are often core memories that are still unavailable, often of the most traumatic instances of abuse; these await full acquisition of support and self functions in order to emerge. But they still overdetermine strong reactions, misattribution of these reactions to present circumstances, and so on. The ability to discriminate between present and past is still inadequate. These strong reactions and stances would be appropriate, perhaps, if they were directed at the original abuse and the abusers. But since the survivor is not yet ready to confront them, he confronts others in the present as if they were the abuser, using self functions that he has only recently developed. Moreover, the new skills are often used in unpracticed, poorly modulated, overreactive ways. More subtle use of these skills (for example, being able to say no in ways that match the intensity of a situation) requires practice and assimilation.

All of this speaks to the importance of remembering the forgotten trauma and regaining the ground of experience. As the self grows more cohesive and capable in the later self-functions phase, the survivor is more capable of tolerating the confrontation with his projections and looking at his own overreactions and overgeneralizations without being flooded with shame or needing to blame the other for attacking him, because he is now in a better position to seek out the underlying memory.

Sensory Disturbances and Blocking

Having had her sensorium flooded with overwhelming affect, and so having been required to dissociate and desensitize herself, the survivor often lacks good sensory contact in one or more modalities (clear hearing, seeing, touching, tasting, smelling), which may limit her ability to sense her own body and physical location. Attention to the basic contact functions (Polster and Polster, 1973; Kepner, 1987) is very orienting and assists reality contact. Particularly in the early phase of healing, I develop small awareness experiments, which help the survivor improve her capacity to hear and see accurately and understand the difference between *guesses* about her experience and what she is *actually* experiencing.

Preset Meanings

Survivors are often predisposed to perceive certain stimuli, or to funnel particular stimuli into predetermined figures (organized awareness against a background). Therefore, they may jump to conclusions about what certain nonverbal cues, statements, or interpersonal configurations mean. Often these are perceived in terms of meanings derived from the abusive context (for example, as signals that presage or predict the onset of some abusive event).

One client learned in her family of origin that certain nonverbal signals from her abuser indicated the next form of abuse she was to undergo. When he licked his lips, that meant oral sex. She was, quite expectedly, sensitive to this "signal" from others in her current, nonabusive context, even when she did not consciously remember the significance or meaning of the cue and knew only that when someone licked his lips she "felt funny." Other clients have learned that certain moods in others presage drunken brawls and violence, or that certain key words are "code" for reminding them of threats made to ensure their silence. When these signals are reacted to in the present, nonabusive context—for example, when the therapist does or says something otherwise innocuous—

the signal may be experienced so vaguely that the client does not even know what she is responding to. She may simply report "feeling scared all of a sudden" or "thinking something that doesn't make sense." Working these events through means slowing down the therapeutic interaction, carefully exploring feelings, images, and sensations, and backtracking so as to discern the details of the event to which the client may be reacting. The process may have to be engaged in more than once.

Disowned Polarities

To maintain some sense of self-cohesiveness amidst the stress of trauma, the survivor had to disown and project many intolerable feelings and gain some kind of self-differentiation and self-definition,[19] so that he could move away from recognition of the abuse, or at least feel less vulnerable to it. Characteristics and qualities are denied and disowned, and this strategy either makes the survivor define himself as *unlike* the abuser or makes him define himself as *like* the abuser so as to derive some sense of power from this identification with the aggressor. Thus the survivor forms a "self" that is reactively defined: never angry, never vulnerable and soft, never dishonest, never trusting, never hurtful toward others, always uncaring and callous, never critical , rigidly religious, and so on. Implicit in these reaction formations, of course, are the disowned aspects of the self illustrated in Table 3.1.

Table 3.1. The Polarized Self.

never angry	⟹ angry
never vulnerable and soft	⟹ vulnerable and unprotected
never dishonest	⟹ dishonest
never trusting	⟹ yearning to trust
never hurtful toward others	⟹ wishing to harm those who did harm
always uncaring and callous	⟹ deeply softhearted
never critical	⟹ critical and wishing to make judgments
rigidly religious	⟹ abused by others' religiosity

The developing child is protecting a still fragile and vulnerable self. These disowned polarities, when they are stirred up or evoked by circumstances, are likely to be projected onto others instead of identified as partly belonging to the self.

Owning faults and failings is a difficult enough task for normal neurotics, let alone for those carrying the burden of shame and trauma. The ability to face up to and own the most unsavory aspects of oneself, including the heinous things one was forced to do or participate in, is difficult for the survivor until he has healed enough to withstand their ownership.

Making Sense

What happens when the survivor tries to make sense (Kluft, 1990) of a reality where she was abused by someone she loved, and who may also in certain ways have loved her? Where her experience was denied, distorted, or explained away? Where she was blamed for being abused? Where she was regularly betrayed? She may create (or receive from the abuser) magical and distorted explanations of reality. These schemas then shape and condition her perceptions and disturb her contact with reality. Most often, they will take the form of child-logic conclusions about the world, and they are often concatenations of what she was told about the abuse by the perpetrator or others: children are bad and must be punished; there is a nighttime Daddy and a daytime Daddy, and they are different people; Mommy will die if I tell; they are nice and I am bad; I deserve what is happening; it's punishment; and so on.

Phase and Reality Functions

It is our understanding of the developmental process in healing that will allow us to make clinical choices about how to intervene in projections and reality distortions. It is useful to look at the acquisition and working through of reality functions within the different phases of healing.

Support Phase. Many survivors can tolerate little if any confrontation about their projections or distortions. Such interventions are experienced as abandonment, criticism, or messages that they are bad or have done something wrong. Any suggestion or recognition that they have negative or problematic aspects of self is immediately channeled into the retroflective core of shame and self-diminishment, which obviates the possibility of any ownership. It is merely introjected, in keeping with the traditional role of compliance with abusers, or it creates distrust and defensive rejection of the therapist.

Early Self-Functions Phase. The self at this point is still a fragile formation, and the retroflective core of shame is not yet undone, but the survivor is experimenting and acquiring boundary and feeling functions. Therefore, there is a tendency for the survivor to polarize and react strongly, rejecting anything perceived as "dangerous," (that is, like the abuse). At this stage, he may experience any suggestion that his perceptions are inaccurate or overdetermined as blame. He may "feel abused" by such interventions, either withdrawing or becoming angry. He may cling to the newfound "victim" identity to counter the still weighty and unworked retroflective core of shame, guilt, and negative beliefs about himself. Confrontation about projections or perceptual distortions by the therapist may replicate still unknown memories of trauma and bring about strong emotional reactions. At this stage, however, the base of support built in the previous phase of healing does allow some gentle exploration of perceptions and curiosity about how the history of trauma may have contributed to the survivor's seeing a situation in a certain way. Similarly, the survivor values self-knowledge and understanding and from this perspective is quite willing to look at his "rough edges" and blind spots as they relate to others, particularly as he becomes aware of repeated difficulties in interactions or relationships and begins to reconsider the possibility that he has something to do with their creation.

Later Self-Functions Phase. The availability of the self functions makes for a sense of self that is stronger, more able to tolerate a range and variety of stimuli, and more able to encompass self-knowledge rather than be flooded, overwhelmed, and shamed by it. Now the survivor can be confronted more directly with his distortions of situations and his overreactions to others. He can also look at disowned aspects and fragments of himself. This tolerance and this ability are markers that the self-functions phase is approaching resolution.

Undoing, Redoing, and Mourning Phase. The survivor who is working through this phase of the healing process is in a position to tolerate his grappling with his disowned characteristics and feelings, as well as the deeper or more traumatic core memories that influence his perceptions of others. Moreover, he *must* do so in order to free himself fully from the past. Negative aspects of self can now be confronted and recognized because the survivor is now anchored in other aspects of self and so feels less overwhelmed by shame (the feeling of self-diminishment) than he would have been before. As the survivor *feels* less like a victim, he *needs* less to polarize with others by labeling them "abusive" or to "revise" interactions so that he is never to blame for anything. This defense itself can be worked through in therapy and confronted as a once useful crutch that will now impede growth.

Projection onto others can sometimes cover memories of the survivor's own perpetration of abuse, either because he was forced by the circumstances of the abuse or by the abuser or, later, as he acted out his abuse on others. In this phase, the survivor's memories of his own perpetration of abuse (if it has occurred) can come forward, and the guilt, grief, shame, and anger can be dealt with because these feelings are now part of self functioning.

Reconsolidation in the Self-Functions Phase

Reconsolidation is a reformulation both of the figure of the perceived self and the ground of one's perceived life and world. It therefore involves both poles of the organism or environmental field. The survivor's perception of self continually grows and expands as each new self function is mastered and as the survivor experiences herself as increasingly able to meet and encompass the challenges of healing and of life. The self becomes a different self, although this may not be fully appreciated until the end of the self-functions phase. Another important healing task for the survivor is to enlarge her perception of life context and the world so that it becomes large enough to hold and integrate what the survivor has discovered about her life, about who she is and who she is becoming. This reconsolidation takes place by focusing on spiritual and philospohical understanding, which we will discuss first.

Spiritual and Philosophical Integration

Spiritual and philosophical interests become an increasingly important framework throughout the self-functions phase. Whether through twelve-step programs, traditional sources of religious practice, social ideologies (such as stands against violence) organizations that support survivors, classical meditation, or "new age" practices of healing, most survivors find some compelling need to develop a transcendent spiritual or philosophical framework. The reality of trauma and abuse, with its horror, hideousness, and inexplicable quality, simply cannot be held and made sense of within the individual person: How could this have happened to me? What did I do to deserve or cause this? How can I make sense of these senseless events? What meaning does this have for my life? How do I reconcile myself to all my suffering, all the years I have had to put into healing while others got on with living? How do I live with all that I have had to give up, all the normal life I have longed for but that doesn't seem to be mine?

These questions are inevitable, for we are meaning-making creatures at our most fundamental level. And, certainly, these questions can be answered from an existential or rationalistic standpoint:

We don't know why. It is happenstance. This is simply your life to face. Your existence is what you make of it, how you play the cards you are dealt.

But this, too, is a philosophical framework, which finds a larger meaning: that of the individual wresting meaning from the overwhelming chaos of life. Regardless of the particular framework that is formed, we all need a larger perspective than the individual alone, something that transcends the smallness of the individual self and can hold the existence of abuse and the process of healing and make meaning of it. Spiritual and philosophical interests may be the only thread that a survivor can hold on to in order to have faith that she will pass through the chaos and come out into something better. In the self-functions phase, in addition to serving as a support, a spiritual or philosophical framework becomes a way to form something meaningful out of the hard work of healing.

Very often, the survivor finds some sense of purpose related to abuse; a sense of direction that can make her experience and understanding meaningful to others, as well as to herself. Seeds of this sense of purpose may come from her finding that she can be helpful to others in her support group and that she has something to offer others from her learning, suffering, and growing. She may decide to take a stand on social issues that have some bearing on her own experience (hunger task forces, Women Against Violence, organizations that promote peace or child welfare, AIDS support work). She may also find a sense of purpose in a spiritual context, becoming a healer to help survivors, involving herself in church programs, joining meditation groups, and working on developing a more loving or spiritual approach toward others. She may find that her life direction is affected strongly by this activity and go about looking at ways to change her career in a direction that feels more congruent with her path of healing and her emerging framework of meaning.

Like many stances in the self-functions phase, those developed from the emerging spiritual or philosophical framework may be quite rigid, naïve, or polemical at times. There is no reason yet for us to expect an integrated maturity with respect to transcendence. Nevertheless, these spiritual and philosophical concerns are not merely crutches. They are part of an authentic human need and self functioning. But they are also something from which the survivor derives support, and so when she needs support and needs to fill the gaps in her self-functioning, she may use these interests as part of her defensive adaptation.

Of key importance for the self-functions phase is the way in which transcendent spiritual and philosophical developments assist in the formation of an attitude of love and compassion toward oneself. More than anything else (other than working through the deepest elements of shame and self-denial) development of a transcendent context on the spiritual and philosophical level allows one to forgive and hold oneself in a better light. Love and compassion for oneself are softening. Love comes to be experienced as more powerful than the evil of the abuse. The very fact of our smallness against the larger backdrop—not the smallness of self-diminishment and shame, but the recognition and acceptance of our human limitations—is what helps us diminish our self criticism: If God can forgive, can't I? If what happened to me was random, can't I let myself off the hook?

Therapists who regularly work with survivors must themselves face some way of holding these realities in a larger context of meaning or else face the fact of burnout and numbing from their exposure to them. As in work with the terminally ill or with those dying in hospices, these existential realities cannot be faced regularly without some source of help beyond the self. The therapist who has not seen to his or her own spiritual or philosophical development will probably find that he or she cannot support clients to do so in the context of therapy.

Reconsolidation of the Self-Functions Phase

The core memories that form much of the basis for overdetermined reactions to stimuli must still be worked through in the undoing, redoing, and mourning phase. But as the survivor moves into the end of the self-functions phase, he feels stronger and more capable than at any other time in his life. He has the tools to manage and even enjoy life, and he feels that it really is possible to heal. He becomes balanced between the future and the past, rather than totally absorbed by trauma as the definer of his life. He feels bigger than the abuse, and so the process of assimilating the prior work of healing is experienced as integrating it into the larger self which he has become, rather than as trying to absorb huge, difficult chunks into a small, easily overwhelmed self.

At this stage, some survivors feel that their healing is done. Life is good in most respects, and they may have some denial about the reactions they still have that indicate still unknown material. The suggestion that some things are still unknown may be rejected. Since only time will tell whether this is true or not, I do not find it therapeutically useful to take any position on this issue with clients. At best, I could only predict something difficult ahead, and doing that would undermine the full appreciation and celebration of what has been achieved so far in the healing process. At worst, I would undermine my relationship with the client because she might feel that my pointing out that the journey is not over means that her accomplishments are less valued by me.

In either case, I do not know what really lies ahead. Better to leave the door open for future work if new material surfaces. The survivor must choose the pace of her own healing, and this is not a bad time for her to take a break from therapy and enjoy the fruits of her labors. If she has proceeded this far in the healing process, she is mature enough to take responsibility for her own needs, as well as for her own avoidance and limitations.

Celebration and Appreciation of Accomplishments

At the end of a phase, before the new phase begins, clients frequently come in spontaneously with reports of how well they have handled previously difficult situations, or with some awareness of how much they have accomplished in their healing work. There can be a sense of deep satisfaction and well-earned pride at this passage, as well as deep gratitude for the therapist.

It is important that the therapist join in celebrating, affirming, and appreciating clients' accomplishments. It is often difficult, however, for us to let go of our own perfectionism or self-criticism as professionals and appreciate that celebration is an important task, not only for the client but also for ourselves as healers, and for the client-therapist partnership. As healing progresses, therapy does indeed become more and more a partnership and less a hierarchical relationship. Reconsolidation in the self-functions phase often marks the recognition of this shift toward equality in the therapeutic relationship, which becomes even more figural in the latter part of the next phase.

Chapter Four

Undoing, Redoing, and Mourning

In terms of Gestalt theory, the person, or organism/environment field, is a whole, or *gestalt*, configured in a certain way: a pattern of experience, behavior, relationships, and perceptions. Where this *gestalt* has become fixed (that is, where the organism/environment field has become inflexibly patterned), the person cannot adapt her relationship within that field in a way that accurately responds to her current organismic needs and the current realities of the environment. Aggression[20] must be brought to bear on the destructuring of this fixed gestalt, so that a new and more flexible configuration can be formed, one that supports adaptation, growth, and development.

With respect to the growth of the survivor, there has been a fixed gestalt or relationship of the survivor to himself, to others in the present, and to his abusive history. Gradually, this fixed gestalt has been reformulated by the work on support and by the development of self functions, which provide him with the human context and the organismic skills necessary for aggressive destructuring of the gestalt.

In the Healing Tasks Model, our emphasis is first to reformulate the relational (gestalt) and the self (gestalt) with the memories of abuse, as the increasingly articulated background and source of this work. With these transformations, we can now bring memories more into the forefront of the work. In this task, which I refer to as *undoing, redoing,* and *mourning,* the survivor uses aggression quite directly to stand against what was done to her, defend her own abused child-self, confront the abuser(s) symbolically or actually, take actions she could not take before, speak on her own behalf, and so on. This phase is marked by the destructuring of the configuration (figure) of the hidden abusive history, with its residual introjected thoughts and retroflected actions, and by the mourning of losses in a way that allows completion of the cycle of healing. A new balance can then be experienced. These themes occur repeatedly throughout the healing process, but they become more focal in the later stages of therapy, since they cannot be addressed fully and intensely until adequate support has been obtained and the self functions are developed enough to serve as a foundation.

For example, signs of mourning, such as sadness and retrospection, will appear in early, middle, and later stages of the healing process. But deep mourning cannot be fully engaged in early or middle therapy because it is likely to produce fragmentation of self, depression, anxiety, or even decompensation as the person cannot support the intensity of affect or derive adequate support and comfort from others. Intense affect, such as that which deep mourning involves, cannot yet be tolerated by most survivors, and "grief therapy" becomes retraumatizing because the working-through process has no more supports than the original trauma. With the development of more range and intensity of affect and fuller grounding, grief work is fruitful and can be assimilated.

Similarly, full undoing work, such as experiencing anger and physical rage at the perpetrator (previously retroflected in body tension and anger at oneself) may involve direct expression of feelings, symbolic confrontation with abusers, hitting a bolster or pad, and so on. Such strong feeling and expression usually cannot be supported in the early and middle phases of healing by most survivors. Undoing and mourning work are addressed in appropriate amounts if they can be tolerated by the client in earlier phases but full focus on these themes remains for the Undoing/Mourning phase of healing.

Undoing

Undoing, and its concomitant process of redoing, refers to taking actions in the current environment that could not be taken when the abuse occurred and relating to the past with current skills and capacities. It involves the working through of the "unfinished business" that all survivors carry: the things that could not be said, the experiences that were never described, the feelings that could not be felt or expressed, the events that became directed at the self but should now be turned back toward the environment.

The importance of undoing work is to break the link to the past formed by the traumatic effects on feelings, actions, and self-perceptions. It restores to the survivor a full capacity and range of possibilities with which to meet the environment, his life. It is not about abreaction for its own sake (in my view, there is nothing healing about abreaction understood in this way). It is about experiencing oneself *differently* in relation to the abuse, the abuser, and one's own history, feeling larger and more encompassing than the abuse. The past cannot be changed, but one can "redo" the way one has come to live and cope in the world, and one can stop treating the present as if it were the abusive past of childhood.

This work can take up a substantial portion of therapy. It usually also involves the recollection of particular memories of abuses, the expression of strong emotions and repressed actions, and the working through of what I have termed the *retroflected core*.

Retroflected Core

This aspect of undoing is involved throughout the phases of the healing process, but this long-term undoing work reaches its full intensity in this phase of healing. Since so little action in the original environment was possible, much had to be contained. So little support was available that much was taken on, performed on, or performed by the self. In other words, the self became the actor, the acted on, the display of, and the whole domain of abuse. What was originally an interpersonal event came to be played out as if it were about the survivor *only*. Undoing, in this phase, involves placing back into the interpersonal field those things now experienced as part of the self that were originally part of the interpersonal world but were never articulated as such. Specifically, we attend to the following tasks:

1. Finding forms of expression that allow the survivor to restore the capacity to *act* in the environment on what has been withheld and contained within the organismic boundary

2. Putting abusive behavior back in its original context, working through memories of abuse, and undoing self-enactments of abuse[21]

3. Identifying beliefs, aspects of one's own identity, feelings, and behavior that were taken in from or forced on one by the environment, ejecting these, and symbolically returning them to the environment where they really belong

Table 4.1 shows the elements of the retroflected core. As the examples in the table suggest, the retroflected core is part and parcel of the feelings of shame and low self-esteem that are the common heritage of survivors. Many of these examples, in one way or another, represent some interaction that has been truncated at the interpersonal boundary and turned back toward the self. Others are representations of abusive events that, severed from their context, can be portrayed only when acted out on the self or on the current environment. They contain, in their essence, acts of power that can be liberated in the service of healing and life functioning, but only when the survivor has enough self functions to face the events and take a stand without being flooded or overwhelmed. There are also introjects that must be assimilated by the survivor, and this will require some available aggression on her own behalf. Much must be spit out: beliefs, criticisms, demean-ment of the victim, blame, guilt, shame. In this phase, the survi-vor brings a fuller set of resources that allow her to face these issues more aggressively and assertively, confronting them and working them through.

Table 4.1. The Retroflected Core.

Core Element	Examples
Retroflections	Actions not taken in the original environment and now taken against oneself (anger directed at self; muscularly withheld sadness; tension in legs, as if to run; flaccidity or underdevelopment of musculature, to avoid urges to move sexually)
	Feelings about abuser or abuse turned against oneself (disgust turned to self-disgust; hatred turned to self-loathing; anger turned to self-punishment)
	Things unsaid now said to oneself ("You hurt me" becomes "I am damaged goods")
	Identification with the aggressor (adapting by taking on characteristics of the abuser in the service of self-protection, mastery, keeping back one's own aggressive impulses)
Self-enactments of abuse	Physical symptoms that replicate or communicate abusive acts (bodily pains as somatic remembrance of abuse)
	Enactment of abuse in behavior (interpersonal relationships, therapeutic transference, provocative behavior, sexual habits)
	Identification with the aggressor (self-destructive behavior as a form of acting on the self as one was acted on by the abuser)
Introjections	Names one calls oneself, which were used by the abuser or others
	Feelings created in the abuse (dirtiness, helplessness, shame) now taken to be about the self (I am dirty, I am helpless, I am shameful)

Core Element	Examples
	Beliefs or attributions from the abuser or the family following or surrounding the abuse (I'm a whore, this happened to me because I'm bad, I like being hurt and abused)
Introjections (cont'd.)	Introjected family enacted on the self, in dissociated parts modeled after abusive family members
	Explanations or conclusions made up to explain overwhelming events, often containing elements of magical thinking and preoperational logic (I am evil, therefore I deserve punishment; I was curious, which led to my being abused; it was my fault that I was abused)

Undoing, Redoing, and Core Memories

The term *undoing* refers to the reversal of something done: turning an action in a different direction, which will take the person out of some bind that the action has placed him in. Here, we mean the action of turning expression and behavior back onto the self instead of toward the environment, severing experience and behavior from its context, introjecting meanings.

Undoing work will be engaged with all along the healing path, as the holographic Healing Tasks Model implies, according to the capacity of the survivor to tolerate and manage this work usefully. In the support phase, the work will involve recontextualizations, which allow the rephrasing of self-referred beliefs and behaviors within the abusive context. It is the work of making sense of one's retroflective mode of being by putting it into its formative context. This begins to relieve the pressure of self-blame and self-punishment, which all survivors carry to one degree or another. In the self-functions phase, the undoing work is experimenting with behavior that is increasingly vigorous, establishing better self-other boundaries and sorting out perceptions, a kind of "unbundling" of the tightly retroflected mode of being promulgated by the adaptation to trauma. The survivor increasingly establishes a sense of self in stronger relation to the environment. The client may, for example, experiment with making firm statements to the therapist about his abuser ("He really hurt me, and now I can acknowledge to you that I feel angry about what he did") but may not have all the resources and readiness to symbolically confront the abuser directly. As we move into the present phase, the undoing work is more directly engaged, in the safe context of the therapy room, with the events and persons of the original situation.

With trauma survivors, all of this means that memories of abusive events will be grappled with to one degree or another. For the most part, there are no special techniques that must be employed to elicit memories at this point in the healing process. By now, the establishment of ample support and self functions has provided the ground for memories to develop naturally, as behavior and feelings are explored and experimented with. But even without a focus on memories, experiments can be created that allow the survivor to experience directing movement, voice, words, and beliefs toward the environment, rather than toward the self.

Expressive Work

At this stage of healing, the client now has the resources and structure to tolerate and benefit from more intense expressive work. Expressive work in therapy has often been misused and therefore stereotyped. Its misuse stems from its being employed as an intervention much too early in the healing process, so that it is experienced as overwhelming and out of context.

Because it looks more dramatic than other work, there is often the illusion that expressive work is somehow more powerful than other interventions and therefore (in the faulty logic of reasoning by simile), more healing. In fact, however, the intervention that is more healing is a function of whatever is most assimilable, most readily integrated at the client's current stage of development. There is no absolute scale of interventions that determines their healing effects. Expressive work can indeed be dramatic at times, in the sense of vigorous, full, sometimes loud, and often aggressive.

But its drama should be congruent with the readiness of the client to integrate the drama as a part of the evolving self.

Expressive experiments are used because they give the survivor the actual felt experience of being able to act with vigor and strength on her own behalf in relation to the abuse. Expressive work allows a major reorganization of the field in relation to memories, abuser(s), and current life. It undoes the retroflective pulling in and collapse upon the self and allows full relationship to the environment. This shift is crucial for the survivor's ability to be in balance with herself and her world. It gives her the power to move beyond fear, establish a healthy sexual life, feel fully empowered in relationships, and so on. Some possible forms of expressive experiments follow (notice the grading from lesser to greater intensity as the list proceeds):

• Taking a memory of abuse that has emerged and asking the client to make a series of statements that start with "What I could not say then but will say now . . . "

• Asking the client to write a "declaration to the abuser" and read it aloud to the therapist (or the group)

• Having the survivor stand and give firm, passionate voice to his feelings about what was done to him

• Having the survivor stand up on behalf of a fellow survivor in the group or confront their abuser in a symbolic enactment

• Using empty-chair work to confront the abuser or others who allowed the abuse to take place

• Having the survivor stand up and talk down to the abuser in a symbolic enactment

• Having the survivor call to account all those who were in complicity with the silence about the abuse

• Having the survivor discharge rage through physical expression, such as hitting or kicking a pad, which allows her to experience her embodied sense of capacity and power[22]

- Actual confrontation of the abuser by the survivor (this procedure has been inappropriately promulgated by some therapists in work with survivors, although it has its uses)

As an example of expressive work, I had seen Toni for about two years, during which time we had focused predominantly on self-functions issues: developing good interpersonal boundaries and using them at work, tolerating and developing a wider range of feelings, and clearing her bodily self of the impact of incestuous assaults by her father (manifest in tension, pains, disconnection from her bodily experience, lack of sexual sensation, and the tendency of any bodily sensation to evoke flashbacks and memories of abuse) through body-oriented therapy. Toni had been in therapy before and was also strongly linked to a variety of self-help groups. She had a marvelous network of social and interpersonal support.

As she moved into the close of the self-functions phase of her work, Toni had a confidence in herself at work that she had never felt before. She had taken on greater responsibilities, which required her to be assertive and clearly bounded with co-workers and superiors, and had reclaimed most of her bodily self from the abuse. She was just beginning to focus on reclaiming her sexuality by allowing herself to experience more spontaneous sexual feeling, and by exploring what it meant and felt like to be a woman, something she had shelved years ago as only a vague possibility for her. She felt not yet ready to try dating or romantic relationships, but she was entertaining the idea.

We joked that in terms of her work and friendships, she was very much her adult age, but in terms of "boys" she was about thirteen years old, a considerable advancement for her from her "latency" state of putting sexuality aside. But she felt blocked from moving ahead. As we explored her sense of this block, she was able to describe the feeling of being "held back," which she illustrated by showing me how she felt: as if someone were holding her by the arms to keep her from moving.

When I asked her who was holding her back, she immediately replied, "Of course, it's my father." I asked her if I could hold her arms as she felt her father holding her, so that she could pay attention to what she wanted to do about being held. She agreed enthusiastically.

I firmly held her arms, as she had indicated, while she allowed herself to concentrate on her bodily sensations and allow something spontaneous to emerge. Toni said that she wanted to shake my hands off, and I told her to go ahead. She faced me squarely and then vigorously shook her arms until I could no longer maintain my grip. She stood there breathing strongly, flushed and very pleased with her feeling of power and strength.

I suggested she put her father in the empty chair in front of her and make whatever statements might come to her. Toni faced this task, which earlier in her work with me she had been unable to do, as squarely this time as she had faced me to shake off my grip. She had felt angry at her father before, but she had never been able to say that directly in any form.

"You son of a bitch! I am not going to let you hold me back in my life any more," she began. "I've spent the major part of my life trying to recover from what you did to me. What you did was unconscionable."

Toni, as it turned out, had a lot to say to him. She spoke, and I suggested possible statements and variations. First she called him to account for what he had done to her. She listed the ways he had violated her, how it had hurt and damaged her, how he had lied to and betrayed her, how he had pretended that nothing had happened. She confronted him for his lack of feeling, his callousness, his cruelty, his treating her as if she were nothing more than an object to gratify his needs. She also called him to account for his pushing her to achieve, so that he could find his own self-worth in her achievements.

As her statements went on, Toni grew increasingly angry at her father. She pointed her finger at him, shook her fist, raised her voice, and stayed grounded in her body as she did so. For the first

time, she could experience herself as strong, powerful, individuated, and in command in relation to her father.

Toward the end of this experiment, I observed that she had
quite thoroughly called him to account, and that it was perhaps
time for her to claim her healing and wholeness as *hers*, rather
than in relation to what he had done to her. She understood me
immediately and beamed for a moment before turning once again
to the chair of her father.

"This is *my* healing. What I've done, I've done for *myself*, not
for you. It's been *my* hard work that I'm able to stand here and say
these things to you now. You have no claim over what I've become."

With that, she proudly sat down, and we took time to appreciate
what she had been able to do and how it had affected her.

At the next session, Toni walked in and immediately said,
"That was really important last time. And I have some more of that
to do today." We developed a further symbolic confrontation, but
this time we also had a chair for Toni's mother, since, as Toni said,
"She was part of the picture, too." Although I first directed Toni to
continue her dialogue with her father, there was little energy in that
for her. Despite whatever agenda I had in mind about her unfinished business with her father, Toni turned to me and said, "No, it's
not about him right now. It's about her."

It was Toni's mother who had lied and covered up for her husband when she had to take Toni to the doctor as a result of the
abuse. It was her mother who had emotionally abandoned Toni to
her father when Toni had appealed to her for help. She also confronted her mother for how she had controlled her daughter's
sexuality, by making her dress in dowdy ways so as not to attract
her father too much, and had limited Toni's explorations of boys
and the adolescent social world so that she would not leave the
family and develop a life of her own. She put at her mother's feet
her difficulties in knowing what it was to be a woman, because of
the rotten model her mother had provided for her. Toni had a lot
to say to her. As with her father, Toni was able to do this expressive

work strongly and powerfully. She stayed well grounded in her bodily self as she did, so that she could clearly *feel* what she was.

At the end of this session, Toni felt free from an immense burden. She felt defined and individuated from her parents in a way that she had never experienced before, which allowed her to recognize the degree to which she had been bound and "held" to them by the legacy of the abuse: their betrayal, her keeping their secrets for them and living in service to the preservation of their marriage, even at the sacrifice of herself. The result, over the next months, was that Toni was able to take more risks in developing new projects at work. She could feel more ownership of exploring her feminine side and was able to experiment with clothing that expressed this and to explore and tolerate more sexual feeling.

That this work was highly appropriate to her stage of healing and her emotional readiness was indicated by the way she was able to integrate its impact into her life and thereby experience change. When expressive work takes place too early, however— because the therapist pushes it, or because the available temporary support allows it (such as that found in intensive workshops or treatment programs), even though the client's developmental level cannot support it—the person cannot assimilate it into her life. Either it remains a bracketed and disconnected experience, as when people engage in expressive confrontations in residential treatment programs but find that these have little usefulness in life outside the program, or it makes the client feel dissociated, anxious, or disconnected, as if she has cooperated with the therapist but gone well beyond her own capacity.

With another client, we integrated physical expression into a symbolic confrontation. Noticing that the client was shaking her fist at a symbolic representation of her rapist as she made angry statements to him, I encouraged her to exaggerate this action as she spoke. As she began to punch the air, I slid a softly cushioned footstool over to her and had her punch into it, to emphasize her words. She began hitting and beating the stool, finally able to give vent to her rage and feel fully connected to her body as she did so, linking her angry statements to her physical actions to join her thinking, feeling, and bodily expression into one unitary statement.

An experiment in more purely physical expression occurred with a man who was healing from memories of having been molested and raped by older children in his neighborhood. He had gone through the phases of support and self functions as a natural course of therapy, without ever having had any memories of abuse. It was only in this later phase that he had enough personal solidity and healing to allow these memories to surface. After the shock of recollecting the violent trauma, the symptoms that ensued subsided about a month later. He then came in boiling mad at what the abusers had done to him, at how they had so affected his life without his having been able to recall why. He now recognized that his difficult struggle in therapy to understand what it meant to be a man, and to feel strong in his maleness, had been shaped by how weak and helpless he had felt during the rape.

Now he felt powerful with his anger. During the session he beat pillows, ripped up phone books, yelled, and raged at his molesters until he had expended his anger and could allow himself to soften into sadness and sobs. He could now encompass this entire range of feeling in his sense of what it was to be a man, raging on his own behalf and mourning for his deep losses, without shame or sense of weakness. It was a mark of his readiness and his phase of development in healing that he was able not only to tolerate vigorous feeling and action but also to assimilate these to his sense of self, his life, and his functioning. His self was big enough to encompass this work and use it, rather than be disturbed by it or have to disconnect from it.

Redoing

Redoing means experimenting with actually changing one's responses to the original abuse as it is recalled. In this way, the survivor can take back to his experience of the trauma the skills and capacities he has developed in the course of his healing and experience facing the trauma differently. Things can now be said to the abuser that he was unable to say as a child. Actions can now be taken that he was unable to take then. Help can be asked for and received from someone (the therapist) in the context of the memory and occurrence of abuse. The competent and powerful adult who has developed can come to defend and rescue the child-self who is still "captured" in (dissociated into) the memory, so that the child can be brought back to the present, where he can heal.

As we entered into the undoing phase of work, an incest survivor began to recall previously unavailable memories of being used by family members as part of a prostitution ring. During treatment, this woman had experienced spontaneous recall of incestuous abuse by her brothers, as well as by her father. (It is not unusual, in my experience, for brutal or otherwise more intensely traumatic forms of abuse to emerge only in later phases of healing, when they can be borne.) By this time, her long, hard work at acquiring support and self functions and her capacity for increased expression put her in a very different position from which to face and interact with these newly emerging memories.

I reminded her to stay grounded in being an adult as she began to describe the memories to me. We were able to enact the scene as she recalled it, but with her entering into it as a strong adult who could aid the abused little girl in the memory. Anchored in her hard-won strengths, she enacted the process of pulling a stranger off the little girl (by lifting a bolster, which we made into the abuser for the experiment), kicking "him" out of the room (quite literally, I might add), and then holding and comforting the little girl, whom we had symbolized with a soft pillow. Comforting the little girl, promising her that she would not let this happen again, she said that she would bring her out of this place and time where she had been hurt and into the present, where she could help her heal. We literally enacted this by walking out of the room and into the hallway, reentering the therapy room in the "present," so that we could integrate the wounded little girl into her heart, where she could be properly healed and cared for.

A similar process of bringing current skills and capacities into a past recollection, but with a slightly different emphasis, occurred with a woman who found herself recalling a previously known memory of being orally raped by her father at night, when she was six years old. In this incident, her father caused physical damage that had required her hospitalization. Both parents made up a story that blamed her for what had happened to her throat. Again, this was not a new memory, but it was clear that something more had to be done with it, which we had been unable to do before in our work. It was an unfinished figure, demanding something for closure and completion, so that it could be assimilated.

As we explored her feelings, I observed that she was reacting very differently from the way I remembered her reacting before. During earlier recollections of this incident, she had responded with intense fear, terror, distinct somatic sensations of awful pain. Now she was clenching her fists, wearing a grim expression, and feeling a deep disgust in her belly. She agreed that she felt different: angry and disgusted, rather than terrorized and victimized. We created an experiment of reenacting the memory and encouraging her to act from what she was now feeling, to see what she would do differently from what she had done as a small child.

I agreed to act as her father. She lay down, and curled up on the couch as I strode over and towered above her. As I slowly approached her, she began to ball up her fists, and her breathing became firm. Her eyes glared out at me as I came closer. Suddenly she sat bolt upright and shouted, "Get away from me, you pig!" She stopped me in my tracks. Since she was handling herself so well and clearly was not overwhelmed by her actions, I decided to challenge her to stay in her power. In the role of her father, I told her to lie back down; I was her father, I could do with her as I wanted, and so on.

She told me, "Don't you dare try and touch me again! You are disgusting. What you did to me was disgusting. I'll not submit to you again, and if you try anything I'll fight you with all I have."

At this point, she was shaking her fist at me, standing firmly on her legs, without an ounce of hesitation in her. I could not stay any longer in my role, since I was beaming with appreciation for her strength, power, and self-affirmation. I literally shook off the role and clapped my hands in applause: "Brava!" She bowed.

As we discussed this experiment and its results, she reported feeling that she had finally broken the spell that her father had held over her. Before, she had been able to appreciate the truth of what had been done to her, and of how she had been betrayed by her mother as well. Now that she had the support and the resources, *she* was really different, and she could act on her own behalf.

An experiment in redoing is built from the current observation of the survivor's responses and capacities as previously known or new memories emerge. The fact that the responses are *now different* is what creates the possibility for the memory to be *redone* rather than merely *recalled*.

This, rather than the process of abreaction itself, is productive of healing. The reality of the abuse now lives in the *larger context* of a capable, powerful self. It is subsumed by the self. The survivor is now bigger than the abuse.

Confronting the Abuser

The question of whether the survivor should confront the abuser with knowledge of the abuse, as part of the healing process, is a delicate one. Bass and Davis (1988) have given many survivors and therapists the impression that this is necessary in healing. Recent countersuits by people accused of abuse and claims of the harm produced by inaccurate accusations (Loftus, 1993; Yapko, 1994) have also brought this question to prominence. It is probably incumbent on any professional who treats survivors, particularly on anyone who is suggesting a model for treatment, to clarify his or her understanding of this question.

My basic position on confrontation, as described in the last chapter, is not to push for it. I do not believe that confrontation is required for healing to occur, nor do I believe that it is the thera-pist's decision. It has seemed to me that confrontation and legal actions are often urged by therapists who have a political agenda and who believe that healing is not possible without some kind of social action, as if the secret of the abuse must be disclosed on all levels of the system (personal, familial, and social) or else some-thing is left unfinished. I emphatically do not believe this in this approach.

If the question of confrontation arises, it must emerge from the integrity and self-determination of the survivor. For it to be driven by the therapist undermines the essential process of restoring control to the survivor, a process that I *do* believe is critical to healing. In my experience, a few survivors, as they integrated and assimilated their healing, have decided that confrontation was necessary for them. Many survivors choose to inform family members at various points in their healing work, but most survivors I work with do not find this step necessary for their healing.

If a survivor wishes to explore this possibility, however, a num-ber of questions need to be asked. Is she ready to deal with denial by those she accuses, and not feel set back in her own healing? Does she have adequate support from anyone in the family sys-tem? Does she have corroborating evidence that can reduce her vulnerability to being scapegoated or blamed for disrupting the family? Does she appreciate the impact that this will have on oth-ers whom she cares about? If the questions surrounding confron-tation are explored carefully, the survivor can make a decision that emerges from her integrity, rather than from impulse or social pressure.

Mourning

Sadness and mourning are pervasive in the experience of survi-vors, and so understanding and working with these phenomena is an intrinsic part of any therapy with survivors. Sadness and mourning are threads that run throughout the therapy process with survivors: it is the result of confronting the reality of abuse to ones life and self, acknowledging the deep losses such abuse has entailed, and it is the entry point into the completion and recon-solidation process. Mourning becomes most figural as the person feels himself supported adequately in the interpersonal relation-ship with the therapist. Sadness and mourning may not have any content initially but must be given space even so.

Mourning is an essential and legitimate function, which al-lows us to complete the cycles of life. By mourning, we acknowledge our wounds and losses, connect our hurt and sadness to real and important events (without which it is misconstrued by us and by others as depression), and seek comfort and community for our healing. It is through mourning, in the safety of the holding en-vironment provided by the therapist or group, that the experi-ence of ourselves as the "hurt child within" can finally be soothed and healed. Sadness and mourning, like other pervasive issues in the healing process, will be approached differently and have different sources according to different points in the heal-ing process.

Mourning in the Support Phase

Even before memories emerge, clients may find themselves over-taken by unexplained waves of sadness, which neither they nor the therapist really understand. Such feelings, which on the sur-face appear groundless, can leave the client feeling disturbed, neurotic, or crazy. In the Gestalt approach, our theory insists that such organismic experiences are always in relation to some-thing, even if that something is not apparent in the present con-figuration. Therefore, I allow the client room for as much of his sadness as he can usefully tolerate, and I validate that this feeling has meaning, even if we do not yet know what it is about. I do not try to connect the sadness to abuse or to any other events that are unknown, but I do say, "I believe that you have ample reason in your life to feel sad."

As clients experience the first memories of abuse, or new memories that expand the scope of what they knew about before, feelings of mourning and sadness now gain a focus. Once they are through the shock of such memories and have begun to accept that something indeed happened to them, they are now dealing with real and profound loss: the loss of the world and the self as they have known these things. The implications of assimilating the reality of abuse and trauma into one's experience become readily apparent. The image of childhood that the survivor has formed, with the trauma dissociated from the picture, has been providing a false but rosier picture from which to create a life narrative. Whatever security derived from this false picture is now gone. Everything feels in flux. Everything seems to be falling apart, and there is no clear sense that anything better will emerge.

This loss in the present, as memories emerge, mirrors the previously unfaced loss and mourning that occurred in childhood from the abuse itself, which the abused child dissociated. Now it can be seen because the context of support is now here, and it must be *felt* if the survivor is to understand what must be healed.

At this phase of healing, however, the survivor often finds himself in despair. Knowing feels horrible. Such a response is a natural reaction to waves of previously unfelt sensations, reactions to trauma, anxiety, and so on, which accompany the previously unavailable memories. Moreover, the survivor does not have enough experience yet with the cycle of such events. He has not felt how integration and assimilation of the truth will eventually leave him stronger.

The therapist is the main frame of support at this point. The therapist's assurances that the client's disturbance, sadness, grief, and even despair are natural and normal responses to such recollections, and that this is a cycle that he will get through, as others have, is what helps the client stay with the process, so that he can come out the other side. What is needed is assistance from the therapist to help the client be as grounded as possible. The therapist must grade and pace the process so that the client can face his mourning in assimilable chunks instead of falling back into numbing or dissociation. The therapist needs to support the client in finding ways to distract himself appropriately, so that his feelings do not seem endless. With persistence and consistency, the survivor eventually does come out the other side of the cycle of mourning, and the mourning is what helps him assimilate the reality of the abuse.

Mourning in the Self-Functions Phase

Because the focus in the self-functions phase of healing is on developing the specific skills and capacities for managing contact, the nature of what is being mourned for tends to become more specific. Instead of feeling the broad, pervasive mourning and sadness that the survivor experienced in the support phase, she becomes acutely aware of how her upbringing and the abuse have denied her the acquisition of important life skills.

As the survivor grapples with learning about boundaries, learning to tolerate and manage feelings, learning self-support and self-care, and so on, she feels acutely what she did not get, what no one helped her learn, how little help in the task of growing up was available to her, and how impoverished her interpersonal environment was. The development of self functions is hard work. "Why should it always be so hard for me, when normal people don't have to struggle so much?" is a frequent question. "I have to learn everything from scratch!" is another frustrated comment. Particularly in the first half of the self-functions phase, when so much of the healing work seems to lie before them, survivors often feel this keenly: "How much of my life has been lost to this!"

Certainly, this awareness can evoke anger about the past, and this is useful for helping the survivor mobilize and differentiate herself and find her fighting spirit. But this recognition also opens the survivor to mourning for the loss she has experienced in relation to others who had childhoods and parenting that gave them the skills they needed to grow up. The childhood that she never had and never will have feels like an irreversible deprivation. It cannot be gained by "reparenting" in therapy. It is a loss that must be grieved, no matter what contemporary family she has creatively formed for herself.

At this phase, there are two common difficulties with allowing the natural course of mourning to take place. One difficulty is the retroflective tendency to turn elements from the abusive environment back on the self. Many survivors experience the recognized lack of self functions as self-blame such as "I am lacking." The habit of blaming the victim is so well introjected that it does not occur to them to put this lack in context: "The abuse and neglect I experienced left me with significant lacks" or "They deprived me of a chance to have something that others easily have." At times, the predictability of self-blame is preferable to the unknown experience of grief and mourning. This stance is also held to as an avoidance of sadness and hurt that feel overwhelming and bottomless. The other difficulty involves using anger as a life stance, to generate a sense of security and a rigidly protective boundary. Survivors who do this have great difficulty with mourning because mourning requires them to soften, seek comfort, and exist in a condition that they feel as weak and vulnerable. They avoid this by becoming rageful at life, angry at God, jealous of "normal" people, angry at the therapist if the therapist is not himself a survivor, and so on. Both modes allow the survivor to avoid the process of mourning losses by sticking to the security of what is familiar: self-blame and inadequacy, on the one hand, and rigid boundedness and rejection of others, on the other. Nevertheless, we must appreciate the creativity in which each of these modes is grounded, for each mode of contacting the childhood environment had great survival value in its original context. Self-blame and inadequacy kept the child from challenging the "powers that were" and perhaps bringing on worse punishment, or it meant that the child could not be brought low by the abusers because he or she had already brought himself or herself as low as could be. Anger and rigidity of boundaries were very useful for other survivors in keeping people away from the wounds and challenging the abusers. In both cases, the work is the same: to experiment with the novel, the unfamiliar. This in itself is a self-function task: to broaden the capacity for taking risks in the safety and support of the therapeutic environment. The self-blamer experiments with the risk of blaming others and allowing some of his grief to emerge. The hyperbounded person learns to experiment with softening into sadness, without labeling it as weakness, so that she can claim this feeling as legitimately hers.

Mourning in the Undoing, Redoing, and Mourning Phase

What characterizes mourning in this phase is *fullness*. So much more intensity of feeling can be tolerated at this point that deeper grieving can occur in the course of the expressive and redoing work. Sobbing, wailing, shedding deeply felt tears, and giving other expressions to grief are more likely to be experienced as cleansing and relieving than as overwhelming, as they once were. As one client put it, "I feel like I'm finally dredging the bottom of the well."

Mourning may occur spontaneously, as a punctuation to experiments expressing anger, or it may be part of expressive experiments involving loss more directly (for example, confronting an abuser with everything that was taken from one as a result of the abuse). The therapist now stands as witness, as part of the grieving community, as a fellow human sharing in the grief of life's difficulties.

The grief that can emerge during this phase of the healing process is often focused on the same themes as in the self-functions phase: grief for lost childhood; compassion for one's suffering as a child; deep regret for hurts inflicted on others as a result of one's own limitations, wounds, and reactivity; mourning for the amount of one's life that has been spent under the pall of or in recovery from one's victimization as a child; and, certainly, grief for lost innocence. There is no way to avoid the existential reality of these losses. They can only be mourned. But what makes mourning resolvable at this phase is that the losses can be mourned fully. They can now be held within a transcendent spiritual or philosophical context of meaning, which places them in a framework of understanding about life and life's purpose. The survivor is now open to the simple, essential human comfort of the therapist's acknowledging presence, and to the human community of supportive others.

Chapter Five

Reconsolidation

Reconsolidation, defined accurately but somewhat abstractly, is the reorganization and growth of the organism/environment field. To state this a bit more concretely, it involves the reorganization and growth of one's perceptions, one's sense of self, and one's understanding of the larger world and one's place in it, as well as reorganization and growth in how one makes meaning of experience. Reconsolidation comes about because one has made contact, in Gestalt terms, with something new (or perhaps with something old, which had become stale or useless). Having actively met and engaged with some experience that one's previous organization could not adequately hold, and having grappled with it in a way that changed one's relationship to it, one assimilates this experience so that it results in one's growth.

This cycle of contact–assimilation–growth is basic to Gestalt therapy's understanding of human process. Virtually all of human experience is movement through this cycle. Interruption or modulation of the cycle results in experience that in one way or another is problematic. In other words, either we make contact in such a way that something new and nourishing can come into our field and be assimilated for our growth or we make contact in such a way that something in the cycle is unfinished and so is insufficient for our growth. If healing, as we have said, is a process of reestablishing normal growth and development, which have been set awry by trauma, then reconsolidation can be seen as the final integrative step, analogous to the digestion and use of nutrition or the detoxification of what is not nourishing, that completes any particular cycle of healing work so as to make for true growth.

Why, in the context of healing from abuse, do I use the term *reconsolidation* instead of something more traditional, like *integration* or *assimilation*? Certainly, this process is going on for everyone all the time. We are constantly assimilating and integrating new experiences into our field, constantly growing and developing in at least some ways in the course of life. But for survivors of abuse, what must be grappled with and assimilated provokes a much more major destructuring of the ways they have come to be organized. What must be assimilated has major repercussions for the survivor's sense of self, sense of his or her environment and history, and course for the future. Therefore, I use the term *reconsolidation* to mark the magnitude of the reorganization that takes place in healing from abusive trauma, and to emphasize the way in which this reorganizational process is increasingly felt as a consolidation of everything that has gone before. With each completion of a cycle, each consolidation and reconsolidation, the survivor experiences himself as increasingly strong, increasingly stable and emotionally coherent, increasingly big in relation to the abuse, and increasingly part of something larger than himself that makes his history meaningful. Nor is it the survivor alone who is being reorganized in the reconsolidation process. His relationships, work life, community, and so on, are also being affected by the changes. Thus reconsolidation is a reorganization of the field, of the organism *and* the environment as a whole.

Transcendence and Reconsolidation

A significant aspect of healing from trauma, which I see as part of the reconsolidation process, is the emergence of a transcendent perspective. I do not wish to imply a necessarily deific or religious outlook, although that may be relevant to a particular survivor. From the perspective that I will define, transcendent meaning also includes existential and atheistic outlooks, which may also organize experience from a larger perspective than the individual's. Transcendence, used to refer to *the largest possible context of meaning*, includes any framework that goes beyond the individual and social contexts.

This term may be emotionally loaded for some readers, either in a predetermined positive direction or in an overdetermined negative one, but it is the only term that captures enough of the elements that seem important to the reconsolidation process. Before we see how reconsolidation occurs within each phase of healing, let us spend a moment understanding as deeply as we can what transcendence means. A transcendent perspective, by its very nature, encompasses all boundaries and levels of the system that it holds and gives meaning and direction, in some overarching way, to human concerns. The transcendent context of meaning could be an ecological one, which embeds us in the interconnected webs of relationship and interrelationship of biological communities. It could be the principle of randomness, which organizes in its chaotic way a framework for understanding the events to which we are subjected in the course of life. It could be a theological understanding, which gives meaning and direction to life events through a deity. It could be an understanding of life as a path of learning and development of the soul through whatever occurrences we find before us, causative (karmic) or random though such events may be.

Without some kind of transcendent context, it seems difficult if not impossible for the survivor to complete the cycle of healing. As part of the reconsolidation process that occurs over the course of healing, the survivor must shift her experience of trauma from one that fills the field of awareness to one that occupies a less predominant place. Unless traumatic events can be put into a perspective that subsumes the personal and even the social levels of a system, the survivor will find nothing large enough to encompass and hold the aberrant quality of the trauma. As the healing process advances, the shift from being a captive of the past to arriving in the present as a self (characteristic of the self-functions phase) requires having some sense of meaning that imbues past, present, and future with significance and direction. And as the survivor finds passage through the later course of healing, it is difficult for her truly to let go of trauma and its impact without also seeing her life in a context much larger than the trauma and her individual self.

In the usual phenomenological frame of reference, we tend to orient our experience from the center outward, as represented by Figure 5.1. The arrows represent our perceptual orientation (they are not intended to imply any kind of force) as we make contact in our field with different levels of our system. From the developmental perspective posited in the Healing Tasks Model, we would say that human growth and development encompass the polar processes of embeddedness in the field and differentiation from the field (see Wheeler, 1991). Over the course of development from infancy through adulthood, we go through an interplay of polar processes. On the one hand, we derive increasing support and interrelatedness with ever more encompassing aspects of the larger field in which we are embedded. On the other hand, our increasing sense of differentiation includes both a differentiated self and a differentiated layering of the more encompassing systems in which we are embedded. We experience ourselves first as embedded (as in the support-task processes) and then as figures

Figure 5.1. Phenomenological Orientation in Development.

From the center outward

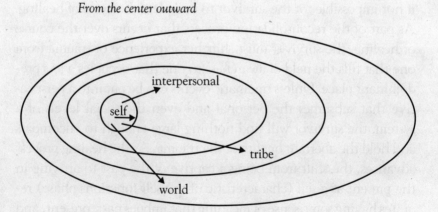

against that supporting ground, and then as bounding the larger ground and identifying with it against the ground of both individual and system. The newborn infant is predominantly of the field, with the relationship of self to support being one of seamless interconnection (if the environment is responsive to the infant's changing needs). Increasing individuation within this context of support proceeds as motor behavior and capacity (self function) develop. The toddler and preschooler increasingly extend the sense of field-embeddedness and identify themselves predominantly with the family level of the system—*my* family, *my* mommy, *my* brother.

We could trace this development of phenomenological perspective from adolescence ("my tribe"; see McConville, 1995) through young adulthood (where "my tribe" is translated into "my nation") and on into adulthood ("my world"), although perhaps only a few of us get as far as true identification with the global boundary of the field. Perhaps another characteristic of increasing maturity, as understood with this model, would be the capacity (self function) to shift perspectives, so that one can view things from various levels of the system within the field, as well as from the various perspectives of the other individuals with whom one has contact. This developmentally sound use of projection, as the capacity to imagine and include differing perspectives, is a hallmark of higher-order growth and development.

By now, of course, the reader will recognize this description of development as what occurs in a context that provides both support and challenge, in reasonable amounts. Where one or the other is missing or oversupplied, the gaps and creative adjustments that ensue will produce difficulties of one kind or another, and development will be truncated. The Healing Tasks Model describes the "corrective" processes that attempt to restore the developmental course for adults who have experienced childhood abuse, but similar models of developmental healing could certainly be generated from this outline of development and from the comments contained in the model presented here.

The transcendent perspective, by contrast with the phenomenological frame and orientation, does not simply entail the next outward boundary, in a kind of linear expansion of the field. It is different *dimensionally*. It imbues the field *as a whole*. Figure 5.2 is an inadequate but perhaps useful attempt to picture the shift of perspective that transcendence represents. The transcendent frame is a context that holds *us*, rather than what we hold or even *can* hold as individuals.

The Reconsolidation Task by Phase of Healing

The task of reconsolidation—as is true for other Healing Tasks—is a necessary process within each phase of healing. Of course, reconsolidation will have a different focus as the course of healing progresses, and as the survivor's growth requires ever more complex integration and assimilation of the growing field. In the sections that follow we will examine this task as it would be expressed in each phase of healing.

Figure 5.2. Spiritual Context in the Field.

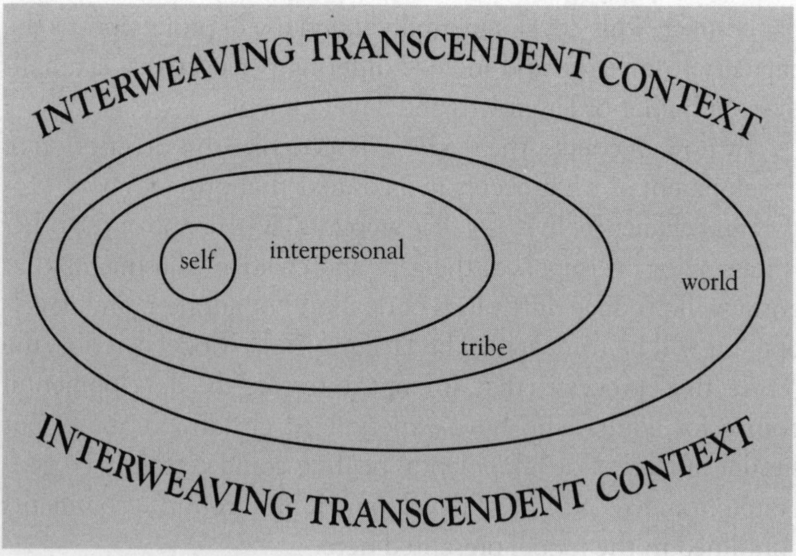

Reconsolidation in the Support Phase

In the early or support phase of healing, reconsolidation centers on including the abuse as a reality in one's life and coming to grips with one's identity as a survivor. For some, who do not develop full memories but are left at this point with impressions or intuitions, what is now being included is the possibility that abuse *might have occurred*. Their task is to tolerate the sense of uncertainty while allowing for the possibility that abuse might have occurred, so that it can be explored. These aspects of reconsolidation involve a kind of enlargement of the self because one's boundaries must expand to hold previously excluded memories of trauma or the possibility that trauma took place.

Reconsolidation also means assimilating the *impacts* of this acceptance, including mourning, shock, anger, hurt, and other reactions to the traumatic reality. This phase of healing is probably the most difficult one because fewer resources are available than in later phases for grappling with the emerging reality of abuse. The steadiness and consistency of the therapist and the frame of systemic and interpersonal support are the main resources at this point, unless the survivor has come to therapy with self functions and support already strongly developed.

The process of reconsolidation in the support phase certainly can generate feelings of anxiety and grief, but relief is also experienced as well. Energy that was tied up in keeping awareness of abuse outside the experienced self is now freed up, and the acknowledgment of the previously hidden factor of abuse leads to a better understanding of one's symptoms and life patterns. The experience of life as a struggle may be lessened for a period as the feeling that things now make sense is experienced. Moreover, much more support may be available now than at any other time in one's life.

Transcendence may go through a number of twists and turn in this phase. For some, preexisting religious or philosophical beliefs form a sustaining and integrating force for reconsolidation in the support phase. Anything that provides a more encompassing framework can help put the difficult reality that is being assimilated into some kind of perspective. A believing Christian has a metaphor of redemption through suffering, as well as the arms of Jesus and the bosom of Mary to seek solace in. The Buddhist has a philosophy that acknowledges the reality of suffering for all beings and gives a means of detachment, centering, and service to others as a way of transcending the suffering. The "new age" person usually has some essential belief in life experience as part of the development of the soul, and so abuse can be held in a framework where it can be seen as part of the path of learning. The feminist may use the framework of feminism to see her personal trauma as part of a social phenomenon shared in one way or another by women in general. Faith, prayer, and other spiritual practices (Wilson, 1989), as well as social action, helping others, and twelve-step programs, are all manifestations of self-transcendent resources that aid the survivor through the support phase.

The support phase can bring on a crisis of spirit, however. If spiritual or philosophical beliefs have been used as part of one's bolstering against the acknowledgment of abuse, then the assimilation of memories leads to a destructuring of belief as defense. The person who has used religion to create a rosy perspective will have to struggle as her limited spiritual viewpoint deserts her in time of need. The feminist who has avoided her own personal pain and vulnerability by throwing herself into "fighting for women" will now have to assimilate the experience of weakness, perhaps wondering why feminism is not supporting her to feel more powerful. Others may recognize that their strong belief in God did not save them from being abused. They may remember nights spent in vain praying that God will make Daddy stop, take the violence away, or rescue them from their family. The feeling of betrayal by God can be quite profound for some survivors at this point, as their simpler and more childlike ways of understanding deity and their relationship to deity are destructured by the disappointment of their expectations. Simple notions of God, simple notions of social philosophy, and simple notions of spirituality cannot stand up against the complexities of life and the reality of personal suffering. Thus the support phase may engender a reorganization, not only of one's sense of self but also of the larger meaning and context in which one feels embedded.

Some survivors have rejected any transcendent belief as useless or harmful. Those who were abused by ministers, priests, or nuns, those who were abused by fundamentalist families, and those who were abused by religious cults will often have abandoned anything spiritual in order to experience a boundary, a distinction of difference, from their abusers. Until transcendence is experienced as something emerging from oneself, rather than imposed on one or distorted by others, it will not be a particularly useful or important feature of healing. If it does become important, however, many of these survivors will begin to explore or develop their own transcendent spiritual or philosophical contexts as they gain a clearer, stronger sense of themselves over the course of self-functions work. The abusers will no longer be experienced as the purveyors and controllers of spiritual meaning. Spiritual meaning will be greater and larger than the abusers, just as it is greater and larger than the survivor. By identifying with the transcendent, the survivor eventually experiences himself as allied with something greater than those who harmed him.

Reconsolidation in the Self-Functions Phase

The self-functions phase is fundamentally about the survivor's acquiring a sense of agency and capacity. This acquisition involves hard work for the survivor-therapist team, and increasingly challenging self functions are faced as the foundation of the self's capacity grows during this phase. The changes produced for the survivor are sometimes not figural until the end of the phase, when the work and life in general are felt as having become easier.

What is reorganized in this phase is the relationship of the survivor to his past, to himself, to his current environment, and to his life. This is no small reorganization! The close of the self-functions phase marks acknowledgment and reconsolidation of the most major shift in the survivor's experience and organization since the assimilation of the abuse and its meaning.

Over the course of this phase, the survivor moves from feeling absorbed by and swamped in the past to being able to stand in the present and *face* the past. The acquisition of self functions (capacities) and the increased ability to make contact with the world are significant shifts in the survivor's orientation to himself, to others, and to his history. In the self-functions phase, reconsolidation often marks the sense of oneself as capable of mastery, with a growing sense of competence and power in one's life and in relation to the memories and history of abuse. Reconsolidation is often felt as a kind of celebration and appreciation. The ability of both client and therapist to rejoice in these changes is important.

As already noted, it is not uncommon for survivors to punctuate the end of this phase by terminating therapy or deciding to take a break. This, too, is part of reconsolidation in this phase. It serves growth because it often helps the survivor experience using the hard-won skills and capacities to live life with satisfaction, independently of the therapist. We can think of it as analogous to the "young adult" phase of development, in which children must move away from home and live on their own for a spell, to confirm that they can do it. And the therapist, like the parent who must let go as the later-adolescent child moves into the world, must trust the survivor's improved self-regulation and resilience in dealing with mistakes. As therapists, we must reorganize ourselves and move out of the position of providing the judgment and reference point that the survivor may have lacked, and which we may have provided legitimately in an earlier phase. The reorganization here is indeed of the field (organism and environment), including the therapist.

The larger field, including friends, family members, co-workers, and so on, is also reorganizing as the survivor relates differently to others in all her life contexts. Not infrequently during reconsolidation within the self-functions phase, the survivor sets limits with others that she has never set before. She carefully examines relationships that have been based on co-dependency and her own compliance. She finds herself no longer willing to engage in one-way relationships, with herself in the role of listener and helper. She is no longer willing to put up with abusive work situations, and so on. Entering into marital therapy, getting divorced, challenging the unhealthy aspects of friendships, and making other shifts in the field are not uncommon at this point.

One of the ongoing tasks of reconsolidation—developing a framework of transcendent meaning—has been present in one form or another during the self-functions phase but is now felt as more significant in the survivor's life. Whatever larger and transcendent meaning the survivor has evolved for himself is increasingly experienced as a resource, as the ground of his being, and as something that puts trauma into some kind of perspective that makes it less central and dominant. This reorganization of the trauma means that emerging memories, flashbacks, and so on, are held against a much larger background than ever before and so are more easily assimilated and integrated into the self. Transcendent meaning, at this phase, often acquires shades of a mission, of putting ones learnings and beliefs to use, doing something to fight injustice and abuse. The self's sense of capacity is extended from the personal to the transcendent sphere.

Reconsolidation in the Other Phases

The last two phases—undoing, redoing, and mourning, on the one hand, and reconsolidating, on the other—are discussed together because the reconsolidation process at the end of the third phase quite organically becomes the fourth and final phase of reconsolidation, often without a distinguishable boundary. At the end of the third phase of healing, the process of reconsolidation involves encompassing the whole of one's experience up to that point. This is a larger integration, an assimilation of healing as a whole. It often takes years and is mostly done outside psychotherapy.

As therapists, we are privileged whenever a survivor shares any part of this reconsolidation with us, since it is shared by choice rather than from need. We have completed our task with the survivor, and now the mourning process shifts to our being able to let go of our role with the survivor, honoring our dedication and struggle as healers, and being willing to allow a true and whole parting of the ways. Often during the undoing, redoing, and mourning phase, previously disowned aspects of spirituality will be confronted and worked through. The individual's relationship to transcendence is for the first time fully her own.

In the reconsolidation phase, abuse is integrated into one's personal history, now definitively in the past. It is experienced as meaningful but not especially dominating of one's life and perspective. Final reconsolidation of oneself in relation to survivorship does not happen all at once. It occurs with each piece of therapeutic work over the whole course of therapy. But as the healing process comes to a close, there may be a more profound letting go of one's identity as a survivor, and life goals can begin to come more into focus. This development cannot be brought about by affirmations or fiat. It is a result of hard work and of acquiring a mature perspective on the meaning and place of the abusive experience in one's life.

Mourning in the Reconsolidation Phase

In this phase, the closing of the cycle of healing is felt. Mourning and sadness are experienced more in the form of honoring and completion. This phase marks the passage and letting go of something that has been significantly defining in one's life. The sense of loss here is usually more existential than personal: the survivor's focus is on recognizing the pain and hurt of her abuse as *a part* of her life, and of life in general. But her focus is more on what she has learned and gained in her passage through the pain than on what is missing from her life.

Only when we have the capacity and support, both internally and in the field, to mourn deeply and fully can there be true resolution, true letting go, and a real completion of the figure of abuse. Mourning is the essential expression of grief and regret. Ultimately, it allows us to move on.

The Question of Forgiveness

One of the issues in healing from childhood abuse is the question of whether the survivor must forgive the abuser. I believe that much of what has been said about this issue has emerged more from a political stance of healers than from the needs, orientations, and phenomenology of the survivors engaged in their own healing. For example, therapists whose own transcendent orientation stems from a Christian-based theology, wherein the practice of forgiveness is a central concern, may insist that forgiveness is an essential element of healing, without which the survivor is not truly free to move on. Similarly, therapists who for theoretical reasons (another kind of religious belief) see lack of forgiveness as a sign that the survivor still has unfinished business, or is in some way still fixated on the abuse, will pathologize the absence of forgiveness as "incomplete resolution." This is similar, in my mind, to a feminist therapist's insistence, for reasons of political activism, that the survivor's healing cannot be complete without confrontation of the abuser, or a family therapist's insistence that healing is not complete without some kind of family meeting.

As therapists, we must be mindful not to project our own beliefs and needs—religious, scientific, or political—onto the client instead of joining in an *experiential investigation* of what would be correct for that survivor. Or, to put it another way, *my* dogma, in the Healing Tasks Model, is that the healing process is an exploration brought about by the experimentation and dialogue of therapy and of life, and that the survivor is the one who ultimately determines the proper direction of his or her own healing path.

That said, it is my experience that forgiveness is not a *requirement* for healing, although it is often intrinsic to the healing path for many survivors if by healing we mean an outcome by which the survivor has reoriented herself to the abuse as past, has been able to encompass the abuse as an aspect but not the whole of her nature, has been able to profoundly let go of the abuse through the process of mourning, and has a larger context of meaning in which her life (including the abuse) takes place. These things may indeed be facilitated by a transcendent spiritual or philosophical viewpoint that includes forgiveness, but many survivors do finish their healing (if any process of life can actually be said ever to truly finish) without forgiving their abusers.

What else, then, shows lack of resolution that might help to guide client and therapist toward assessing whether something may indeed be unfinished? Most of the survivors I have worked with, who had varying beliefs and orientations, at least found a place of *becoming at peace* with their histories and life experiences, as shaped by the abuse. I expressly do *not* mean that they were neutral about abuse (their own or others') or no longer had feelings about it or took political or social action to fight abuse. One can feel deep empathy for the hurts of others and honor the reality and existence of one's own pain on the personal level and yet be grounded in something larger and beyond one's individual self. Becoming at peace is *not* denial or dissociation, like minimization of pain before memories are known or grappled with. I am reminded of an old Zen story: before enlightenment, there are a rock, a tree, a mountain; at the moment of enlightenment, there are a ROCK, a TREE, a MOUNTAIN; after enlightenment, there are a rock, a tree, a mountain. The overwhelming realization that came with enlightenment is now integrated and experienced as intrinsic to reality.

Survivors do express the experience of reconsolidation with words like *forgiveness, neutral, reconciled, detached, at peace,* and *serenity.* Having healed from abuse, the survivor faces the same life difficulties and crises that everyone must face (loss, aging, death), as well as the mystery of being and life's joys and successes (which can actually be *more* difficult for survivors to face, because they are more experienced in dealing with great difficulties than great joys so early in life). But the whole point of the process of growth is that we become ever more encompassing of our world, more differentiated and mature in our perceptions and responses, more connected and in contact with self and other, more able to face new challenges with depth, resonance, and heart.

The four essential healing tasks have been discussed in detail in chapters two, three, four and five. Table 5.1 is included at the end of this chapter to provide a summary of these tasks as they are seen within each stage of healing.

Table 5.1. Summary of the Phases and Tasks of Healing.

Support Phase	
Support	Establishing the therapist as support*
	Establishing the therapeutic environment*
	Establishing systemic support*
	Validating abuse and feelings*
Self Functions	Developing grounding skills
	Managing stimulation
Undoing/Redoing/ Mourning	Encouraging additional systemic support as new memories emerge
	Testing therapist's support and holding capacity
Reconsolidation	Assimilating reality of abuse history
Self-Functions Phase	
Support	Managing stimulation and affect levels
	Continuing basic grounding skills
	Using therapist for grounding
Self Functions	Boundary functions*: Developing functioning and awareness of interpersonal and bodily boundaries
	Experiencing functions*: Making choices about managing the intensity and pacing of any kind of experience (in therapy, at school, at work)

	Self-Functions Phase (cont'd.)
Self Functions (cont'd.)	Feeling functions*: Broadening the range and intensity of tolerable affect
	Reality-perception functions*: Sorting out projections and distortions; overlaying the present on the past
	Self-support functions*: Learning self-care and self-nurturance
Undoing/Redoing/ Mourning	Testing self functions with higher-risk experiments
	Doing memory work, with emphasis on identification of necessary self functions
	Reworking missing self functions in the context of memories
	Improving client's tolerance of both sides of an issue, and of own negative qualities
	Improving client's tolerance and ownership of projections
Reconsolidation	Emerging transcendent perspective

	Undoing/Redoing/Mourning Phase
Support	Validating feelings of loss and sadness, even if they exist for no apparent reason
	Validating emerging memories, even if fragmentary
	Working on memories as they contribute to validation and as current self functions allow
Self Functions	Experimenting with expressions of affect
	Undoing, with focus on current relationships (speaking up, standing one's ground, being active, checking out guesses)
Undoing/Redoing/ Mourning	Experimentally reenacting* of scenes of abuse; symbolically or actually confronting abuser, using new skills and capabilities
	Bringing back from the past* those parts and capacities of the self that were left there
	Allowing core memories of abuse to emerge*
	Working on retroflected core,* returning self-referred behavior and attitudes to original abusive context

Undoing/Redoing/ Mourning Phase (cont'd.)	
Reconsolidation	Further development of transcendent perspective

Reconsolidation Phase	
Support	Using spirituality as support
	Supporting client's emerging identity as a survivor
	Encouraging assimilation of the reality of abuse
	Possible reaching of hiatus in therapy
Self Functions	Affirming sense of mastery and strength
	Diminishing intensity of symptoms
	Reaching the point of saying, "I can handle it"
Undoing/Redoing/ Mourning	Using transcendent framework meaning to encompass abuse
	Finishing memory work
Reconsolidation	Integrating abuse into larger life meaning*
	Redefining the self as larger than survivorship*
	Affirming abuse's meaning within overall life purpose*

*Indicates figural task for the respective phase.

Chapter Six

Assessing the Healing Process

Once the clinician is familiar with the Healing Tasks Model, the next question is, "How do we know which phase the client is in?" With a clinical model that accounts for the layered, interactive nature of developmental phases, it can be difficult to determine the specific phase, because significant tasks or processes appear and reappear at different phases. For example, clients must work on self-functions tasks, such as boundaries, throughout the course of healing. What distinguishes someone in the support phase who is working on certain boundaries from someone in the self-functions phase or the reconsolidation phase?

We are also interested in the survivor as a person. Each survivor comes to the formal process of therapy with different resources and different capacities. Each one has adjusted creatively in his or her own way to the presence of trauma. Even though we see commonalities among survivors, such as symptomatic patterns like anxiety, flooding, and dissociation, every person brings his or her own resources to managing them. It is important to acknowledge what clients bring with them as they face particular phases of development, for this is what they can draw on in their passage through those phases.

For example, two clients both appear to be in the support phase. They are both working on establishing support and trust with the therapist, learning grounding skills for managing dissociation and anxiety, and struggling with the meaning of memory flashes of abuse (which were unexpected and do not fit into their pictures of who they are). One of the clients has few friends and

no preexisting transcendent viewpoint within which to understand crisis and difficulty. She can tolerate little or no emotion
without dissociating. She does, however, have a rich creative side,
which has found an outlet in drawing and journal writing, and
these serve as tremendous releases of inner feelings for her. The
other client has a strongly supportive spouse and a budding sense
of spirituality, which gives her an understanding that crisis is part
of spiritual growth. She has always been able to challenge others
(a boundary skill) when she disagreed. Clearly, the preexisting
support and self functions that each of these clients brings to the
support phase will make for a different passage through that phase.
One client will have more support available through her spiritual
viewpoint, her spouse, and her ability to manage issues of trust and
mistrust actively with her therapist. The other client will need to
go much more slowly, learning to develop support and safety for
expressing her trust and mistrust along the way, but will have her
creative expression as a resource. Both clients will be working on
other issues as well in the support phase, such as tolerating feelings, grounding, and accepting the reality of the abuse. But even
these tasks may be faced differently as each survivor approaches
these issues with her own particular resources.

Similarly, two survivors enter therapy and are both apparently
in the self-functions phase. One has built up support in the course
of recovering from alcohol addiction, through rigorous involvement in Alcoholics Anonymous. She has attended support groups
and developed a spiritual outlook. She has also developed a basic
tolerance for feelings but has little capacity for grounding herself
on her own, without calling a sponsor or appealing to her group
for support. The other client has managed to pass in more intro-
verted fashion through the process of grappling with first memories of abuse. She has read widely in the survivorship literature and
worked with exercises and journal-writing methods to learn how
to manage feelings and memories. She meditates regularly to center and ground herself, as well as to support her transcendent connection. Both clients appear to want to work on developing

boundaries, and both need to learn more about being able to deal with feelings. These are concerns of the self-functions phase but each client will need to backtrack a bit to "loop in" the foundational concerns that belong to the support phase, to have the basis for moving through the self-functions phase. The first client may need to develop more self-support, such as grounding skills, and learn to use them to tolerate feeling waves better, without resorting to other people to keep her grounded and present. Breathing, body contact, and meditation will be helpful to her. The second client has many inner means of support but has not taken the risk of building interpersonal support. In her isolation, she has no one to reach out to when the going gets rough, and her isolation heightens her feelings of shame and unworthiness, since she does not know or see that there are others like her who are struggling, too. A support group, work on developing friendships, and so on, will be essential to her for developing self functions.

In what follows, I provide an experimental summary Healing Tasks Checklist of many of the features already described in this text. The checklist can help guide the clinician in assessing the course of healing for a client. The features presented here seem best to mark the phases of healing. The checklist is based on the adult population typical of those who come to me for help: mostly women, urban and suburban, between the ages of nineteen and fifty.

The checklist is much like an interview schedule. It should not be seen as a scorable assessment device. It is intended as a way to organize clinical thinking. It has content validity, and its items are drawn explicitly from the model as presented. It appears also to have clinical validity and utility. Its cross-validity and reliability are currently unknown, given the American Psychological Association guidelines for psychological instruments.[23] Some of the items may not turn out to distinguish one phase of healing from another, and they may not be of equal weight in the determination. My intent in presenting a clinical checklist, rather than a formal assessment device, is to leave room for clinical judgment by the therapist. My interest is not in boxing the client into a particular phase but in providing a guide for the therapeutic process, but the checklist should not be used to supersede clinical judgment.

A number of clients have also found the checklist useful in looking at their own process, independently of the therapist's assessment but in conjunction with the therapeutic work. Used judiciously and wisely, in collaboration with the therapist, filling out the checklist can be a useful exercise for clients, to help them spot areas that need development, affirm work that has been accomplished, and focus the therapeutic process. This exercise can be disappointing for clients who wish to see themselves as farther along than they actually are, but for the most part it is very validating. Clients can see what they have accomplished and what resources they bring to their healing. They can see where they need work and they can find gaps in the healing process that are holding them back and creating "resistance." They can gain the sense that there is a process to healing and that it is *finite*.

Since the checklist is meant to be used as an adjunct to clinical judgment, it should be used only by readers who are already thoroughly familiar with the Healing Tasks Model and the foregoing chapters. I recommend trying it out with familiar clients, so that there will be a large pool of data and interactions on which to base judgments. Later, it can be tried with clients with whom the clinician is less familiar. *In any case, the checklist should not be used with a new client before the therapist has had a number of sessions gathering history and observing the client's behavior.* It is not a screening device. It is *not* intended to assess the truth or falsity of memories of abuse, or to determine whether a person is a survivor or not.

I use this checklist to help formulate the data I have gathered about new clients, to help me clarify what I am working on with steady clients when I feel confused in the course of therapy, and to help me understand why we may be getting stuck during periods of impasse. I have often discovered that "resistances" or "stuck" points in therapy with survivors are a matter of neglecting tasks in previous phases, so that the survivor does not have adequate support or self functions to approach a later phase. Sometimes we also need to redo some otherwise accomplished task in the new phase, to meet a higher level of demand.

Using the Checklist

Purchasers of this book have my permission to make copies of the assessment instrument provided at the back of the book *for learning purposes only*. Anyone who wishes to use it experimentally and clinically should obtain the checklist directly from me, to ensure that the most current and clinically useful version is available.[24]

Essentially, the checklist offers two views: Part A is based on what survivors typically look like at the beginning of a particular period of work (although they will also carry these characteristics well into that work) and is intended to estimate the *phase* of healing that the survivor is *currently* in. Part B is a listing of the typical behaviors that mark the accomplishment of the different healing *tasks*. The *combination* of the two views seems to offer a fairly good idea of the phase the client is working in. It also appears to highlight the preexisting strengths a survivor brings to therapy and to demonstrate the tasks that remain, or even those left undone from previous phases, which are preventing movement in therapy. The examples given with some of the tasks are not intended to be definitive but rather to help characterize behaviors and issues representative of the tasks, so as to help the clinician understand the scope of the questions. Above all, the checklist offers a view of the healing *process*.

Marking and Evaluating the Checklist

The basic procedure is to go through all the items and check off those that you can affirm for the client with an adequate degree of certainty, starting with Part A and proceeding through Part B. Make notations and comments as you go along: "Seems to be working on this." "Can do this with most people, but not yet with the boss." These will help you get a much more specific and informed picture of your particular client's healing process. Remember, this is not a psychological test. It is a checklist intended to help organize clinical information and impressions. Your thoughtfulness and consideration are more important than the "right" answers. Remember also that the tasks in Part B are not "steps," and no survivor will enter therapy with the same pre-existing resources. The checklist, like the Healing Tasks Model in general, does not take the place of other clinical and diagnostic considerations. These also must be factored into assessment and treatment.

Using this checklist with clients who carry a diagnosis of Multiple Personality Disorder (MPD) is a more complex issue. One personality may be highly functional and have significant self functions, whereas others are just coming forward and are still immersed in feelings about abuse and trauma. It is difficult to know how to describe the phase or task that is most figural for an MPD client. General experience in treating MPD suggests, however, that it is not necessary for all the alters to be at the same level of development before integration can occur. Nevertheless, the developmental limitations of one set of personalities can clearly hold back the healing process for the whole system, and it is important to know where these developmental needs are within the system. Not all personalities need to share the same level of self functions for healing, since with coconsciousness they can draw on the self functions deposited with particular personalities, but it does seem true that most of the personalities need to have developed support in order for healing to advance. When filling out the checklist for MPD clients, you must find a way to mentally "average" your assessments for the task items. Often the alters who significantly hold the average down are the ones that need clinical attention. Our interest is in using the checklist to get a general impression of the phase of healing, and to help us look at what parts of the MPD system (at least those parts we know about) may be needing work in some area, to allow the whole system to move ahead. If the MPD system as a whole appears to be in the later phases of healing but is still unable to move ahead, we may suspect that there are still hidden parts, whose issues lie at earlier phases of healing, or that there are hidden issues for the parts that are known. The assessment instrument appears in its entirety, without annotations, at the back of the book.

Filling Out Part A

This first part of the checklist describes the features and symptoms typical of survivors at the beginning of the different phases of healing. The vertical columns of items are divided into the various phases (rows) of healing and seen according to the different characteristics typical at the beginning of those phases. For example, the beginning of each phase is seen within the dimensions of general functioning, posttraumatic stress, systemic support, and so on. The phases are presented side by side, so that you can easily compare one phase to another according to the particular dimension in question.

Not all the items within a particular dimension are mutually exclusive across phases of healing, but you are likely to find that one "box" will have the most items checked rather than spread across the phases. The items have been constructed to discriminate among phases, but of course they will be refined as I receive feedback from interested users. If you find that a category—say, general functioning—has checked items spread across all the phases, it is likely that your knowledge of the client is still too superficial for you to discriminate well, or that you need to reread the items to make sure you understand them.

The last row of Part A is for totaling the items checked for each individual phase. After filling out the checklist for a client, simply count the total number of items checked in each column, divide this figure by the total number of possible items in that column, and multiply by 100 to find the percentage of items checked for each phase.

Part A: Identifying the Phase of Healing

Client _____

✔ Check any items that apply for this client.

Category	Beginning of Support Phase	Beginning of Self-Functions Phase	Beginning of Undoing, Redoing, and Mourning Phase	Beginning of Reconsolidation Phase
General functioning	☐ Serious impairment of relationships: family, work, school	☐ Effort focused on developing more stable functioning in one or two areas of impairment	☐ Good general functioning in most areas ☐ Ability to address directly those areas where difficulties exist	☐ Good functioning in relationships: family, work, school
Posttraumatic Stress Disorder (PTSD) symptomatology (numbing, restricted affect, flooding, depression, anxiety, hypersensitivity to cues recalling abuse, avoidance of cues recalling abuse, intrusive recollections, flashbacks)	☐ Predominance of PTSD symptoms ☐ Little ability to cope with PTSD symptoms ☐ Feeling of helplessness predominates	☐ Frequent presence but not predominance of PTSD symptoms ☐ Continued periods of feeling flooded and overwhelmed by memories and waves of feeling accompanied by somatic sensations and anxiety ☐ Emphasis on learning to manage PTSD symptoms	☐ Occasional PTSD symptoms, but with significantly diminished intensity ☐ Application of coping strategies to management of PTSD symptoms when they occur	☐ Rarity or absence of PTSD symptoms

Systemic support	□ Little or no interpersonal or community support □ Tendency to shift between rigid self-support and dependence on others for support □ Some awareness of need for more support, but fear of reaching out, with consequent immobilization	□ Basic sense of support felt from therapist □ Some support with abuse issues found from friends or significant others □ Contact with basic social service systems, as appropriate	□ Increased ability to manage differences and conflict in relationships □ Willingness to renegotiate and/or terminate unhealthy relationships □ Seeking out of a broader, more nurturing network of support □ Working through of therapeutic transference	□ Mutual support and interdependence in relationships □ Little needed from therapist, but contact welcomed and appreciated
Management of affect, stress, and restimulation	□ Poor stress tolerance □ Unpredictable feelings of being overwhelmed that occur often □ Often experiences disruption, disorganization, when under stress □ Lack of coping skills □ Frequent restimulation of trauma	□ Poor stress tolerance but some coping skills □ Tentative stability when dealing with difficult feelings and memories □ Difficulty clearly discriminating between overreactions and appropriate reactions to stressors □ Understanding that overreactions are restimulations	□ General sense of mastery and ability to cope with stress reactions □ Awareness of overreactions to stressors, ability to sort through overreactions or seek help □ Ability to constructively use and assimilate strong reactions to memories	□ Trauma rarely restimulated □ Emotional response produced by remembering trauma, but not associated with disruption or disorganization of functioning □ Ability to experience and tolerate broad range of feelings

Part A: Identifying the Phase of Healing (cont'd.)

Category	Beginning of Support Phase	Beginning of Self-Functions Phase	Beginning of Undoing, Redoing, and Mourning Phase	Beginning of Reconsolidation Phase
Self perceptions and self-care	☐ Feeling of shame, self-critical or self-diminishing thoughts predominant ☐ Comfort, soothing derived from addictive or compulsive behaviors in response to difficult feelings or thoughts	☐ Acceptance of the idea that the sense of "badness" and lack of worth is related to something that happened to them rather than their "nature" ☐ Acceptance of responsibility for dealing with addictive and compulsive patterns	☐ Recognition of shame and self-criticism as habitual processes rather than as "truths" about self ☐ Working through and referring back to abusive context (shame and self-critical and self-diminishing thoughts) ☐ Availability of healthy self-care, self-soothing, and self-comforting as "antidotes" to abusive context	☐ Ability to accept shame as an appropriate feeling in response to violations of personal values rather than as a definition of self ☐ Ability to respect, nurture, and celebrate self
Acknowledgment of abuse	☐ Shifts between denial and belief in possible history of abuse	☐ Acceptance of reality and possibility of abuse but hesitation in moving toward addressing it directly	☐ Acceptance of reality of abuse and willingness to move toward difficult issues associated with trauma	☐ Acceptance and working through most aspects of abuse ☐ Integration of abuse experience into wider view of self

Stance toward survivorship	❑ Denied, limited, highly tentative, or intellectualized acceptance of survivorship, with little or no evidence of its emotional impact	❑ Identification of self as possibly a survivor (or recognition that more information is necessary before survivorship can be affirmed) ❑ Acquisition of basic understanding of relationship between abuse and current experience and behavior ❑ Acknowledgment that past abuse influences current feelings	❑ Acceptance of not knowing everything about abuse, and recognition that it is not necessary to work through absolutely everything in order to have a good life ❑ Power of discrimination, as evidenced by recognition that not everything difficult in life was caused by the abuse	❑ Abuse seen as part of history that influences but does not define self ❑ Sense of opening to new possibilities beyond abuse-related issues
Reality testing (ability to distinguish between past and current experiences)	❑ Inability to distinguish reactions to current circumstances from reactions conditioned or influenced by past experiences ❑ Feeling that present and past are blurred together and poorly bounded	❑ Tendency to be defensive or denying about suggestions that perceptions of current situations may be distorted by abusive past experiences ❑ Frequent appearance of projecting past abusive context onto current interactions, with no awareness of doing so	❑ Ability to recognize when reactions to current circumstances reflect responses or perceptions related to past traumatic context ❑ Ability to begin recognizing, confronting, and understanding ways of having a negative impact on others	❑ Ability to own and take responsibility for negative impact on others without feeling overwhelmed by shame or self-blame ❑ Ability to recognize own human failings and flaws without feeling overwhelmed by shame or self-blame

Part A: Identifying the Phase of Healing (cont'd.)

Category	Beginning of Support Phase	Beginning of Self-Functions Phase	Beginning of Undoing, Redoing, and Mourning Phase	Beginning of Reconsolidation Phase
Orientation to past, present, and future	☐ Sensation of being gripped or flooded by the past ☐ Belief that there is "no future"	☐ Sensation of being less gripped by the past, but still with no strong anchoring in the present	☐ Interest in grappling with and finishing with the past ☐ Sense of "possible future" emerging ☐ Good anchoring in a sense of the present	☐ Realistic and optimistic orientation toward present and future ☐ Integration of past issues
Spiritual perspective	☐ Tendency of traumatic symptoms to overwhelm any preexisting spiritual or philosophical perspective	☐ Movement toward looking to the spiritual or the philosophical for support and understanding in facing the reality of trauma ☐ Beginning of ability to consider abuse in a larger context of spiritual or other encompassing meaning	☐ Heightened interest in spiritual perspective, with possible return to previous spiritual and philosophical involvements or exploration of new areas	☐ Integration of spiritual perspective into viewpoint and life ☐ Understanding of abuse within larger spiritual perspective
Percentage of items checked	(checked items) / 21 (total items) ×100 = ___%	(checked items) / 22 (total items) ×100 = ___%	(checked items) / 23 (total items) ×100 = ___%	(checked items) / 19 (total items) ×100 = ___%

Filling Out Part B

Part B has sections for each of the four healing tasks. Under each task are questions for more specific areas—the subtasks, so to speak. Simply read the items and check those that apply to your client. Note specific areas of concern that come up in the course of filling out the items, and make any qualifications that are appropriate. Most of all, let the checklist that follows stimulate your thinking about the client you are working with.

Part B: Healing Tasks

✔ Check any items that are *true now* for this client.

I. Support Tasks
    A. Trust/Mistrust
        ❏ 1. Aware of having concerns about trust, boundaries (for example, ethical issues or issues of sexual boundaries) and/or your attitude toward working with issues related to abuse and survivors of abuse?
        ❏ 2. Able to express to you concerns related to trust?
        ❏ 3. Able to express to you concerns about boundary violations?
        ❏ 4. Able to express to you concerns, as they arise, about your attitude toward abuse and working with survivors of abuse?
    B. Safety and Containment Boundaries
        ❏ 1. Able to understand and be responsive to the boundaries and limits of the therapy environment and the therapeutic relationship?
        ❏ 2. Able to manage self in basic ways to ensure personal safety (that is, absence of suicidal ideation and doing of harm to self and others; presence of ability and willingness to channel emotions into safe forms of expression)?

These issues, related to the establishment of trust and safety in the therapeutic environment, are the ones that the survivor, particularly at the *beginning* of the support phase, typically cannot engage in without the direct assistance of the therapist. During that stage, making it possible to engage in these issues and negotiate them is the work of therapy. As the survivor gains experience in negotiating these issues *explicitly* with the therapist, rather than indirectly or not at all, as she may they have done in the past, we find that she is able to take the initiative more, so that by the latter part of the support phase we will be checking these boxes off fairly readily. These tasks will be *accomplished* and *accessible to the client*. Clients who enter therapy already able to initiate discussion of these concerns with the therapist probably have more self functions and support available to them than others do, and we would expect a more rapid passage through the support phase for them than for others. They may also be initiating therapy at a later phase of healing.

Safety and containment tasks are typically the most difficult ones for survivors who have a borderline mode of adaptation and for MPD clients. Thus we find that the support phase in general is stretched out with these clients, since these boundaries are repeatedly challenged before they are in any sense "established." To the borderline client, any boundary is automatically experienced as abandonment, rather than safety and containment. It takes some time for her to recognize the consistency of the therapist over time as the holding environment. Other clients find these boundaries supportive and comforting because they know clearly what to expect, and that counters their experience of others as changeable and inconsistent. For the MPD client, the issues of trust are of greater concern, since these clients are often organized to deal with betrayal of trust. There will be much hanging back and testing by alter personalities in the background, perhaps before this hidden process becomes apparent to the therapist.

C. Validation of History of Abuse (the clinician using this checklist should be familiar with the stance taken in the Healing Tasks Model toward the validity of memories and the proper role of the therapist in validating memories; before beginning or assessing this aspect of the work, the clinician should also be aware of the potential for biasing the client's beliefs)

❏ 1. Able to accept support and validation from you regarding importance of his or her feelings, impressions, or memories?

❏ 2. Able to entertain the possibility of a history of abuse, and of his or her own survivorship?

❏ 3. Able to entertain this possibility with relatively little denial, disbelief, disconfirmation, or self-doubt (this ability expected only toward the end of the support phase)?

Validation and recognition of the history of abuse is one of the central concerns and tasks of the support phase. Therefore, we find that clients who either are entering into this phase or are in the midst of it will be cycling between recognition and denial or disbelief. This is the normal cycle of having to assimilate something (the trauma) that does not fit into the previously recognized narrative of one's life story, and it cannot be done all at once. Some survivors, given the increased recognition of childhood abuse in the media, may have a kind of superficial acceptance of their abuse, but it is intellectualized or distant, without any affect about it. This adaptive pattern fits the traumatic memory or impressions prematurely into a kind of introjected identity, taken in wholesale from the environment without true assimilation. It should not be mistaken for true acceptance.

It is important that the therapist have an *accepting*, but *not influencing* position here. It is not the therapist's job to convince the client that she is a survivor. It is the therapist's job to support the *possibility* that a memory, flashback, or impression of something could be true, help the client sort through the experience, help her explore, normalize the cycle of doubt and disbelief, and point to the realities of the client's experience (such as posttraumatic stress symptoms, feelings, and reactions, or the lack of these clinical signs) that she is ignoring or denying, or that may have some bearing on the client's self-validation of the abuse.

As this task is truly accomplished, we find a sense of assimilated acceptance. This does not mean that everything is now remembered; far from it, for many survivors. It means that the reality of trauma and survivorship is part of the client's life space.

D. Systemic Social Support (a "healthy" relationship is characterized as having good boundaries and as being nonabusive)

❏ 1. Able to turn to others outside therapy for support?

	Available?	Healthy?	Unhealthy?
Intimate relationship	❏	❏	❏
Friends	❏	❏	❏
Co-workers	❏	❏	❏
Family of origin	❏	❏	❏
Family of choice	❏	❏	❏
Support groups	❏	❏	❏

❏ 2. Medical resources available, if needed?
❏ 3. Social service resources available, if needed?
❏ 4. Able to use these kinds of support in appropriate and timely ways?

The acquisition of systemic support is part of the general task of developing support. For item D.1, you may find that you will have more than one check mark for a category—for instance, that friends are both an available and healthy support, or that the family of origin is available for support but is by and large an unhealthy choice for support. We find that those clients who come into therapy with a full range of support will move, other things being equal, through the support phase more easily than those who do not. Pay particular attention to clients who seem to be working on the later phases of therapy but who either have few available supports or a number of unhealthy ones. Chances are good that they will go into crisis when stressed (such as by new traumatic memories) or that therapy will become "stuck" as the healing tasks require more risk and support. This is one of the frequent "holes in the fabric" that make healing difficult if they are not attended to. My clinical experience is that most "regression" in healing—that is, the apparent inability to sustain progress, or the recurrence of crisis in therapy—can be traced to insufficient support. It is so against the grain for survivors to reach out for help and take seriously the importance of maintaining systemic connections and interpersonal relationships that these are easily allowed to lapse, even by those who are in the later phases of healing. By far the most common adaptation for the abused person is to pull into herself, not to seek help but to go it all alone. This may be the hardest habit for survivors to break, since doing otherwise makes them feel so vulnerable.

We would not expect a survivor in the support phase to have seen fully to this task. For many survivors in this phase, developing a bare scaffolding of support represents all the resources they can bring to bear. As the self functions develop, survivors can return to this task and take greater interpersonal risks so as to develop wider and richer networks of systemic support. It is important to keep in mind just how much a client has developed this task, however, since it has proved to be one of the most influential factors in apparent "resistance" to later-phase work.

E. Basic Self-Functions as Self-Support
    1. Able to manage stimulation and intensity of feelings and responses with any of the following basic tools?
    ❏ Relaxation methods

❑ Grounding methods (for example, sensory awareness of body and environment)
❑ Breathing
❑ Self-comforting (for example, attending to and
appropriately responding to own needs for food,
rest, relaxation, exercise)
❑ Others (for example, psychotropic medication,
internal "safe space," journal writing)
❑ 2. Able to use these basic tools with your coaching?
❑ 3. Able to use these basic tools without your coaching
(on own initiative)?
❑ 4. Able to use contact with you for self-grounding in
the present (through eye contact, verbal expression,
and so on)?

These tools, developed during the support phase, form the
ground for coping with difficult feelings and memories. Clients who
do not appear to have any way of managing these things are typically in the early part of the support phase. Clients who appear to
be focusing on the later phases but have little capacity to use
grounding methods will need to backtrack and fill in this gap as
greater challenges are faced in the normal course of the healing
process. Survivors who can use grounding methods on their own
initiative are probably working in the self-functions phase, or they
have been able to develop a broader range of self functions because
of their life circumstances before they faced the support-phase tasks.

F. Reconsolidation Task
❑ Sense of self redefined to include possibility of abuse
in childhood?

As most of the previously reviewed tasks are accomplished,
the survivor will appear more or less organized in relation to her
identity as a survivor. She may be disturbed by the memories

themselves but will derive some stability from the fact of her survivorship itself.

II. Self-Functions Tasks
   A. Boundary Functions
      ❏ 1. Able to manage *interpersonal* boundaries competently?
        ❏ Able to say yes or no as the need arises?
        ❏ Able to withdraw appropriately from potentially dangerous or problematic situations?
        ❏ Able to refuse, modify, or question your interventions in accordance with own feelings and needs?
        ❏ Able to have some flexibility in interpersonal boundaries instead of maintaining a fixed stance (consistently guarded and rigid, or uniformly compliant)?
      ❏ 2. Able to manage *bodily* boundaries competently (for example, by making and expressing choices about whether he or she wishes to be touched, and how)?
      ❏ 3. Able to manage *sexual* boundaries?
        ❏ Consents or refuses according to own wishes?
        ❏ Makes realistic assessment of a situation's safety and appropriateness?

Boundary functions are essential before the survivor can be in a position to competently negotiate interpersonal relationships, prevent reabuse, and manage the ambition and enthusiasm of the therapist's interventions. When evaluating this task clinically, consider it also from a historical standpoint, since some survivors at certain points of development may appear rigidly bounded, but the opposite has been their customary stance. Toward the middle or later parts of this phase, some survivors seem to become quite rigid about their boundaries, in a kind of reaction formation to their previous lack of boundaries. I have found that survivors in this position are not able to develop more flexible and situationally responsive boundaries until later in the self-functions phase.

B. Experiencing Functions
   ❏ 1. Able to make useful choices for managing the *grading* (intensity) of any experience (including therapy, work, school)?
      ❏ Usually does not overstimulate self with activity, entertainment (TV, movies), or reading that leads to feeling stirred up, anxious, and out of control?
      ❏ Knows when a particular memory of topic is too much to deal with, given current support, and takes appropriate action to reduce intensity?
      ❏ Knows when a particular topic, experiment, or level of work in therapy is too difficult or over-stimulating and is able to express this?
      ❏ Tends not to take on too much work on the job and is able to express workload needs to supervisor or employer?
   ❏ 2. Able to make self-respectful choices for managing the *pacing* (frequency) of any experience (including therapy, work, school)?
      ❏ Knows when to take a break from focusing on issues related to abuse and when to focus instead on other things in therapy?
      ❏ Knows when it is time to move back toward difficult subjects, so that these are not avoided?
      ❏ At work, makes appropriate use of breaks to relax?
      ❏ Makes appropriate use of sick days, vacation time, and so on, to meet health-related needs, spend time with family, or take time for self?

As the capacity increases to make healthy choices for managing experience within assimilable limits, so does the capacity to work with increasingly difficult traumatic memories, as well as to face greater life challenges in general. The increasing sense of competence that the survivor has as she moves through the self-functions phase is partly a result of this increased capacity: "I have what it takes to face whatever I need to face."

C. Self-Support Functions
    ❑ 1. Knows how to self-soothe (for example, by eating when hungry, resting when tired, refraining from self-criticism for perceived mistakes)?
    ❑ 2. Able to act toward self in loving, caring ways (for example, by praising self for a job well done, preparing a tasty meal for self, "being lazy")?
    ❑ 3. Seeks adequate medical care in a timely fashion?

These constitute some of the basic capacities for self-care that contribute to making healing possible. Others are certainly possible, and you are invited to add to this list as you assess your client.

D. Feeling Functions (an "integrated" feeling is experienced as appropriate to the situation, and as originating in the self)
    ❑ 1. Experiences a variety of feelings over a range of *tolerable* intensity?

	Integrated	Tolerated	Disruptive	Absent
Sadness	❑	❑	❑	❑
Anger	❑	❑	❑	❑
Vulnerability	❑	❑	❑	❑
Joy	❑	❑	❑	❑
Disgust	❑	❑	❑	❑
Pride	❑	❑	❑	❑
Happiness	❑	❑	❑	❑
Shame	❑	❑	❑	❑
Excitement	❑	❑	❑	❑
Love	❑	❑	❑	❑

    ❑ 2. Able to work actively with strong feelings as they emerge, so as to tolerate and assimilate them?
    ❑ 3. Able to tell when emotional reactions are stronger

than the current stimulus warrants and are more related to events in the past?

❏ 4. Able to use this awareness to modulate strong feelings reactions?

In checking off the preceding chart, you will check *Integrated* if the feeling is available, well tolerated, spontaneous, and *owned by* the person; *Tolerated*, if the person can bear the feeling but has to work at managing it; *Disruptive*, if the experience of the feeling is uncomfortable or significantly disturbing; and *Absent*, if the feeling is generally unavailable to the client. Try to check only *one* of these categories for each feeling.

The capacity to have a range of available feelings, and to tolerate and manage having them, is crucial to facing traumatic memories, which by their nature contain strong feelings, as well as to facing life fully, in all its complexity. This list is not intended to be exhaustive but only to highlight some commonly problematic feelings. The positive feelings listed here are often as difficult for survivors to tolerate as the negative ones, but are essential to the survivor's ability to live a good, satisfying life healed of pain.

E. Reality-Perception Functions
   ❏ 1. Able to have some sense of distorting or projecting onto others or external circumstances?
   ❏ 2. Generally aware when some response may be over-determined (that is, influenced by some background factor related to the history of abuse)?
   ❏ 3. Generally able to perceive situations and others in graded ways (that is, able to avoid extreme polarizing, categorizing, and labeling), so that people who are angry are not necessarily labeled "abusive" or "abusers," and so that people are not seen as either "trustworthy" or "untrustworthy" but are seen as possibly displaying both qualities at different times?

❑ 4. Able to sort out personal sensitivities from external circumstances (for example, by understanding that *feeling* attacked does not necessarily mean *being* attacked, and so on)?

You can use the examples given in parentheses to determine whether to check these items or not. No one is perfect, but our interest here is on whether the survivor can *generally* sort these issues out. As the survivor's sense of personal competence increases through the development of self functions, and as she has a firm experience of being validated with respect to the reality of the abuse, she becomes more able to face how she may be overreacting or distorting situations, without feeling overly shamed for admitting it. It becomes a fact of survivorship that until the whole of the truth is known, it will influence her from the background to misperceive people and situations, or to overreact to relatively innocuous situations. The rigidity spoken of before can now be worked with as well, and responses to boundary issues can become more flexible and less reactive as the client is better able to discern the difference between the perpetrator of the abuse and the flawed human beings in her current world.

F. Reconsolidation Tasks
  ❑ 1. Beginning to see the larger question of how history of abuse fits into life as a whole (that is, beginning to see how he or she has grown and developed with respect to the abuse, and how he or she may have developed personal strengths from the experience of having been abused)?
  ❑ 2. Beginning to use a spiritual or philosophical framework to encompass the abuse in some larger context of meaning (that is, beginning to understand how the experience of abuse and healing has guided his or her transcendent development)?

This is an important part of healing and growth. It commonly begins during the self-functions phase of healing. Much of it may occur spontaneously, outside therapy, or it may form part of the discussion and relationship with the therapist.

III. Undoing, Redoing, and Mourning
   A. Reality Perception
      ❑ 1. Able to tolerate considering both sides of an issue?
      ❑ 2. Able to tolerate looking at own "shadow aspects" (own negative or self-alienated qualities), as encountered in projections, without becoming overwhelmed by shame or self-blame?

Although this work starts in the self-functions phase, survivors become increasingly able to tolerate what it entails. The survivor becomes more competent, more resilient, and more able to accept her own humanness without shame, as well as others' human failings without such a sense of betrayal.

   B. Undoing and Mourning
      ❑ 1. Able to manage and *usefully assimilate* higher-intensity undoing and redoing (experimental reenactments and reworkings of scenes of abuse, symbolic or actual confrontations with the abuser, use of new skills and capacities with memories and reenactments of the original abusive environment)?
      ❑ 2. Working to bring back from the past those parts of the self and those capacities that have been left there (child-self left behind, possibility of saying words that were left unsaid, possibility of taking actions that were not taken, possibility of now offering recognitions—for example, that abuser was weak and stupid, rather than powerful and cunning—to abused child-self)?
      ❑ 3. Able to mourn the losses caused by the abuse and

its effects in a way that brings some sense of closure (as opposed to a way that is overwhelming)?

❏ 4. In process of returning internalized or self-destructive attitudes and behavior to original abusive environment (self-criticism as introjected words of abuser, self-punishment as acting out what abuser did, dissociated behavior revealed as replication of abuse, self-cutting as abuser's threat, promiscuity as reenactment of gang rape, and so on)?

❏ 5. Allowing core memories (those that are most traumatic and most difficult to face) to emerge, and working them through?

❏ 6. Facing and reowning sexual life?

These items are more likely be checked off for survivors who are doing later-phase work, but some (items 2 and 4 in particular) are also touched on in the course of the self-functions phase. Again, you must look at what parts of this task are *phase-appropriate* in order to know whether checked off items mean that healing has been accomplished, or whether attempts at accomplishing this task are being made without the necessary support and self functions.

Memories of abuse have been worked with all along in the healing process, but now the survivor is able to tolerate and fully benefit from direct and intense therapeutic confrontation with the past, without fragmenting or dissociating. Therapeutic reenactments of scenes, which allow the survivor to say what she could not say at the time, act on her rage, and otherwise experience using her hard-won capacities and powers against the original abuse, now become integrative rather than damaging. Moreover, problematic patterns of self-criticism, self-punishment, and interpersonal behavior are now seen increasingly as part of an interpersonal *context* related to the features of the abusive environment.

Some survivors have not had the personal and interpersonal field for core memories to emerge into until now. These may be memories of the more violent acts by the abuser, or of witnessing others being harmed, or of scenes that have been too highly charged to be known before now.

Issues of sexuality, which for many survivors have been "on hold" until enough of the trauma was resolved, can now be worked on more vigorously. Less of the trauma is held in the body, and there is less that is unknown that could be triggered by sexual stimulation.

IV. Reconsolidation

❏ 1. Integrating abuse into context of larger meaning?

❏ 2. Affirming meaning of abuse to life purpose?

❏ 3. Redefining self as larger than survivorship?

❏ 4. Celebrating healing (for example, by taking pride in resolution of abuse-related issues, feeling excited about moving on in life, and so on)?

❏ 5. Attending to completion and closure of the healing process (for example, by moving toward assimilation and integration of work in therapy, setting new goals, and/or terminating therapy)?

❏ 6. Continuing to develop the bodily self (for example, by showing more interest and involvement in physical movement, exercise, martial arts, and so on)?

Work on the first four items has been growing and developing recursively over the course of the healing process. I encourage you to make annotations to the items that you check, identifying which phase of development these tasks are really referring to. For example, celebration of accomplishments in healing occurs often as a marker of moving from one phase to another. It is a healing task seen throughout the healing process. The remaining two items are not checked until the survivor is truly in the reconsolidation phase. They are the work of this phase, so to speak.

A therapist is graced if he or she is able to see the reconsolidation phase through with the client. Often therapy ends as the undoing, redoing, and mourning phase comes to a close, and re-consolidation is part of the survivor's own on-going integration work which they do quite well on their own.

Understanding the Results

The section that follows presents guidelines to help the clinician interpret the results of a checklist that has been completed for a client.

Part A

Common patterns for the results are as follows:

- Most items checked (percentages higher than 50 percent) are within one particular phase, with low percentages (10 percent or under) of items checked for all other phases. This pattern suggests that the client is at the beginning of the relevant phase of healing.

- Percentages appear more or less distributed between *two adjacent phases*, with low percentages checked for all other phases. This pattern suggests that the client is in the middle of the *first* of the two adjacent phases. For example, if the highest percentages fall within the support and self-functions phases, we would expect the client to be working in the middle or later part of the support phase, with aspects of the self-functions phases already being addressed.

Part B

Our first aim is to look over the checklist and note what task items are checked for the client. These represent the client's particular strengths and resources. Every client has his or her own particular strengths and has found access to at least some environmental resources, which can be relied on in the course of healing.

Pay particular attention to tasks that are unchecked when all the other evidence suggests that the client's healing is in a later phase. These represent "holes" in the fabric of healing, which will probably cause difficulties in later phases. Some of the items in Part B are more appropriate to one phase of healing than to another. These are particularly useful for cross-validating indications from Part A.

Parts A and B Combined

Looking at Parts A and B together can help you confirm the determinations suggested by part A alone:

- The more *tasks* checked off within a particular section of Part B, the more likely it is that the client has reached the corresponding *phase* as indicated by Part A.

- When fewer than half of the *tasks* are checked off within a particular section of Part B, the client is likely to be working in the early part of the respective *phase*. The unchecked items are a helpful guide to directions in therapy.

- When only a portion of the tasks is checked off for a phase in Part B, but when the corresponding phase in Part A is mostly checked, it is likely that the client is working in the early part of that phase.

- When the pattern for Part A seems split between two adjacent phases, the items checked on Part B for the corresponding tasks will help suggest which phase is the more likely focus for that client.

These appraisal items can be very helpful to us as clinicians, and to survivors, as we focus our work and form realistic expectations. They can also serve as markers of progress, which is very important in a healing process that can seem interminable as the survivor is thrown back into earlier feeling states and easily loses perspective on what has been accomplished. It can be disappointing for a survivor to realize that she is not as far along as she wished to be, but the checklist can also remove the pressure for her to do the wrong tasks at the wrong time.

Chapter Seven

Memories and Remembering

The question of traumatic memory in general, and so-called false memory in particular, is inseparable from the nature of memory and of human experience itself. Therapists and survivors, as well as the public at large, have been assailed in recent years by extreme positions on every side of this issue. The debate is fueled by a veritable media frenzy, which has latched on to this question as a cause célèbre of the moment. The real and very complex truth of this issue has often been lost.

The debate has often been framed in absolute terms, with voices on each side lending themselves to positions that defy common sense but make good press. On the one hand, there are some who wish to assert that every last detail of any recollection of abuse, or even the belief that one was abused, must of necessity be true. For them, to do other than stand fully behind every claim of abuse is to invite revictimization and give haven to perpetrators. On the other hand, we have the purveyors of false memory syndrome, who wish to parlay research showing that memory in general is suggestible to changes, under certain circumstances, into a denial of the validity of recollections of abuse and even of psychotherapy. For them, to do otherwise is to risk destroying lives with false accusations of heinous crimes.

Both positions neglect the complex reality of the survivor's world and do nothing to help survivors appreciate the complex nature of their experience, which includes memories and recollections, meanings, and confusion. Nor do these positions help society appreciate the web of denial and avoidance spun by perpetrators.

It does not help to oversimplify these complex issues. Nevertheless, we must find a place to stand and face them.

The solution offered here is neither to take a position so neutral that the client receives too little support nor to focus on pursuing memories of abuse or looking for abusers behind every symptom. The focus here will be guided by our understanding of the developmental process of the healing in which we are engaged. What we focus on with respect to memories is shaped by our understanding of the essential tasks of healing, and of the context in which healing takes place. With this approach, some of the problems involved in memory work and recollections will turn out not to be what they seem to be when the focus is on memory itself instead of on the healing process.

The Question of Trauma and Memory

As the dust settles, at least a bit, some outlines of the psychological realities behind this issue are beginning to emerge. Some consensus on a considered and reasonable stance for therapists also appears to be emerging. There are no absolute answers to the question of false memory (or of memory in general, for that matter), but at least we need to be informed about these issues as they appear before us in the very human problems that we deal with day to day in our consulting rooms.

An interim report by the American Psychological Association (1994) spells out five conclusions on the matter of adults' memories of childhood sexual abuse. Despite the well-known differences among committee members, I believe that they can help to restore a basis of reason as we approach an issue whose flame has been inordinately fanned by the distortions of the media:

> Controversies about adult recollections should not obscure the fact that child sexual abuse is a complex, pervasive problem in America that has been historically unacknowledged.

Most people who were sexually abused as children remember all or part of what happened to them.

It is possible for memories of abuse that have been forgotten for a long time to be remembered, although the mechanisms by which this might happen are not well understood.

It is possible to construct convincing pseudo-memories for events[25] that never occurred, although the mechanisms by which this might happen are not well understood.

There are gaps in knowledge about the processes that lead to accurate or inaccurate recollection of childhood sexual abuse [American Psychological Association, 1994, p. 9].

A similar conclusion is reached in the executive summary of a report by the British Psychological Society (1995):

Complete or partial memory loss is a frequently reported consequence of experiencing certain kinds of psychological traumas including childhood sexual abuse. These memories are sometimes fully or partially recovered after a gap of many years.

Memories may be recovered within or independent of therapy. Memory recovery is reported by highly experienced and well-qualified therapists who are well aware of the dangers of inappropriate suggestion and interpretation.

In general, the clarity and detail of event memories depends on a number of factors. . . . Although clear memories are likely to be broadly accurate, they may contain significant errors. It seems likely that recovered memories have the same properties.

Sustained pressure or persuasion by an authority figure could lead to the retrieval or elaboration of 'memories' of events that never actually happened. The possibility of therapists creating in their clients false memories of having been sexually abused in childhood warrants careful consideration, and guidelines for therapists are suggested here to minimize the risk of this happening. There is no reliable evidence at present that this is a widespread phenomenon in the UK.

. . . The ground for debate has also shifted from the question of the possibility of recovery of memory from total amnesia to the question of the prevalence of recovery of memory from total amnesia [British Psychological Society, 1995, p. 3].

These two sets of independently reached conclusions restore some balance to the discussion of memory for abuse, acknowledging the reality of amnesia and recovery of memory for childhood events, traumatic and otherwise, as well as for the possibility that distortion and false memories can occur under some circumstances. They also provide a stable position from which to discuss the issues of therapeutic work with memories for childhood abuse and the complex concerns we must keep in mind as we consider the Healing Tasks approach to working with memories. By implication, at least, these conclusions would also apply to other types of abuse, although this is not specified.

It might be useful to summarize some of the issues being considered and what we do know about abuse and memory to better understand what we are facing, and to review the resulting treatment concerns when approaching the emergence of forgotten traumatic material. My intent here is not to be exhaustive, nor is it to present a rebuttal to accusations of false memory or to detractors of therapy; this rebuttal has been done cogently by a number of other writers (Bloom, 1995; Cronin, 1994; Herman, 1993, 1994; Lawrence, 1994; Whitfield, 1994; Robbins, 1995; Rockwell, 1995).

Traumatic Memory and Forgetting

All memory appears to be reconstruction from encoded impressions. It is subject to distortion, misremembering, and even pseudomemory, yet we have a basic trust in the essentials. The main difference in memories of abuse is the great difficulty of obtaining corroboration. Perpetrators of abuse often deny criminal acts, and unless others have been similarly abused by them, it is often difficult to obtain corroboration. Nevertheless, survivors often do obtain direct or indirect corroboration of abuse, in the form of medical documentation or agreement from family members and others. That many survivors do not have corroboration does not in any way discredit their claims. The question of corroboration comes up in three contexts. The first is the legal context, where doubt about the validity of childhood memories raises reasonable doubt in regard to evidence for criminal acts. The second (Yapko, 1994) is the context of the family and the impact on family members who are accused of abuse by adult children. The third context is therapy itself, with the need to minimize the potential for harm by therapeutic methods.

Traumatic memory is different from narrative memory (Van der Kolk and Van der Hart, 1991). Narrative, or autobiographical, memory is a construction of recalled events meaningfully organized in relation to ourselves. Some experiences take more processing to assimilate, but most life experiences, by and large, are readily integrated into this narrative construction. Traumatic experiences, whether due to war, rape, disasters, or childhood abuse, are by their nature discrepant from the flow of our narrative construction. They do not fit. This is why reconsolidation is such an important and recurring issue in healing from abuse and trauma. The survivor must reformulate his narrative sense of self, his construction of the story of who he is and what his world is, repeatedly as new material emerges and is therapeutically worked through. It is precisely the unprocessed, unintegrated nature of traumatic memories that results in their often being forgotten, denied as meaningful, or held aside as discrepant and uncertain. They do not fit into the narrative flow of remembered life until they are worked with and processed.

In a phenomenon known as delayed memory, memories of abuse in childhood can indeed be forgotten and then remembered years later. A number of studies have demonstrated this, including one by a leading scientific proponent of false memory (Loftus, Plonsky, and Fullilove, 1994), in which 19 percent of women with histories of sexual abuse reported forgetting the abuse for some period of time. An even stronger study (Williams, 1994), of women with *documented* sexual abuse in childhood who were interviewed seventeen years after the abuse occurred, demonstrated that 10 percent of the total study population reported having forgotten the abuse at some time in the past, while 49 percent did not recollect the abuse at the time of the interview. Others (Briere, 1992; Herman and Schatzow, 1987) have suggested similar conclusions. Proposed mechanisms for forgetting include the following:

- Repression (material is dynamically held out of consciousness)
- Denial (material is partially known but rendered without meaning and significance)
- Dissociation (events are split off from normal consciousness)
- Disorganization of consciousness at time of event (impressions are blurred, vague, or fragmentary)
- State-dependent learning (events recalled only in a similar state, and so there is intrusive recollection with stress or similar stimuli)
- Encoding problems (traumatic events are not stored in the same way as normal memory)
- Processing problems (traumatic events are not processed fully and so are not accessible by narrative means)

These are all theoretical constructs to explain the mechanism of forgetting. It is unclear which *mechanisms* best explain the phenomenon of delayed recall of abuse, but its reality is not in doubt. We should not confuse theoretical discussions of whether repression exists with the fact that forgetting and delayed recall do occur, regardless of the mechanism producing them.

Validity and Accuracy of Reports

Traumatic memories are probably subject to some of the same inaccuracies that affect any other memories. But the special nature of trauma, as well as the age of the victim and the circumstances of the trauma, can make traumatic memories more accurate in some ways and less accurate in others. One of the classic phenomena of Posttraumatic Stress Disorder (PTSD) is the flashback: the intrusive, intense reliving of a traumatic incident. Flashbacks and intrusive recollections also point to the unintegrated, raw nature of some traumatic memories, which may be more photographic and detailed than most other forms of memory, which are more like abstractions of events.

Nevertheless, the circumstances of abuse render distortions of their own. Children perceive from their own unique perspective. Consciousness may have been so scattered by the violence of events that memory is fragmentary, impressionistic, or kaleidoscopic. Drugs given by perpetrators may have distorted perceptions and therefore the material that is later remembered. All of this must be considered, sorted out, and sorted through as the *whole* picture emerges. We must ask what is *essential* in the recollection, and we must always differentiate between what we conjecture or interpret and what we know.

In the debate over false memory, proponents of false memory syndrome have focused on the fact that a traumatic memory may not be perfectly accurate. But *any* form of memory (including the memory of what we had for breakfast) may be inaccurate, while its core or essence may be quite in line with reality. It is certainly legitimate for *clients* to question the accuracy of their *own* memories. They are the ones who have to live with what they are recognizing.

The issue is confused even more by the difference between what is required for veracity in legal circumstances and what may be required in psychotherapy. If a survivor does choose to initiate legal action against a perpetrator, corroboration of the accuracy and validity of recalled memories is probably essential, and clinicians who support clients in taking legal action without corroboration are probably not acting in their clients' best interests. In the personal sphere, however, everyone has the right to determine his or her own truth. In a noncoercive atmosphere, where the therapist is interested in the client's experience and does not have an agenda about the reality or unreality of childhood abuse, the client will probably question the accuracy and validity of his or her own impressions. Clients know what is vaguely or confusingly recollected. They know what they have very clear memories of. They know what is consistent with other facts and with continuous memories. They know what they are willing to be uncertain about until, with adequate support from the therapist, enough of a pattern emerges.

We infantilize survivors and clients when we act as if they are not capable, in the proper frame of mind, of discernment and discrimination with respect to their own experience. There is something patriarchal and diminishing in treating clients as if they are like children—or, worse, "like women" in their inability to bring mature (read "masculine") reason to bear on their experience. I see no need to diminish the capacities of either women or children, notwithstanding the cultural bedrock on which such diminishment stands. Even toddlers have been able to report accurately on trauma that happened to them as early as twenty-eight months of age, when they were given leeway for their verbal and cognitive capacities and for their tendency (just like an adult's) to focus on details that had relevance to them (Sugar, 1992).

I have the same concern that Yapko (1994) does about supporting family relationships. But I must remind him that it is not *our* decision, but the client's, to determine the proper relationship with the family of origin. It is quite surprising to me, but many of my clients maintain relationships, even at great emotional cost to themselves, with parents who were perpetrators of abuse. Those who decide for themselves to break off contact with family members generally do so not just because they have recognized that they were abused but also because chronic patterns of emotional abuse persist in their relationships with them, or because contact with them so overwhelmingly triggers intrusive memories and feelings that the contact is clearly detrimental.

The outlandishness of a memory is also not disproof. Until quite recently, reports of incest were considered outlandish and unlikely by therapists and the public at large. The Holocaust was unbelievable to the American public until Allied troops liberated the concentration camps and photographed the horrors. Yet there are people who still deny the existence of the Holocaust. As the evidence for the existence of ritual cults mounts (Feldman, 1995), will we require photographs of human sacrifice and videos of ritual rapes before we believe survivors? Freyd (1993) notes that outlandish reports have at least a psychological truth, so that meeting such reports with doubt closes down the attempt to express this truth. Others, including myself, do not find reports of ritual abuse outrageous at all. It has been part of human culture since time immemorial, just like abuse in general (rape, warfare, torture, and religious cultism). We have only to look at the mounds of human skulls in Cambodia, and the "ethnic cleansing" through torture and rape in Bosnia, to realize that what we see all too often as wholesale genocide may be occurring in small groups as ritualized murder. Clinicians would be advised to look more deeply into this area before dismissing memories of ritual abuse from the realm of possibility.

Suggestibility and False Reporting

We know that pseudomemories can be created under certain conditions in the laboratory. We do not yet have any evidence that this occurs in therapeutic contexts, but it is not hard to imagine that some conditions would make it more possible.

Coercion. The field of psychotherapy includes a wide range of people and professions, from nondegreed counselors in drug- and alcohol-treatment programs to masters- and doctoral-level practitioners in social work, medicine, psychology, nursing, and education. Like other people, therapists have their own sociopolitical and philosophical axes to grind about various issues. They have their own biases and rigidities with respect to their personal development and the limitations of their personal world views. They are as subject to the winds of culture, to what is popular, to common ignorance, as anyone else. Some are themselves survivors of childhood abuse, in the early phase of recognizing this fact, and may tend to see abuse everywhere. Some are in denial of their own childhood trauma and will not see it in others, even in those who are sitting in front of them. Some are or have been perpetrators of abuse, with a clear stake in denying or minimizing their actions. Coercive circumstances could be created by any therapist. Any of the following actions would bias a client's interpretation of his or her experience or be otherwise detrimental:

- Ascribing a one-to-one correlation to symptoms and abuse
- Denying the reality behind all memories of abuse
- Promulgating simplistic answers or solutions
- Seeing abuse around every corner
- Ignoring abuse
- Overdiagnosing abuse
- Refusing to take symptoms or memory impressions seriously
- Urging alienation from the family of origin
- Urging contact with the family of origin at all costs
- Fostering conditions of strong dependency

Recollections of abuse occur spontaneously, without coercion or suggestions by therapists. The therapy room is not the place for coercion or pressure to assume a particular viewpoint on the issue of abuse. Neither is it the place for interrogation, doubt, or judicial investigation. It is a place for *support* and *exploration*, so that clients can determine the meaning and validity of their experience *for themselves*.

Suggestibility. The special atmosphere of therapy does foster possibilities for suggestibility. We take advantage of this in therapy when we utilize the trust and relationship that we have developed with a client, to support her in considering new possibilities, shifting how she thinks about something, or experimenting with new behaviors. Nevertheless, there is no evidence that I am aware of that memories of abuse are actually created by therapeutic suggestion, although extremely biased methods of interviewing or hypnotic induction could make this possible with highly compliant or suggestible clients, at least to my mind. I have not heard any legitimate reports, however, that actual memories of abuse have been created by any circumstances in the therapeutic context. It does seem reasonable to consider that false *beliefs* that abuse took place can be prompted by therapists, through suggestions that memory impressions or symptoms be *interpreted* in particular ways.

But, again, and particularly if the atmosphere we create is noncoercive and collaborative, it is infantalizing of clients to suggest that they are not able to sort through their experiences for themselves. In therapy, we *suggest* all sorts of things, which clients refuse all the time: different ways of looking at life problems, interpretations of process or experience, reframing of attitudes and symptoms. Asking a client whether he thinks he was abused, making inquiries about life history or symptoms, does not a memory make. And it is our job to inquire; therapy is itself a special kind of inquiry. But inquiry alone does not create memories and cannot produce the symptoms of PTSD or dissociation. Similarly, there is no evidence that reading the literature on abuse creates memories, although such reading may be the essential support that allows previously undisclosed memories to emerge.

The other concern with respect to suggestibility involves special techniques of memory recovery, such as hypnosis, body-oriented explorations, and dream work. That these techniques could render a client more susceptible to suggestion does not invalidate their use. It only means that clients must be informed about the possible effects of the techniques involved, and that therapists must use special care, so that their language does not imply more than is actually known or experienced by the client and the possibility of questioning what emerges is open. It is the therapist's job to work with the client so that he can determine his own truth, in this type of therapy as in any other therapeutic endeavor.

Two broad guidelines for therapists and the public have been put forth by the American Psychological Association (1994):

- Therapists must approach *questions* of childhood abuse from a *neutral* position. There is no single set of symptoms showing that a person was a victim of childhood abuse.
- The public is advised, when looking for a psychotherapist, to seek a licensed practitioner who has training and experience in the issues for which treatment is sought.

It is crucial to note here the recommendation for *neutrality* in approaching *questions* about abuse. By this is meant that when clients ask whether their symptoms mean that they were abused, or whether a dream or a visual impression means that they were abused, the possibility must be neither confirmed nor denied.

But this does not mean that we should approach emerging *memories* neutrally. A survivor in the early stages of recollecting delayed memories of abuse requires more than neutrality from the therapist. She requires support and validation that her *experience* is meaningful (this is not the same as confirmation). We must be willing to be in a position to affirm though not to confirm; that is, to help generate the field conditions necessary for remembering to occur.

The *minimum* conditions I laid out earlier regarding the process of validation were

- The environment is receptive and does not deny or minimize.
- The environment is willing to hold and look at any possibilities.
- The environment is not coercive and does not press for a particular view or version of the truth.
- The environment must be able to support holding fragmentary, conflicting, or unclear impressions over time without doubting them and without prematurely assigning meaning

to them, until a pattern of truth and meaning can be discerned by the client.

We must be able to affirm the client's experience, to trust that there is validity and truth in it, even if we do not yet know what is factual. With all of this in mind, we are in a position to approach issues of memory and remembering with appropriate cautions, but without replicating the doubt, denial, legalistic interrogation, coercion, and lack of support and validation that survivors have so often experienced. Perhaps now we are in a position to look at the broader question of memories and remembering in therapy.

Approaches to Traumatic Memory

As we look at issues of memories and remembering for trauma survivors, there are basically two questions. The first is how we approach memories of abuse and trauma as they emerge during the course of therapy. The second is how we access memories of trauma for therapeutic purposes. Our answers to these questions are structured, of course, by our theoretical assumptions about what is healing of abuse. Much of my approach to these questions has been presented in earlier chapters, since the holistic and contextual nature of this model requires such embedded discussion. In this chapter, I will try to elaborate on the way we approach these questions from the Healing Tasks Model and discuss some of the differences from earlier approaches.

The predominant approach to trauma has been based on the abreactive model inherited from early work in hypnosis and early psychoanalysis. In a field that has often tended to focus on abreaction of the traumatic memory as the central concern of therapy, the main question therapists often have in working with abuse is how to help the client remember—how to access memories, how to manage them when they are accessed, and so on. For survivors, too, the questions often seem to focus on how to "get at" memories and how to get through them as fast as possible. The idea of containing in oneself such a legacy of unknown and therefore un-controllable impressions is so abhorrent that the survivor, under-standably, often wants to "get it over with" as soon as possible.

It is my experience that the orientation, from either therapist or client, of "getting through the memories" tends to be iatro-genic. The abreactive model seems to produce a relatively high degree of problems. Clients feel overwhelmed much of the time, therapists are dealing with constant crises by phone or in ex-tended sessions, therapy is felt to be a monumental and insur-mountable task, and so on. Remembering and memory work are certainly essential parts of healing from childhood abuse, but are they the central focus? Or are they part of a larger framework of understanding? As one survivor put it, describing her conversa-tion about therapy with a fellow survivor, "The therapist tends to focus on whether we have more memory back after a session, but we tend to focus on whether we are *more ourselves* rather than *less* ourselves after a session. A lot of times, *more* memory leaves us feeling *less* ourselves."

In the Healing Tasks Model, the point of therapy is *healing,* which is to say becoming more whole. The model is developmen-tal and is person- and process-centered rather than centered on content (such as memories). We must evaluate our methodology in therapy on the basis of how it is affecting the person involved and how it fits into our understanding of human development in general. The assumption here is that remembering in itself is not healing; how the process of remembering and working through traumatic events assists in reinstating the proper course of devel-opment and growth *is* healing.

The abreactive model is an inheritance from pre-Freudian the-ory (Janet, 1890), which essentially viewed psychological therapy as a process of evoking repressed traumatic memories and reliving them with enough intensity that they no longer needed to be re-pressed and stored. The idea was that such stored memories were like contents under pressure. In this nineteenth-century steam-boiler metaphor, the pressure needed to be relieved by releasing the valve. This could be done through such techniques as hypnosis, therapeutic interpretation, or confrontation, but essentially it involved intensely recalling the trauma, with all its incumbent emotion, so that it was virtually relived. Clearly, the idea is not without some validity, in the sense that pent-up (retroflected) feelings may be experienced as "inner pressure," with somatic consequences (one of which is high blood pressure), and "blowing off steam" can make one feel better, but it does not necessarily promote healing and wholeness.

Freud's rejection of the seduction theory, and his revision—that neurotic symptoms are caused by fantasized wishes *of the child*, rather than by actual seduction by parents or others—quite simply meant that there was no trauma to be released. It never happened; it was merely a fantasy produced by the libidinal urges of the child, and so the hidden, screened wishes had to be sought out in their disguised forms through interpretation of symptoms, dreams, and fantasies (Miller, 1984). Other early psychoanalytic thinkers, notably Ferenczi (Dupont, 1988), maintained the belief that trauma is often a central part of psychoneurotic disturbance. They believed this in spite of the Oedipal dogma that dominated psychoanalysis.[26]

With the impact of the women's movement and the post–Vietnam War studies of the delayed effects of battle trauma, therapists began to take clients' reports of incest and sexual abuse more seriously (Herman, 1992). But, as practitioners dealing with what we began to believe was *actual* trauma and incest, we looked to the pre-Freudian theory of Janet, which took the reality of trauma seriously, and we saw his abreactive method as the solution. This meant that, no matter what phase of therapy the survivor was in, the purpose and focus of therapy was always and singularly to *evoke remembering*, as if when all the steam was finally let out of the boiler and no further memories had to be held away from consciousness, therapy and healing would be complete.

When practitioners are guided by the abreactive model, they tend to emphasize the process of recalling, even reliving, memories as the main focus of therapy. Of course, many competent clinicians using the abreactive model in working with trauma have come to use it within a context guided by more sophisticated clinical understanding than the model alone would suggest. When it is used naïvely, however, therapy itself can become "abusive" in that people are forced to relive the same traumas without any more coping skills than they had as children, or in ways that simply repeat the traumas without bringing anything new to bear on them. Thus they experience recollection with the same modes of coping that were used to deal with the original abuse: desensitization (numbing), dissociation, and denial, instead of more integrated, mature, and varied modes that would allow them to assimilate their memories. To understand the true implications of abreaction, we need to understand the meaning and place of remembering in the healing process, and of not remembering in the original coping with trauma.

Importance of Remembering and of Not Remembering

To understand the purposes of remembering, we must first have an appreciation of the purposes of *not remembering*.[27] In my view, the survivor of abuse comes to repress or dissociate abusive experiences because the experiences are contextually unbearable. They are overwhelming and flooding. They threaten one's sense of self-cohesiveness, and there is inadequate support in the environment. In other words, *the field conditions of the original trauma made it impossible for the child to maintain the full continuity of experience without risking survival and self-integrity.*

In this sense, not remembering is a *creative adjustment* to a difficult organism/environment problem (Perls, Hefferline, and Goodman, 1951) in the truest sense of the term. It is the solution of adjusting one's own internal awareness (by repression, the splitting of consciousness in dissociation, compartmentalization of affect and somatic experience from its cognitive meaning) instead of being able to receive respite or care from others or being able to affect the environment in any way on one's own behalf. It is the best possible solution, given the resources available.

This is why pure abreaction, in and of itself, can be harmful. If the current conditions are not experienced as different (with more available possibilities, resources, and support) from those under which the abuse originally occurred, then remembering becomes simply a review of what was intolerable in the first place. The results are dissociation, decompensation, increased depression and hopelessness, and other signs of worsening symptoms—in short, iatrogenesis.

This is not to say that recovery and healing from abuse is a pleasant process, even when guided by a developmental and contextual model, as I propose here. Unfortunately, in the course of working through abuse, the person will inevitably feel quite uncomfortable at times. But it is not bad to *feel* bad when one is coming to grips with bad things. To feel bad is a normal response to bad things. The reality of having been abused is existentially painful. It is a wrenching, saddening, hard truth, one that must be lived with and assimilated, at times with great difficulty.

It is not good, however, to become hopeless or suicidal, unable to function in life, or psychotic. These reactions indicate that what is being dealt with is being experienced as intolerable and must be coped with, even if coping means absolute withdrawal into depression, obliteration, or fantasy. We should try to have the process of healing avoid retraumatization, as much as possible. Loss of functioning should be viewed as a sign that we are missing something essential to the healing process.

We must also distinguish existential pain from decompensation (such as fragmenting or depression) as much as we can. Significant worsening of the clinical condition of the client is feedback to the clinician and the client that they are pushing too hard, or that support or self functions are inadequate. Such occurrences are unavoidable in the difficult course of working through abuse, but they should be taken as important feedback, so that the process of therapy can be adjusted. These episodes are *not* about the survivor. The survivor is not resistant, weak, sick, and so on. They are *contextual statements* about the severity and nature of the abuse, about the time-honored coping methods that worked for this person at the time of the abuse, and about the therapeutic need to attend to developing other skills and resources that would allow the survivor to cope differently. The lens of therapy must be shifted from remembering the abuse to looking at the whole context of the person who is remembering.

Trauma Forgotten and Recalled

Traumatic memories, even when a person has completely dissociated or repressed them, appear to emerge through a contextual process—that is, the configuration of the present organism/environment field lends itself to recollection. A number of configurations commonly evoke the recollection of otherwise forgotten memories.

First, the field now offers support or capacities that the person has not had before. Traumatic memories may emerge spontaneously just as life is finally going well for some people, and precisely because life *is* going well: they finally have enough of the right kind of support and resources that difficult memories are affordable. Love exists, help is available, someone will catch them if they fall apart, money is adequate, and so on. This is much like what might occur naturally in the course of therapy when memories emerge because of improved conditions in the field, and so it is natural that this would occur in nontherapeutic contexts as well. Similarly, people develop self functions naturally in the course of life and learning—having children, becoming more capable adults, going through a course of therapy, and so on. It is no wonder that people sometimes have a number of courses of psychotherapy, or are a number of years into recovery and sobriety from substance abuse, and only then find traumatic memories coming back to them.

Second, developmental demands may evoke otherwise well-cordoned-off memories because certain capacities are called on that are linked to those memories. The developmental demands of the life cycle often call on capacities that have been avoided or undeveloped because these are closely connected with the episodes of abuse. For example, a young man reaches his twenties, the age of developing true intimacy (Erikson, 1968), and a love relationship demands that he move deeper into intimate territory than he has allowed himself to go before. This development taps into his feelings of anxiety, distrust, and fear of being hurt, which are rooted in the avoided traumatic events. Or a woman becomes pregnant with her first and very much wanted child but begins to recall the rejection and neglect with which she was treated as a child, in contrast to the love and caring she feels toward the baby she carries. The executive who is promoted and given more responsibility must summon true self-confidence, rather than the facade she has been operating with, and uncovers a deep well of shame and self-loathing, as well as memories of the emotional abuse that formed it. A woman in her late thirties has felt the call (which often occurs at this age) to develop her spirituality, having previously scorned religion and the Deity, and recalls being fondled by her priest.

Third, stresses in the field, or other life events, cause memories to be more easily triggered and recalled. Certain stresses, emotional states like depression (Kuyen and Brewin, 1994), and retraumatization (rape, a car accident, illness) can also force dissociated memories into awareness. Anxiety and hypervigilance may sensitize survivors, so that memories are triggered by stimuli that were also part of the abusive situation. Depression wears down ego strength, so that memories are more easily elicited by otherwise innocuous events. Physical illness and its unavoidable feelings of helplessness may evoke remembrance of times when the person was helpless during abuse. Car accidents and the resulting shock, dissociation, or physical pain may evoke other times when life was similarly threatened, or when pain was created in the course of beatings, incest, and the like. Situations like rape or sexual harassment may evoke otherwise forgotten instances of childhood rape or molestation.

What is important here is to recognize that the conditions of the *field*, of the person and the environment *together*, are what foster recollection. Survivors do not necessarily remember because they are "ready." Sometimes they are not at all ready, but circumstances of the field insist. Sometimes "they" are ready (their internal resources are adequate), but the support of the environment is not adequate. I have seen cases in which therapists who had treated survivors for years, without having any recollections of abuse in their own lives, suddenly had such memories evoked in the course of some developmental life event (such as having a child). I have also seen cases in which car accidents and the pain of physical injuries opened a Pandora's box of recollections when there were few supports or resources for the survivor to deal with what was emerging, and a major life crisis ensued.

The Cycle of Remembering

The experience of remembering forgotten childhood trauma tends to follow a predictable sequence, and appears to be wavelike in nature. It is useful for both therapist and client to know this because knowing normalizes the process and reassures one that no matter how difficult remembering is at first, one will get through it. Understanding the cycle of remembering also gives some indications of where a survivor can become stuck in the process, and thus of how to support him better to keep him moving through it (see Figure 7.1). Being mindful that the Healing Tasks Model is a *guide*, not a prescription for the client's experience, we can look at some of the typical concerns and problems that survivors face as they confront emerging memories.

Emergence of Memory Fragment and Shock

It is a common fact in work with survivors that the recollection of almost any new traumatic memory (or previously known memories that have been severed from their affect but are now

Figure 7.1. Cycle of Remembering.

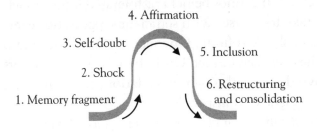

4. Affirmation

3. Self-doubt

5. Inclusion

2. Shock

6. Restructuring
and consolidation

1. Memory fragment

recalled with the affect) results in at least some experience of shock. Even the most therapeutically experienced survivor, who has already recalled quite difficult or traumatic memories, will have a sense of anxiety and dislocation as otherwise unknown memories, even less traumatic ones, emerge. This is a natural consequence of the emergence of an experience that was originally fragmented from the stream of consciousness because it was perceived in a context of insufficient support. When first recollected, such an experience comes forth "as if" still within that original context. It is only by working it through, holding this recollected figure against the present ground and the present context instead of the original ground, that the survivor can embed it in the present context (which, ideally, includes support and self functions that were not originally available).

Memory fragments themselves frequently do not emerge in recognizable form unless some degree of support is available. Because most memories for survivors do not emerge in full-blown "cinematic" form,[28] the problem is holding the fragment of memory, whether image or feeling or intuition, long enough for more impressions and data to be collected and to inform the initial recollection. Moreover, disconnected fragments do not always make sense. They are not always connected in logical or linear fashion, and they may contain impressions from more than one event and time. It takes considerable support to stay with this process of gathering such fragments until a more complete gestalt can be formed.

At the point in the cycle where a memory fragment is emerging, shock often cannot be held or tolerated long enough for the cycle to take its course. With sufficient support, however, the experience of shock is finite. One moves through it, and the next part of the cycle can be met. Until then, however, the person may try to avoid shock through dissociation, numbing, or keeping memories vague or nonspecific.

External support for allowing the emergence of memories is essential as the person moves through periods of doubt and insecurity. If the therapist challenges the survivor in the shock phase with a distrusting or questioning stance, it may replicate familial denial of abuse and collude with existing repression, denial, or dissociation. The result is that the material may be rerepressed, or trust in the therapist may be significantly damaged. An open stance—"I believe this is important, even if we don't yet know what it means" or "Yes, it could be true" or "You don't have to be certain for us to look at and talk about it"—is the minimum requirement from the therapist at this stage. Nevertheless, the therapist should not go beyond what is known or what the client feels he or she knows.

One survivor may demand full and logical proof before she will allow herself to attend to a memory fragment. Thus she effectively stops the process of recollection before enough is gathered for any feelings to emerge. Another may shame herself immediately upon any recollections—"I'm making this up"—and so prevent any gestalt, any coherent whole, from emerging. Still another may distract herself or be deflected into other activities to prevent fragments from emerging. Attention to adequate support, helping the person ground and slow down and stay with the process, reassuring her that this is a cycle and that this too shall pass—all these will help the survivor move through the emergence of memory and the response of shock, so that the cycle can continue.

Remember, these interruptions and avoidances are not pathological. The experience of having traumatic memories emerge can be horribly frightening and uncomfortable; survivors may literally feel sick. In lieu of grounded and supported ways of coping, disconnecting modalities of coping will be used as the "best possible" available means.

From Shock to Doubt

Shock is a normal reaction to trauma, and to the remembering of forgotten trauma. Shock is experienced both because of the charge of affect that the memory carries and because of the phenomenological jarring that we experience whenever something novel forces a reconfiguring of the gestalt of our experience. Whatever continuity of life narrative and sense of self and world we may have, previously unrecollected memories will jar us as they emerge, to the extent that they do not fit into our narrative construction.

Most traumatic memories have a particularly deconstructing effect on the narrative gestalt we have formed for ourselves. As a natural consequence, the more divergent an emerging memory fragment is from our existing gestalt, the more shock and disbelief there will be. The process of doubt is a natural one, part of the process by which novel experience is gradually assimilated and the gestalt of who we are and what we are about is reorganized.

Doubt holds things at a distance, where they can more slowly be known and examined. But because of the tendencies toward shame and self-diminishment, many survivors turn the process of doubt into *self-doubt*. They manage difficult recollections by casting stones at themselves, rather than at the recollection. This retroflective mode of contacting shifts the direction of the contact away from the emerging memory, which is too overwhelming to make direct contact with and toward oneself, where at least one can control both halves of the conversation.

Survivors often shift back and forth between shock and self-doubt. It is normal and expectable to cycle between shock and self-doubt for a period of time, since it takes working and reworking to be able to truly assimilate difficult or horrible memories. Often the best stance, both for the therapist and for the survivor at this point in the cycle, is to be willing to hold anything as a possibility and trust that more will be understood as the cycle continues. It is not desirable to become too analytical or to ask for "proof " at this stage, since this closes down the openness required for experience to be reorganized. Since doubt is a natural part of the cycle of remembering and accommodating, its occurrence is not a signal of the invalidity of the emerging memory. It is part and parcel of the natural sorting-out process. Often reassurance from the therapist is needed to help the survivor hold this awareness through the cycle.

From Doubt to Affirmation

Eventually, the survivor can begin to affirm that what has emerged has at least *some* kind of truth in it. What emerges may not be a complete memory. It may be confused with other times or occurrences, or it may have some misinterpretation or fantasy mixed in. Most survivors with whom I have worked appear to be quite capable of discerning for themselves whether a recollection has some truth, or has some aspects that seem distorted, unclear, or seen from a child's viewpoint and therefore exaggerated in some ways, or is a straightforward recollection of what happened. What constitutes an adequate criterion is ultimately up to the client, but therapists have a legitimate place for input at this point. Mostly, the therapist's role here is the work of clarifying what the image, sensation, or other fragment is.

The more vague or fragmentary the impression or recollection, the more support is required to hold it until the picture grows clearer. When recollections are more clear and unitary, whether in the form of "snapshots" or whole scenes, they are more easily affirmed and available to therapeutic work.

Inclusion and Consolidation

This is the stage of remembering when the therapeutic work appropriate to this phase occurs. *Inclusion* means that support and self functions are brought to bear on the process of reorganizing the gestalt, the figure and ground of experience. Problems here occur mostly when the person hurries on to the next memory, without giving proper time for the work of inclusion and reconsolidation. Rather than find an organic pace for experience and for assimilation, the survivor models his pacing on the abuse itself—too much too fast—and then blocks it out and goes on to the next thing. Application of the principles of pacing will aid in the inclusion and consolidation process of remembering. For inclusion and consolidation to take place, time must be spent on talking about the impact of remembering: what it means, what feelings it generates, how it changes the survivor's understanding and viewpoint, and so on.

Over time, some survivors come to understand that they have their own typical problematic places in the remembering cycle. This understanding allows them to predict and normalize their problems and empowers them in their process of remembering. One woman, for example, may feel the emotional impact of a new memory and find herself in the normal process of questioning, but her perfectionism may require her to have such high standards of proof that she has great difficulty affirming the memory's validity. Initially, she will require a lot of support from me to move into even tentative affirmation. Eventually, we will be able to understand that her demands for perfect evidence are her way of keeping horrible truths at arm's length. We can allow this tendency to serve her if we acknowledge how it contributes to her slowing the pace of her remembering. As she appreciates the function of her perfectionism, she can take her demands for perfect evidence less seriously.

Purpose of Remembering

The Healing Tasks Model takes a significantly different approach from that of the abreactive mode toward memories, remembering, and the process of working through recollections. Our question is not *how* to remember, but what makes it *possible* to remember. Figure 7.2 illustrates this approach.

Figure 7.2. Not Remembering.

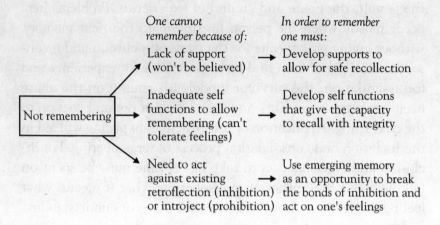

	One cannot remember because of:	In order to remember one must:
Not remembering →	Lack of support (won't be believed)	Develop supports to allow for safe recollection
	Inadequate self functions to allow remembering (can't tolerate feelings)	Develop self functions that give the capacity to recall with integrity
	Need to act against existing retroflection (inhibition) or introject (prohibition)	Use emerging memory as an opportunity to break the bonds of inhibition and act on one's feelings

Our assumption is that amnesia and repression (the blocking of memory) and dissociation (the fragmentation of identity or of experience so as to keep elements of memory divided up and unorganized) occur and must be maintained because the survivor lacks the necessary support or self functions, is not in a position to take powerful actions on his own behalf, is unable to grapple with the pain of the reality of his losses, or lacks a larger framework in which to integrate memories. The filling of these gaps, through work with the Healing Tasks Model, would make remembering possible, manageable, useful, and assimilable.

In the Healing Tasks approach, memories and remembering are dealt with in different ways according to the phase of healing that the client is in. We assume that the purpose of remembering is not to "release" the trauma as such but to serve the organism in the larger task of *becoming whole*. Rather than seeing therapy as serving the process of remembering, *we consider what purpose the act of remembering serves for the person at this time*. Recalling trauma serves the survivor in different ways for different purposes in different phases of healing, and for different tasks in the process of healing.

In this model, the therapist uses the phase of healing as a guide for directing the work with the memory being presented. Table 7.1 gives the outlines of how presented trauma memories are framed and how the therapeutic work of the moment is directed. The interventions given are only examples, to give the reader the flavor of the approach, and the creative collaboration between the therapist and client can generate many other possible directions. It should be apparent from the chart how the process of remembering is contextualized by the healing tasks being addressed.

Table 7.1. Working with Memories by Phase of Healing.

Task/Phase	Therapists' Orientation
Supports	Fostering interpersonal and systemic support
	Holding and speaking of the possibility of what is being remembered
	Seeing remembering as important in how it serves this healing task
	Possible Interventions:
	Framing ways of supporting the client to be able to speak of memories
	Attending to how memory may comment on trust and safety in the therapeutic context
	Validating the possible truth of memories
	Normalizing the anxiety and distress of entertaining memories
	Educating client about the cycle of remembering
	Focusing on how to maintain contact in bringing up difficult things
	Developing grounding skills as a support for talking about difficult things
	Encouraging only as much recollection as support and self functions allow
Self Functions	Seeing how remembering highlights self functions that need to be developed and experimented with

Task/Phase	Therapists' Orientation
Self Functions (cont'd.)	*Possible interventions:* Using memory to identify a needed self function, which is then developed and experimented with in the present context Using memory as a stimulus for practicing specific skills (grounding, tolerating greater affect) Supporting client in reclaiming parts or capacities left behind in the trauma In later self-functions phase, pursuing memories that may lie behind symptoms
Undoing, Redoing, and Mourning	Helping client exercise acquired self functions in the context of recalled traumatic events Undoing introjects (beliefs tied to the trauma) Undoing retroflections (actions withheld during the trauma) Mourning the impact and reality of the trauma *Possible interventions:* Having client reenact memory in therapy, exercising acquired self functions (confronting the abuser, setting boundaries, standing up to the abuser) Supporting the undoing work (saying the unsaid, acting on retroflected impulses) Having the adult client, who can now stand up to the abuser, enact the rescue of the child from the trauma and integrate the child into the present time and the present self Helping the client reject beliefs forced by the abuser or by the family, explicitly or implicitly Supporting the client in recalling a memory and allowing feelings to emerge
Reconsolidation	Seeing how memories fit into larger context of the survivor as he has become through healing *Possible interventions:* Developing "I" statements that emphasize the larger context of self or a spiritual viewpoint ("As I remember how nothing made sense to me after the abuse, I can appreciate how much sense my life makes to me now")

Task/Phase	Therapists' Orientation
Reconsolidation (cont'd.)	Appreciating how memories become part of the client's larger context of meaning now that he is bigger than the abuse
	Emphasizing how emerging memories contrast with current experience

Remembering in the Support Phase

In the early phases of the healing process, the remembering of childhood abuse is seen within the context of how it serves the development of support (trust, safety, interpersonal connection, ability to speak one's truth) and the experience of validation. Early on, survivors often feel significantly overwhelmed by traumatic memories. They lack the support and self functions required to cope with recalling events of such magnitude and emotional impact as childhood abuse.

For the therapist to push for abreaction and deep remembering at this phase, it not only risks retraumatizing the client but also misses the purpose of memories at this particular phase. From the Healing Tasks Model, we can view most of the memories that emerge and are offered to the therapist in the support phase— through feeling states, dreams, vague wondering, indirect questions, proffered fragments, or full cinematic descriptions—as serving the early-phase needs. These needs are to receive empathic support, to develop the conditions of safety, to find help (if indirectly) in tolerating the difficult feelings that often accompany such recollections, to speak the unspeakable, and to hold elements of memory so that their validity can eventually be explored. When a memory is offered, I am likely to attend to it *just enough* for some useful support work to take place. I may not encourage much detailed remembering except as the survivor herself requires it. To paraphrase Winnicott's comment (1960) about "good enough" mothering, what is good enough *remember*ing for the particular developmental needs of this client at this time?

Exactly how much I encourage more detailed recollection depends on the kinds of resources that this particular survivor has and on my collaboration with the client on what she is needing from the process of telling me about the memory. Recalling memories becomes, in Gestalt terms, an *experiment*, which the client and therapist frames together, so that we define its boundaries and operations as clearly as possible.

One client may express the purpose of telling me about the memory as "to be heard." To allow for the experiment in being heard, I school myself to be the hearer, the listener. This relieves me of my ambitious need to be "helpful" and frees me to give the client what he needs. It also teaches the survivor that he can control a difficult situation so as to manage the type and level of stimulation he will expose himself to, and so it builds this basic self function into the therapeutic process.

Another client may be more focused on getting to the point where she can speak of difficult things. Our experiment will be geared to creating the conditions that make the memory speakable. Casting off the "just listening" mode, I become more active and interactive, exploring the client's difficulty in speaking, articulating the prohibitions and introjects behind her silence, exploring her muscular tensions and constrictions of voice, and so on. I may frame an experiment in exaggerating the "can't speak about it" mode, using this exaggeration to reveal more about the inhibition. We may develop a cognitive map of the possibilities that lie between the extremes of unspeakability and shouting it all out: saying one word, whispering, drawing pictures, making statements, crying out, shouting it from the mountaintops. Then we may use our map to experiment with actions that feel more possible than others.

Still another client may say, "I feel so overwhelmed by fear. Help me deal with my fear as I tell you what I remember." Our experimenting will be more focused on his aim of dealing with fear, and the recollections themselves will be used more as a stimulus than as a central focus. For example, I may suggest an experiment in which he says just one sentence about a memory, and then we pause and work with grounding and relaxation or breathing processes until he has managed his fear. Or I may suggest that he talk until the fear seems too strong, and then I will work with him on observing the fear as a wave and letting it wash through him until he is in its trough.

All these experiments are typical in the support phase. Framing the purpose of the work allows the therapist to attend to specific issues and not get sidetracked into abreaction or other phase-inappropriate work. As a collaborative way of working, it also allows the survivor to control and specify the work, a very important feature for people who have experienced the helplessness and lack of control that go with abuse.

The following vignettes offer fuller examples of approaching memories or impressions as they are presented in the support phase of healing.

> Bob came into therapy because of what appeared to be a memory fragment of being fondled by his mother. It had emerged in the course of a personal-growth workshop, but he could not bring himself to speak of it directly. If he spoke of it, it might "become real."
>
> He was not sure he wanted it to be true. When he thought of it, he felt overwhelmed.
>
> "If I take it seriously," he said, "I'll have to change everything I've thought about my life and myself."
>
> I encouraged him to move away from "the whole thing" and move toward it only when he felt able to. I asserted that what was important to me was not his telling me about the "memory" but his learning to respect and honor his own rhythms and pace and find his own integrity in his process. I reinforced this theme by noting when he was not respecting his own signals (body tension, spacing out, and so on) to move away from talking about "the possibility." Over the ensuing sessions, Bob was able to touch on and move away from this material, so that he could gradually deal with the images, the sensations and feelings, and the impact of such a possibility. He felt more in control of this process, by contrast with

his very predominant sense of being helpless and not at all in control when he recalled the memory fragment itself. He began to recognize the feelings of helplessness that had dominated his childhood, as well as his passive sexuality with women.

Marion was quite withdrawn and anxious. In the course of a session, she mentioned a dream fragment in which her father was looming over her and unbuttoning her nightdress. In the dream, she felt very small. After relating this dream, Marion looked down at the floor and appeared to shrink into her chair.

I commented on this and asked her what she was feeling about having shared this dream with me.

"I feel afraid that you'll tell me that I'm just imagining that something happened, that you'll think I'm bad for even dreaming such a thing."

I told her that, on the contrary, I appreciated the trust her "dreamer self" was showing in me to be willing to bring such an image to therapy. I said it was an act of courage on her part to take the risk of being rejected by me.

We explored how much shame she felt about even entertaining the possibility of incest by her father, let alone relating it to me, and how this shame would usually have kept her silent. We eventually experimented with some statements that felt right to her: "I was made to feel that I was the bad one, so I wouldn't speak of my experience."

By the end of the session, Marion felt that she could explore the possibility of something happening to her as a child, and that I would not reject her or minimize that possibility if she began to speak of it.

Charles rather glibly rattled off an account of his drunk father flying into a rage and beating him severely because Charles had made too much noise. He was taken aback when I caught my breath at his account, placed my hand on my chest, and said, "What a terrifying thing for such a little boy."

We sat for a moment in silence, and then Charles said, "I never expect any genuine sympathy for me, for what I went through as a child. No one reacted as if what happened was anything unusual." Tears came to his eyes as he spoke. Then he sat silently, thinking about what he was feeling.

After a time, I said, "So you learned to treat it glibly, like it was no big deal."

He nodded. "Maybe I can take it seriously if you do."

In the early part of therapy, Frank felt compelled to try to describe an image of his uncle leering at him. It felt to him like the prelude to his remembering the actual event of being molested, although he did not have any memory of such an occurrence. Each time he tried to picture the image, he became overwhelmed by fear and panic and dissociated from his body.

My approach with Frank was to focus on how he became ungrounded and unsupported by pulling his breath up into his chest, disconnecting himself from his legs, and losing eye contact with me. We generated an experiment to help him support himself in dealing with difficult feelings. We had him briefly bring back the image of his uncle leering and, as the feelings mounted, shift his attention to grounding himself by moving and feeling his legs, settling his breathing deeper in his body, and staying connected to me through eye contact.

We repeated this experiment a number of times, shuttling between the image and the processes of grounding, until Frank felt less overwhelmed by the image. Eventually, Frank found that he could manage himself well enough to hold the image longer in his mind's eye. He began to see more details in the image, which let him discern it as a true one, not imaginary.

Remembering in the Self-Functions Phase

For the client in the self-functions phase of healing, my emphasis shifts to looking at how memory work serves the identification and development of the skills necessary for effective contact. I am still relatively unconcerned with how much is remembered; I will urge more detail and expression of affect as this phase develops and the survivor has the resources to bear fuller recollection. I am more concerned with what the memory tells us about the capacities that need to be acquired, the skills that were left behind or given up in the service of survival, what needs to be strengthened in the survivor and owned as part of the self so as to meet the world differently. As more self functions are in place, the survivor has more of what is required for full remembering and abreaction.

When a survivor remembers standing by numbly as his brother was brutalized, I may take from this memory an indication that the traumatic context left him unable to know his own internal feelings. I will then work with the theme of knowing feelings in the here-and-now process. We may explore the way he shuts down and minimizes his breathing so as to dampen his bodily sensations and affect, how he makes his face like a mask so as not to express anything, and how this prevents him from knowing his own feelings. We may then try bringing back the memory of his brother being beaten and work to maintain the client's breathing, loosen his mask, and so on, until he begins to feel his pain, his sadness, and his anger at what he witnessed. I may suggest that he make statements: "I feel so bad for you, Eddie, for what you had to endure," or "I am no longer standing numbly by as I acknowledge what happened to you, Eddie." If the boundary and contact capacities are adequate, we may talk about his writing or calling his brother and talking to him, conveying his feelings directly to his brother. In the early part of the self-functions phase, I am likely to extract from the memory the self function that the memory or impression shows as being in need of development and generate experiments, as in the following vignette.

> Lillian began to relate an episode of remembering the crushing weight of her father on top of her and being unable to push him away physically because this would only have made him angry and violent. I notice her withdrawn, collapsed posture and decided to bring her out of the memory, and into contact with me and with her present process, by observing this to her and asking her to attend to her posture as she talked.
>
> Lillian exaggerated this posture somewhat, to feel more clearly what she was doing, and I asked her to look at me as she did so, assuming the posture in relation to me and making statements to me from that stance. We spent some time exploring until we formulated some key statements: "I am pulling back from you" and "I am pulling back into myself because I can't do anything with you."

I became interested in how we could experiment with her reclaiming the capacity to push people away, as appropriate. Too ambitiously, I suggested that we explore how she could push back, and thereby reclaim her arms. Lillian withdrew further into her collapsed posture.

"This is far more than I could even conceive of doing right now," she said.

I realized how far I had strayed beyond the appropriate boundary of our work, and I suggested some alternative explorations, at lower gradations of intensity.

Our collaboration finally resulted in her experimenting with emerging repeatedly out of her collapsed posture and making statements about her experience in the moment: "I am just trying to feel what it's like for me to move toward the world instead of away from it." "This feels dangerous to do, but I think I can handle it." "I am beginning to feel that it's okay do this with you, but I don't think I'd feel safe yet doing it with others."

Before we finished the session, I asked her if there was anything she could say now about the memory she had started with. She reflected on this for a moment, and then she said, "I'm going to learn how to not feel helpless anymore, like I did with Dad back then."

Later on, as the survivor has more competence and capacity, we can use memories more actively. If Lillian had been farther along in her development of boundary functions, she might have been interested in, and able to support, generating the movement of emerging out of her collapsed posture and actually pushing outward with her hands as she made statements, perhaps statements directed at people in her current life with whom she had assumed a passive or helpless posture. Later still in her healing, close to the undoing work, we might have found a useful and assimilable experiment in directing a similar movement at the memory itself: "I'm not lying here helpless now, Dad." "I can push others away now and control my space, Dad, like I couldn't do with you then." In the undoing work itself, the same memory might have been worked with by her physically pushing a bolster away as we enacted the memory in the therapy room.

It would probably be enough for a client in the earlier part of this phase to dip into the feelings that were originally numbed and perhaps shuttle between these feelings and some present grounding, so that he could learn to tolerate them. For a client working more actively on reclaiming a wider array of tolerable feelings, our orientation toward a memory fragment would be to reclaim the feelings that the client had truncated and become numb to during the original trauma. For someone in the later period of this phase, tolerance of the feelings should be high enough for a much fuller reclaiming of affect: staying with it longer, staying with its intensity, taking a stand in the feelings and expressing them in some way. We might also encourage this person to look at situations and places in current life where certain feelings have been numbed or unavailable and to experiment with feeling more in those situations.

Another aspect of self-functions work on memories concerns the process of reclaiming parts of the self from the past, aspects of the self that were disowned, repressed, or unfinished when the abuse occurred. These could be feelings, capacities, knowledge, or even alternate personalities. The point is to reclaim for the present what was left behind but is essential to growth. For example, one client's recollection of being abused in a basement and then suddenly finding herself upstairs, acting as if nothing had happened, alerted us to a discontinuity. As we explored this, she said, "A part of me never came upstairs. She was left behind, hiding down in that basement, so I could go on." We worked with imagery to "go back downstairs," but this time she did not have to go alone. I could go with her and protect her from her abuser. We found the part of her that she had left behind and brought her upstairs, out of the house and that time and place, and we worked to assimilate her into the client's present self.

Similar work may be done to reclaim capacities that one gave up or set aside in coping with a trauma. One may need to reclaim one's capacity to speak, call out for help, stand up for oneself, say no, state what is real and what is a lie, and so on. The information contained in the memory alerts us to the missing skills and capacities and helps us develop the appropriate experiments.

Toward the middle and later parts of the self-functions phase, the survivor has many more options for creative adjustment and coping and can therefore tolerate direct elicitation of memories. It then becomes more appropriate to use techniques of memory recovery for material that continues to be unavailable to conscious recollection. With the higher degree of coping that is now available, the survivor is in a position to tolerate the feelings and stress of hidden recollections, able to sort out impressions, and less susceptible to suggestibility and inadvertent coercion by the therapist or the method of retrieval. As we saw, in the Healing Tasks Model material is "forgotten" because the field cannot support the person's keeping it integrated as part of the life narrative. But as the field is able to support and hold much more than was possible before, the recollection of many otherwise too disturbing events is now possible. At this point, survivors find it useful and possible to pursue symptoms that may indicate forgotten memories. They are prepared to face what they would have been unable to face before without sacrificing self-integrity.

This phase of healing can therefore be a fairly grueling period for client and therapist alike, since the tableau of suffering and cruelty is now laid out before us. Not uncommonly, the core memories now emerge. It is as if the wisdom of the organism keeps the more difficult work for a time when support and self functions can provide a framework for it. This seems particularly true with ritual abuse, child prostitution, and group rape of a child, or when the child was forced to perpetrate torturous punishments and similar horrors. Pacing and self-care are important for both the survivor and the therapist. They are essential so that the client continues to have a life, which she has won back by her own hard work, and is not taken over by retraumatization. The urge is often to press on, in order to "get it over with," but every time I have yielded to this urge, either in myself or in my client, I have regretted the effects.

Practitioners can look to a range of approaches, according to their styles of therapy and healing work and the needs of their clients at particular times. All these approaches require specialized training. My intent here, however, is not to present a manual of memory-recovery techniques but to mention the possibilities of using them in the context of the healing tasks.

Modes of "remembering" that are based on the ability to recall a whole event in linear, cinematic form are only one way of recovering traumatic memories. Traumatic memory is often disconnected and fragmented, so that it will be emotionally manageable. It may appear in the form of symptoms, transferential feelings, enactments in the interpersonal world, bodily sensations, a sense of knowing, fears, phobias, dreams, symbolic images, and other fragmentary and indirect forms. Most memory recollection involves working with the *given* material and reconnecting it to the larger ground and the sense of continuity and meaning that render it intelligible. In other words, memory recovery is not so much a search for deeply buried treasure as an archeological search, starting with clues on the surface, for what has been there all along but is hidden just below. I saw a television show recently on how archaeologists searching for ancient villages in the southwestern United States look for shards of pottery that remain on the desert surface. Sometimes shapes and topography of the land also suggest village walls buried just below the surface. Memory work is often like this: pursuing clues so that details can begin to emerge and a cohesive picture can be created.

Using Dreams. A number of clients I have worked with have found significant clues to forgotten memories in material from dreams. One survivor had repetitive and detailed dreams of childhood molestation, which he was convinced were "just dreams" without factual meaning until they were confirmed by another person who had witnessed the actual events. Images and situations from dreams should not be taken as verbatim reportage, although they can be as noted; they should be considered carefully by client and therapist together for the intermixture of factual and symbolic content. Dreams are not evidence of abuse. They present

starting places and means for exploring the client's phenomenological world, which *may* lead to the uncovering of previously
forgotten material. Dream material, or any other material suggestive of memories of abuse, should never be forced into too literal
a representation by either the client's or the therapist's need for
certainty.

Using Artwork. Often clients engage in spontaneous artwork,
which may reveal clues to childhood abuse. Artistic representations
are quite often intermixed with symbolic representations and so are
taken as starting points for exploration, rather than as literal records of abusive episodes, although they may in some cases turn
out to be exactly that. The phase of healing, and the client's own
responses to her artistic expressions, give the indications for how
they are approached.

An early-support-phase client brought in drawings of a child
being fondled and manipulated by the arm and hand of an adult
male. No face or body of the perpetrator was visible. I asked her
what this meant to her, and she explained that it was merely artistic musing; she only wanted to show me an example of her artistic side. I indirectly probed a bit more, but it was clear that this
was how she viewed her productions, and she was not interested
in exploring them. At that time, she had no notion that she might
be a survivor. In fact, she had rejected this possibility despite the
presence of dissociative symptoms, anxiety, and sexual inhibitions.
Her presenting the drawings seemed to be a testing of my response
to them, rather than an offering of their content. There was
enough useful work for us to do together anyway without the need
for memories of abuse. Only much later in therapy did she herself
begin to conclude that something had happened to her. Remembering the drawings, she brought them in again, and this time our
exploration of them evoked considerable spontaneous recollections of previously forgotten sexual abuse, which began to make
some sense of her symptoms. Thereafter, artwork became a regular
part of her attempts to recover memories of abuse and of her working

through and expressing her feelings about the abuse and about herself, as art therapy is more traditionally used.

Using Enactments. Another way of recovering memories is to work through interpersonal events that appear to evoke emotional reactions for the client beyond what the circumstances warrant. Transference reactions are of course quite similar. Careful sorting through of such situations, to discover exactly what the client may have been reacting to, can fuel experiments that may evoke clearer impressions of abusive incidents.

Using Body Symptoms. Because of the fundamentally bodily nature of sexual or physical abuse and emotional experience, much memory is encapsulated in somatic symptoms (pain, tension, postures, vague or odd sensations, and so on). Experience severed from its context loses its coherence. The recalled bodily sensations of trauma, severed from any recollection of the trauma itself, become free-floating symptoms unrelated to any organized meaning. Fear without an object becomes anxiety. Sadness without an object becomes depression. The sensation of being tied at the wrists and ankles can appear as chronic joint pain or as chronically cold hands and feet. Bracing against unexpected physical blows becomes a rigidly guarded posture. The pain of being hit becomes headaches or other bodily pains. Emotional hurt becomes physical hurt. If these things are explored and experimented with therapeutically, enough elements from the mosaic of memory may become available that abusive episodes can be recalled. Exploration of bodily sensations, recontextualization experiments, and the recovery of feeling all contribute to the recovery of memory.

Using Hypnotic Methods. Hypnosis has been the technique most commonly used to encourage the recollection of forgotten childhood abuse. It has also been the most criticized for its potential to introduce false memory and distortion through suggestion (Yapko, 1994). These criticisms merit careful consideration by those who use hypnosis to assist recall; Bloom (1994) gives some excellent guidelines for its proper use. My own criticism is of hypnosis as an abreactive technique. Used properly, hypnosis does appear to have the ability to elicit memories (questions of accuracy aside) that can bypass the client's developmental readiness to receive them consciously. The resulting intense reexperiencing of an abusive episode may go well beyond the capacity of the client to cope with the feelings, sensations, and recognitions that are evoked. Hypnosis, like any other therapeutic technique, must be grounded in a developmental understanding that shapes the clinical judgment of the practitioner.

Using Outside Sources. Another source of data is found outside therapy. Survivors I have worked with have gleaned much useful information from research into medical records and police files (confirming the arrest record of a grandfather for drunkenness and lewd conduct, for example), from interviews with relatives and neighbors, and from school records and similar sources. These can often help pinpoint the age at which something seems to have happened and help narrow the focus for recall work in therapy. The information gained can also provide the ground for symptoms experienced in the present (for example, a woman with throat constriction, and whose childhood medical records describe chronic throat problems, is later able to see these problems as due to oral rape).

Remembering in the Undoing, Redoing, and Mourning Phase

When the tasks of this phase become figural, the support and self functions that have been developed are used in working with the memories more fully and deeply and in actively pursuing memories that may lie behind symptoms. The therapist must be aware of this shift in emphasis as part of the developmental process. Even here, however, our emphasis is not just on abreaction for its own sake. We encourage fuller feeling and more acknowledgment of detail and intensity in this phase, not to have the client relive the trauma, but to help him engage with it as a full person. The purpose here of the client's engaging with the memory is existential: to meet what happened to him as a full human being, embedded in a different context, with all the resources, feelings, insights, and talents at his disposal, and to do what he needs to do (rage, mourn, say goodbye, take a stand, make new vows and dedications) as a conscious human being.

As memories present themselves in this phase, we look for places where it is appropriate to engage the survivor more fully in the context of the memory. Since the client is well enough anchored by now in his present self to resist the urge to dissociate into the past, he is able to meet and challenge the abuse and the abuser and therefore change his experience of the memory. The undoing of beliefs that have a frozen, unexamined (introjected) quality often becomes possible as memories are worked with.

One survivor believed as a child that she could control when the abuse took place by her thoughts, although she could not control being abused altogether. She could remember concentrating intently on the next abusive act her brother would commit on her each time she was abused, and she remembered that she was always right. Only after she also remembered watching him abuse a cousin of theirs did she recognize that she had merely learned the abuser's ritualized sequence of abuse. The recognition that, despite her belief, she had exercised no control and had been helplessly subject to the whims of the abuser allowed her to mourn more fully and to forgive herself for not having prevented the abuse. She recognized how helpless children are, and she now had to see herself as a child. Paradoxically, she could also appreciate how creatively she had turned being controlled by a pattern into the belief that *she* could control the pattern, maintaining a vestige of illusory power to hold on to.

Not every memory becomes an expressive event. In this phase, many memories emerge and are simply passed through: recalled, experienced, acknowledged, and mourned. It is enough that there is now a person who can truly encompass them, rather than be encompassed by them. This is all that is needed to finish what could not be completed in the original situation: to evoke the experience of being helpless and alone, against the new ground of being capable and connected with another; to acknowledge now, because hope is alive, the truth of how truly horrible one's child-hood was; to give up one's grandiose fantasies and beliefs[29] in the face of seeing how truly helpless one was as a child; to be able to mourn the truth instead of avoiding it.

Memories become disconnected from awareness and from narrative history because they are memories of an unfinished situation. It is our shared sensitivity and perceptiveness as client and therapist, our seeking out in collaboration what needs to be finished, that helps us discern what is needed for the resolution of a memory. We can then create appropriate experiments: expressive experiments, dramatic reenactments, or simple dialogues between one human being and another.

Chapter Eight

Enactment and Recontextualization

Survivors not uncommonly find themselves behaving in ways that seem inexplicable or compulsive, or that do not make sense in the present. They may have symptoms (somatic sensations, phobias about otherwise innocuous objects, sexual preferences) about which they feel much shame, and patterns of interpersonal behavior that they repeat even though these get them in trouble. Therapists working with survivors frequently find that such behaviors and feelings resolve themselves only when specific episodes of abuse are recalled and worked through. For example, one woman's obsessive image of canned goods made sense when she finally remembered being raped in a basement storeroom. She had concentrated on the canned goods on the shelf in front of her, in order to dissociate from the horror of the event.

For others, the issue is not that the history of abuse is forgotten but that events have not been connected to current experience in a meaningful way. This may be because family members or the abuser minimized the events, or because the survivor has coped with the difficult nature of the event by holding it off as if it were separate and isolated from the rest of experience. This was the case for a young man who had a fairly clear memory of regular beatings and emotional violence from his alcoholic parents, and yet he held this as "all in the past," as if it had no meaning for him in relation to his present guardedness in relationships and difficulty in tolerating intimacy. This phenomenon has come to be known as *reenactment,* or enactment of the original trauma in posttraumatic symptoms. Indeed, enactment of the original abuse in behavior, interpersonal style, and symptoms (Miller, 1984) is often a significant aspect of the survivor's functioning.[30]

The process of reenacting the trauma in behavior is most directly seen in children. Burgess and Hartman (1987), for example, describe how young children display erotic behavior with a therapist or a caretaker that essentially mimics the sexual abuse they have been subjected to. This is not at all dissimilar to the way in which children act out other events, punishing their stuffed animals in the ways they were punished, or acting out parental conflicts with schoolmates.

Right Figure, Wrong Ground

Any behavior severed from its context almost always appears unusual or inappropriate. Enactment of trauma, and of our responses to the trauma, becomes decontextualized when the context cannot be spoken of or otherwise communicated and known, when there is no listener or receiver of the communication, and when there is inadequate systemic support for the enactment to be recognized as an effect of a trauma. The trauma may also be actively denied and repressed by the system the child is embedded in. As time passes, events are seemingly left behind.

When the child matures and gets farther away from the initiating event, enactment becomes acting out, acting out becomes symptom or character style, and symptom or style often becomes hidden behind shame and guilt. The adult survivor is then left with a set of present experiences that have become severed from their original context. In Gestalt terms, we would say that they are *figures held against an inadequate ground*, that is, a ground that is not inclusive enough to make them "good gestalts."[31]

Without an adequate context or ground, enactments may seem self-destructive, strange, or sick and are often labeled that way by clinicians and survivors. It is often pathologized by clinicians or seen as resistance rather than taken as a schematic of what occurred in childhood but has been severed from its context. This tendency perpetuates the victim-blaming experience common to much of the survivor's life history, and the clinician loses the opportunity to discover the hidden truth in the structure of the survivor's life.

For many survivors, enactment may be the only access to what happened. Many people have all the symptoms we would associate with abusive histories, or they carry some sense of knowing that they are survivors, but they have no visual or "cinematic" memory of such events. Some survivors never do get clear confirmation of their abusive histories. Others may get full-blown memories or flashbacks only after years of work on support and self functions. Therefore, it is crucial that the therapist have ways of using such symptoms and behaviors as part of the working process, rather than ignore or pathologize them (as perhaps the client is already doing).

Recontextualization

One does not need to know the actual history to formulate statements that hold current processes against the ground of the possible past. For example, noting the repeated difficulty one client had in talking about her experience, even in the smallest ways, I worked with her to explore the qualities of her silence, her sense of struggle with it, and her wish to break it and talk fully with me. I formulated a number of statements for her to make, to see if they experientially "fit" her experience: "I was made to not talk about what happened to me as a child." "What happened to me as a child is unspeakable." "I was made to keep quiet about the abuse." "It's too horrible for me to speak of." Each statement had a slightly different nuance for her. She was eventually able to find the statement that most characterized how she felt in the present as she struggled with her silence. This woman was in the early support phase of her healing. To have her silence make sense and be identified as an effect of something that had been done to her, rather than as her "resistance," was tremendously validating. Validation moved

226 Healing Tasks: Psychotherapy with Adult Survivors

her away from struggling with herself and toward challenging the abuse. She could not do that in her childhood, but it was necessary now if she was to reclaim her power as an adult.

Thus, the therapist works first with the survivor to describe and capture the quality of her present experience and feeling, so as to reflect it as accurately as possible in the formulated statements. The statements use as much of the known history as possible. The idea is to take experiences or thoughts that are seen as being about the self and reframe them in a context that experimentally includes significant others and, possibly, historical events. For example, free-floating anxiety may be an enactment of having been frightened and terrified by an abuser, or of having been threatened with some future harm, so that the person is always anticipating new events with terror. Trying on statements like "I was frightened by him" or "I was made to wait in terror of what would happen, as I feel I am waiting in terror now" can help give free-floating anxiety a real focus and thus lessen the secondary anxiety about the feeling itself.

Listening to Symptoms and Experience

As survivors I am working with describe their current life experiences and attitudes toward themselves, my thinking is often guided by this question: In what context would this experience or symptom *make sense*? I spend time listening for nuances of experience, and getting detailed reports of how a person experiences a problem or a symptom, so that I can make hypotheses about the possible context.

Here are some examples of symptoms and of what they may be enacting. These are only *possibilities*, however. The detailed information provided by the survivor and the clinician's knowledge and intuitions about the particular client are the best guide in thinking about symptoms as reflections of actual *events*, rather than as symbols of internal conflicts, as they have often been interpreted. The emphasis here is on *experience* and *experiment*. We must view any interpretations as starting points, not definitive analyses of experience.

Symptom	*Possible enactment*
Silence, inarticulateness	The unspeakable; secrets; the taboo of not saying; having been made to be quiet
Somatic pain	Pain of abuse, torture
Tensions, sensitivities	Abusive acts (throat sensitivity and having been strangled, circulation problems and having been tightly tied); body structure and posture as protective poses related to physical assault
Transference, countertransference reactions	Quality of the relationship with the abuser (caretaking of the therapist, or acting as the abuser toward the therapist through identification with the aggressor)
Anxiety, depression	Feelings one had as a child that could not be recognized; fearfulness and loneliness experienced at that time
Low self-esteem	Being made to feel bad
Phobic responses	Fear of objects used in abuse; fear of circumstances of the abuse (fear of crowds as related to gang rape)
Eroticization	Confusion of sexuality, aggression, and interpersonal contact by the abuser

Somatic pain and discomfort are common among survivors. I work to develop a more detailed and experientially based description of the sensations involved (see Kepner, 1987). The survivor may then discover what the pain actually *feels like*: an ache, or a burning and searing sensation, or a crushing weight. From such experientially rooted descriptions I might develop some statements for the survivor to try on, collaborating with her to find the wording that best resonates with her feelings and feels like a good fit with her experience.

Description	*Possible statement*
A place that hurts	"I am hurting inside."
	"I am hurting inside about what happened to me."
	"I have places in me that have been hurt."
A vague ache	"I ache about what happened to me."
	"Some distant hurt calls to me to be known and understood."
	"There is something aching and unclear, which feels important to me to get to know."
A crushing weight	"I was crushed by what was done to me."
	"His body weight was crushing to me when he hurt me."
	"I've carried the crushing weight of what was done to me all this time."

Similarly, the exploration of anxiety can help develop more detailed understanding.

Kind of anxiety	*Possible statement*
Fear or terror	"I was terrorized and frightened by others." "What happened to me was terrifying." "Growing up in my family was frightening and terrifying."
Waiting for something bad to happen	"Bad things were done to me, and I never knew when they would happen." "I am waiting fearfully to know about the bad things that happened to me as a child."
Tense drawing in of the whole body	"I am trying to protect myself from what they did to my body." "I drew in from fear of what they were going to do to me."

My thinking is always shaped by what I know about the client, in addition to what he is saying or describing, his phase of healing, and what he can tolerate or entertain, given his current capacity and our relationship. With clients who idealize me and are likely to introject what I say as automatically true, without testing it against their internal experience, I am very cautious about offering statements at all. I may do so only after we have worked to get them well grounded in their own experience and able to clearly discern the internal sensations that confirm or disconfirm a recontextualization as a "good fit."

With a client who has no detailed memories, or perhaps only a vague sense of knowing that she was abused, I tend to offer statements that do not extend too far or assume too much beyond what we already know. With clients who are well into the phase of undoing, I am more likely to offer recontextualizations that are more emotionally charged, and whose language about what might have happened is more pointed and graphic. This assumes that their self functions are able to encompass more charged emotional experiences and memories, and that their boundaries are adequate for rejecting such phrases and images if they are not fitting. Like all therapy, the process of working with recontextualization requires creativity, subtlety, empathy, theory, and experience. It is not so much a technique as an art.

Recontextualization Experiments

The therapist's role in working with enactments is to help identify and articulate possible enactments in the behavior and experience of the client, and to formulate such interpretations as *experiments* for the client to try on as a means of restoring her to her context. It is crucial that this not be done with raw interpretations. We cannot tell our clients what their experience is *about*. Rather, we can offer a rephrasing of their current process and experience as possible *figure-ground relationships*, searching for the "felt shift" (Gendlin, 1978) that signals a meaningful reorganization of experience. I call this a *recontextualization experiment*. We are looking for "goodness of fit" between the client's experience and the statements we develop, to help us formulate experiments for pushing the edge of new growth and development.

A rather straightforward recontextualization experiment occurred during one of my sessions with a woman when we were working on her discomfort with and judgments about her body. By this point, we already knew a fair amount about her family history and about how she had been exposed to her father's rages at her mother about sex, and to his shaming of my client's sexuality as she approached adolescence. The client was well along in the self-functions phase of her healing. She could tolerate and utilize directed attention to her body. As we focused on her body, which for her was anything from the neck down, she verbalized her thoughts to me:

"It's bad down there."

"The body is bad."

"It's not nice."

I took some time to explore with her the degree to which these statements reflected an actual *experience* (felt sensation) of her body versus *thoughts about* her body not based on a sensation. She was able to discern that the statement "It's bad down there" referred both to a sensation of discomfort, which she labeled "bad," and to a thought about her body, not particularly grounded in a current experience. It also referred to her feeling of shame. From the data we began to gather, I offered her a number of "I" statements in which I attempted to capture some of the flavor of her experience and thoughts of her body, but placing these in another interpersonal and historical context:

"I feel bad when I pay attention down there."

"I was made to feel bad about my body down there."

"My body was called *bad* by my father, and now I feel bad about it."

"I had to be nice so I would not be made to feel bad about myself."

"I made myself be nice so I wouldn't be bad and sexual like my father was."

At first, she was unable to say these sentences for herself. She preferred to hear me say them to her, so that she could simply listen and compare them to her felt experience. Then she discarded some of the statements as not relevant to her immediate experience. She suggested alterations in phrasing or wording that felt like a better fit to her. She was able to take the resulting statements and say them—first to herself silently, then out loud to me—with increasing affirmation and emphasis:

> "When I feel my body, I feel how badly I was shamed and mistreated."
>
> "I became a nice girl so he wouldn't make me feel bad about my body."

The result of this experiment was that she felt free of some of the shame and self-judgment that she carried about her body. She could begin to experience these as having been derived from a judging and critical other, rather than as a feature of her own badness. She could also feel how her commitment to "being nice," and therefore not a sexual, feeling body, was a creative way of not identifying with her father's badness and protecting herself from further shaming by him. This shift of figure and ground allowed her to begin actually feeling and exploring her body, including her pains, tensions, and discomforts, in terms of her actual experience and sensations, rather than her judgments and thoughts.

Recontextualization in Various Phases

Recontextualization of symptoms, in terms of how they may be enacting early abuse or the familial environment, is a stabilizing force during the early support phase. Survivors in this phase of healing frequently find it too overwhelming to say the offered statements for themselves, even silently. They often prefer to listen to the therapist say them, with the opportunity to edit, suggest restatements, and assimilate the impact of what they are hearing.

With clients in the self-functions phase, recontextualization not only is a validating reorganization of figure and ground but also can become a springboard for experimenting with new skills and capacities. For example, the client in the early support phase may simply experience the validation that comes with identifying his difficulty speaking about himself as having been made to keep silent about what he felt. In the self-functions phase, he has the support to experiment with speaking up. Here, we might develop an experiment in which the client speaks of his current feelings and explores and defines the range of feelings that can be spoken of. The purpose would be to develop a differentiated range of "speakability": "I can speak to you of my sadness, but not yet of my fear." "I am learning to speak of more things than I was ever allowed by my abuser." "I make the choice, today, to speak of what it was once forbidden for me to speak of. I claim it as *mine*, to speak of or not, as *I* choose."

With a client in the phase of undoing, redoing, and mourning, I might encourage an empty-chair confrontation with the abuser, about how he was silenced by him, how he feels about that now, what he wishes finally to speak of and challenge him with, and so on. In a similar vein, but within the theme of mourning, we might create a funeral ceremony to honor his silence for the way in which it protected him from the wrath of the abuser, sending his silence to the spirits of the silent waters, so that now he can be free to speak.

Chapter Nine

The Body Process in Healing

The survivor embarking on the journey of healing is in a curious predicament. On the one hand, to acquire the capacity to face and work through abuse and live well in the present, he must enter into his embodied life. On the other hand, to enter into his bodily life is to connect with the part of himself that carries the wounds of the abuse and so feels violated, sullied, hurt, dead, fearful, and overwhelmed. Bodily life, a potential source of strength, is experienced as a clear source of danger. For therapy to be able to address this delicate balance, this essential point of healing, the therapy must have a way of understanding and appreciating body process and body experience in the context of what it means to be human, and particularly in the human life of the survivor.

This chapter is intended to orient the reader to the importance of bodily life to the process of healing and therapy. It is not a "how to" manual, and the examples given here are not meant to be imitated. Body-oriented therapy requires training and experience, as does any other specialized technique of therapy, and its application to survivors requires particular delicacy and care. The techniques described here, including hands-on work, cannot be applied wholesale to survivors in general. For many survivors, the nature of the abuse and the particular adaptations they developed make *any* direct attention to bodily experience impossible until late in their healing process. With these people, I work on developing more indirect connections (say, through exercise classes, relaxation tapes used at home, and so on) and do little in therapy sessions that is other than instructional.

Another concern is the kind of transference process that the particular survivor develops in therapy. Some clients develop a strongly sexualized transference, for example. Their lack of certain self functions (good reality contact, adequate boundaries that would make sexual feelings available to therapeutic processing) means that they probably should not do any body-oriented work that requires proximity or touching from the therapist until the transference is resolved. Otherwise, the intimate context of therapy makes body-oriented work too charged and too intense to be of any use. It may even be harmful. If any body-oriented work is needed and appropriate, it can be done outside therapy (taking dance classes, going to a competent massage therapist, and so on) where body-oriented work is not so emotionally based. Transference issues arising from these outside contexts can then be processed during the therapy hour. At any rate, not a few survivors find that even the thought of hands-on work is completely outside the range of possibilities. Any kind of close contact is felt as terrifying, dangerous, or sexual, and it will promote dissociation and decompensation rather than healing.

The population from which I derive the descriptions of body-oriented work that follow was self-selected, to some degree. I am known in my area for being a body-oriented therapist, and I often find clients coming to me who are already interested in and oriented to this kind of work. Whatever the case, it is essential to obtained *informed* consent, and to collaborate in discovering the kind of work appropriate to the client's focus and phase of healing. We must deal with the full picture of clinical concerns for each *individual* survivor.

The Holistic Viewpoint

Because the Gestalt approach is based on a holistic viewpoint, we look at body process and body experience not as an adjunct to the healing process but as intrinsic to the healing process, for body process and experience are intrinsic to the person. We are fundamentally embodied beings, and we organize ourselves in relation to our experience in the world as much with our bodily organization as with our mental organization. Our experience comes through the senses of sight, sound, taste, touch, and smell. In fact, our cognitive process mimics our embodied experience. When we think, we see images, talk to ourselves subvocally, evoke impressions of smell and texture, and so on. Despite the science fiction fantasy that we could be "brains in a jar" operating as disembodied selves, in reality our "self" is always an embodied one, and the means by which we feel ourselves, interact with others, communicate and make contact in our world and with our own being is to a large part brought about by the fact of our physical existence.

This point is particularly important with survivors of physical and sexual abuse, whose trauma and hurt has been fundamentally physical in nature. Because the trauma is to one's body-self, which is the core of physical and sexual abuse, it is essential to give attention to body process and experience during the course of healing. The bodily self does not have to be assaulted directly before attention to bodily experience and process becomes critical to the process of healing. Survivors of emotional abuse also have had to meet and adjust to trauma through the bodily nature and self. All of us meet, respond to, and adjust to *every* situation with the *whole* of our being, not just with our mental apparatus. We adapt to being yelled at or criticized as much by pulling in our shoulders, hardening our chest muscles, and bowing our heads in shame as we do by becoming self-critical and forming mental concepts of ourselves as diminished and powerless. The content of verbal abuse is also often directed at the bodily self. We are described as weak or ugly, called shameful or dirty, told not to speak up or stand up for ourselves.

Because bodily nature is intrinsic to the self, in Gestalt therapy attention to the bodily nature is often the means by which we work to restore wholeness to the person. This is different from therapeutic approaches that split the person into mind and body and view bodily experience and symptoms only as epiphenomena or side effects of the mind, as related but not centrally relevant. From the Gestalt standpoint, physical being is as important for healing as verbal or mental being.

The Survivor and the Bodily Self

Their bodily nature is usually the last thing that many survivors want to feel or become aware of. Most survivors have little body awareness available to them and may experience large areas of the body as virtually numb. If they do have bodily sensation, it is often painful or otherwise uncomfortable. Sometimes even the slightest attention to bodily experience can provoke anxiety and flashbacks or evoke sensations that recall the abuse. The alternation between the polarities of numbing and oversensitivity is classic in any posttraumatic stress condition, but it has not been adequately appreciated with respect to its basis in embodiment.

The survivor had to disown the bodily self in order to survive with some integrity. To have remained connected to the bodily nature in the course of trauma would have meant remaining inside an overwhelming experience. In the present, to be in contact with the body risks remembrance of the trauma and of the denied and disowned sensations, feelings, and actions that come with it.

In Gestalt therapy, we call this pattern of adjustment *desensitization*. We desensitize ourselves by diminishing our breathing, avoiding attention to our bodily experience, rigidifying our muscles so that we prevent movement, awareness, and sensation, or avoiding movement (such as exercise) that would arouse sensation (Kepner, 1987). One survivor of sexual abuse, suffering from lower-back pain, walked with his pelvis virtually immobile. Even the thought of allowing his pelvis some natural movement brought this recognition from him: "If I allow myself to move, I'll have to feel myself there as well. And then I'll have to take seriously what they did to me." A survivor of regular beatings had learned to tighten up, diminish her breathing, and pull her awareness in from her assaulted bodily surface. She thereby rendered herself an "unfeeling lump," which both helped her cope with the pain of the beatings and, paradoxically, made her into the image of how her parents had treated her.

We can appreciate how much of the survivor's physical action and movement had to be restrained, withheld, and bound up. When our natural impulses of movement—to fight, run, kick, turn away—must be held back, we lose the sense of ourselves as effective, powerful, moving, muscular beings. To hold back our spontaneous impulse requires actual *muscular effort*. It is not just a mental repression. In Gestalt therapy we have termed this *retroflection*, to turn back onto oneself. We see evidence of this kind of retroflection in the way survivors are chronically tense in certain body areas. We see bound-up musculature, graceless and uncoordinated movement, rigidities and misalignments of posture.

Desensitization, retroflection, and disconnection from bodily nature and experience are not functions of personal pathology. They are *creative adaptations*, using the tools at hand, to difficult circumstances. But these adaptations, creative and necessary as they were, create dilemmas for the survivor.

Not Being a Whole Person

Having had to sever and deny his bodily nature, the survivor cannot fully be who he is. Lessening of pain also brings the lessening of pleasure. Protection from remembering also leaves him feeling less physically and concretely substantial. Avoidance of his body leaves him unable to develop physical skills and self functions (expression of emotion, standing his ground, setting physical boundaries, practicing self-defense).

Not Being Grounded

Without a bodily aspect, the survivor has no base, no ground on which to weather and solidify her feelings and experience, because direct perception of our bodily nature is what gives us the *concrete sense* of our existence. Indeed, survivors often report feeling insubstantial, derealized, depersonalized, disconnected, weak, frail, and so on. The survivor may move through life feeling disconnected from the present because she cannot feel her own bodily presence in the world. Moreover, memories of abuse tend to be overwhelming because the survivor has no physical container in which feelings can be held.

Inability to Self-Regulate

How can we know what we really want or need if we cannot feel anything? How can we act on our own behalf if the bodily basis of action is unavailable to us? One survivor did not know when he was hungry because he had so little awareness of his internal organs' sensations. Since he was not particularly organized to eat by the clock, he would go for extended periods without eating. Eventually he would become low in blood sugar and quite cranky. Increased availability of internal body sensations, through body-oriented therapeutic work, allowed him better self-care and a more stable mood, although it also connected him to his feelings of hurt and deep sadness. Another survivor was unable to feel clearly and respond to her physical urges to walk away from situations where she felt her boundaries were not respected. This led her into submitting to sexual advances when she did not want to, tolerating the physical proximity of others even when it felt unpleasant, and so on. Relinking her urges to bodily actions, we eventually experimented with her pushing away and claiming more space for herself in the therapy room, which allowed her to experience more congruence between feeling and doing.

Missing Pieces

Disconnection from the bodily self also makes unavailable the sensory awareness necessary for recovering significant memories of the abuse. Remembering is more like reconstructing than like accessing a recording, and a deadened body cannot support the recollection of bodily trauma. To reconstruct or recreate in the present requires all the building blocks to be there: sensation, muscularity, sight, sound, insight, and so on. Memory is reconstruction, and without the sensations and feelings rooted in our body experience we lack the data necessary to reconstruct an event. The survivor with little bodily awareness is left with disconnected fragments of the memory, which appear only as incoherent symptoms.

Somatic Symptoms and Shame

When the bodily recollection of trauma—the hurt and pain, the feelings of fear and disgust, the sensation of hands holding one down, the blows and so on—is disconnected from any awareness of the events from which it is evoked, then this bodily memory appears groundless, free-floating, without meaning or cause. Thus the bodily self may be experienced only as somatic symptoms, pain, discomfort, odd sensations, tensions, and habits. When we have symptoms or characteristics that have no apparent external cause, we tend to attribute them to some flaw in ourselves. The presence of these symptoms supports the sense of shame and badness that the survivor also feels for other reasons. Without the context of the real events that the symptoms are *responses to*, the symptoms make the survivor feel sick, neurotic, pathological, and damaged.

Therapy and the Bodily Self

Most modern training in psychotherapy is almost exclusively cognitive and verbal in orientation. Therefore, most psychotherapists are unfamiliar with the variety of ways in which bodily experience and process can be attended to therapeutically. Many therapists have rather stereotypical views of body-oriented work. These are usually based on outdated images of pillow pounding, painful massage techniques, or hyperventilation. But such methods are clearly inappropriate to most work with survivors, particularly those in earlier phases of healing.

What kinds of body-oriented work are appropriate with survivors?[32] There are many techniques for working with bodily life. Some focus on the release of tension and on the dissolving of personal defenses, as represented in bodily armor. Others focus on posture and alignment as the "carriage of character." Still others use hands-on techniques to deal with tension, or create sensations of energy flow and warmth to promote a sense of continuity and bodily connection. In my view, however, it is not the techniques that define the therapeutic work with the bodily self; it is the orientation toward what this work *means*, and how we go about it.

Ideally, our purpose is not to work "on" the body as such but to work with the person's *experience of self* as it is *embodied*, to understand the organization of his or her bodily life as *self-organization*, and to open up new possibilities and resources that allow the survivor to have a fuller and more supported sense of being in the world. Whatever techniques we use, we understand them first as part of a process of supporting, heightening, and experimenting with experience of self, with the aim of reclaiming and reorganizing specifically *bodily* experience of self. There are many ways in which we can work toward this aim:

- Experimenting with posture and body structure, to discover stances adapted to the abusive context
- Working with posture or stance to find more support for interactions in the world or more access to feelings
- Exploring muscular tension as a way of protecting oneself in the context of physical abuse
- Working with breathing to create more support for having bodily sensations or for expressing feelings
- Using touch to promote sensations of warmth and energy that gently allow the survivor to reclaim bodily sensations and begin to experiment with living in the bodily space

- Developing awareness of the legs as a part of grounding
- Teaching exercises for stretching and loosening to give the survivor comfortable bodily experience and the sensation of physical presence
- Using hands-on techniques to release chronic tension and help the survivor find a different and more open experience of self
- Helping the survivor find different ways to hold himself or herself physically and thereby gain greater strength and competence
- Using movement to expand possibilities for grace and flow and help the survivor reclaim bodily life in a new way
- Encouraging care and nourishment of the body, through exercise, diet, warm baths, and so on, to promote care and nourishment of the *self*

The particular person, the kind of therapeutic relationship, the stage of healing, and other factors will influence what we do. One survivor may find any awareness of bodily life overwhelming, while another finds awareness of nonabused body areas relieving and grounding. For one survivor, an exaggeration of a posture may evoke a traumatic memory, but it could mobilize another to stand up for herself. For some survivors, hands-on work is too intrusive or evocative or is experienced as too sexual to tolerate beneficially, while for others it may be a key to leading them gently and supportively toward discovering their bodily life. Body-oriented work clearly demands care, training, and knowledge.

Attention to body process and experience with survivors involves a delicate balance. We must always ask what kind of body-oriented work would be useful to the survivor's growth at a particular time. What phase of the healing process is the survivor in? What does that say about the kind of body-focused work that would be helpful?

Figure 9.1 shows one possible continuum of body-oriented work. Note the *graded* way in which work with the body can be part of any particular phase of healing, and of the particular tasks being developed during that phase. Like the other aspects of healing, healing the bodily self is a developmental process, and the work must be appropriate to the particular phase of development where the client is focused.

Figure 9.1. A Continuum of Body-Oriented Work.

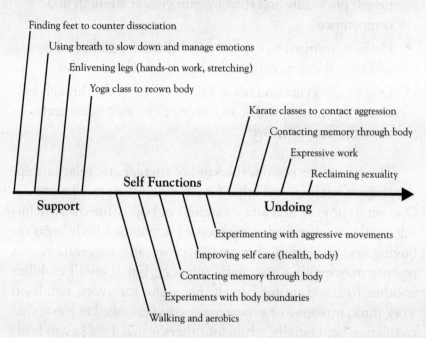

Contributions of Body Process to Support

Typically, the survivor in the support phase is at odds with her body, which is experienced as a mass of anxiety and symptoms, if it is experienced at all. Yet, the bodily self is the potential source of grounding that will help the survivor weather the process of healing. Connecting with one's body experience in this phase requires judicious and careful work.

Orienting and Reality

In the support phase of healing, survivors often feel disoriented and easily affected by feelings and interactions. They are unable to withstand many stresses and strains, such as even talking about the trauma, and are often in poor contact with themselves and the environment. This is in part because survivors have learned to disconnect and dissociate themselves from their body to avoid feeling what is being done to them during abuse episodes. This highly effective strategy becomes an enduring method of coping with any negative experience.

To the body-oriented therapist, dissociation is literally a way of leaving the body. We can actually observe how the dissociating person pulls all of her awareness, as well as her energy, into her head. The rest of the body appears wooden, devoid of animation. In even more severe dissociation, the person pulls all of consciousness and energy still farther up, so that the eyes appear empty, distant, or glassy.[33] The person describes feelings of being far away, disconnected from reality, disembodied, and so on.

Dissociation is highly effective in avoiding unpleasant feelings and sensations, but a body with its consciousness "evacuated" is unprotected and vulnerable. Dissociation avoids *immediate* unpleasantness, but it actually leaves the survivor in *more* of a victimized position.

Thus it might seem that our aim would be to get the survivor fully in touch with her body—and, indeed, this is the long-term goal. But we must find ways to make this safe enough so that it becomes a skill, instead of the privation of an adaptation that has had high survival value.

I once worked with a survivor who was "going away" in her eyes. She would describe "spacing out" as we talked about certain subjects in therapy. I observed how, on the bodily level, this seemed to involve her defocusing her eyes. I showed her what this looked like by doing it myself, and then I noted her doing it every time it happened after that. As she developed more awareness, I worked with her on *re*focusing, which she said made her feel more present and connected with what was going on. But she entered our next session furious at me.

"Now I can't space out so easily! It's all so real now. You took it away from me, and I don't know what to do with being so in touch!"

I apologized and assured her that I did not intend to leave her without resources for coping. My intention had been more modest—to develop her awareness of *how* she spaced out, so that she could choose to be more in contact—and I was quite chagrined to see how effective our intervention had been.

We worked then on how to manage her increased capacity for feeling and contact. But if I had thought to work with her originally on developing ways to *manage her experience* as she refocused, it would have been a more appropriately graded experiment. Fortunately, the strength of our therapeutic relationship helped us correct my omission. It is also important to remember that connecting to one's body connects one to the place where physical and emotional feelings are experienced, and so this kind of connecting may evoke traumatic memories. The support-phase survivor can manage only a limited degree of exposure. Thus we must ask, "How can this survivor begin to connect to her body as a *support* for grappling with the reality of her abuse?"

Another client felt herself to be "a walking head." We began to explore how we could help her connect with her body so that she could have "more of her" available for grounding and support. Scanning her body—"looking down from inside" while still in her head—she reported that any awareness of her chest, diaphragm, abdomen, and pelvis made her very anxious. She could not imagine contact with her body as any kind of support in these circumstances.

It is very difficult to get back in touch with a long-ignored, numbed, or dissociated part of one's bodily self just by *thinking* about it. In fact, thinking about it maintains one's sense of detachment and distance, precisely because it is not the same as *experiencing* that part of oneself directly. But experiencing what has always been associated with trauma takes much care and support to be useful. Therefore, we collaborated on a process whereby she could begin to reclaim "everything around all the bad stuff."

We did this by my using verbal instructions and gentle touching (with the client's careful and continual consent, to make sure she had full control over the process) to *support* this new attention to and contact with herself in a way that was safe and agreeable. This is what hands-on body-oriented work means: the establishment or reestablishment of fuller bodily *self-contact* through the therapeutic use of touch, no matter what the technique. Whether the form of touch uses gentle movement of body parts, "energy work" to promote sensations of inner connection and warmth or flow, "release" techniques to provide support as the client discovers how to let go of chronically held body areas, our interest in hands-on work in this context is to support *self-contact*. Without such a framework this or any other kind of body-oriented technique does not bridge the disconnection of one's experienced self from "the" body. It remains *body* work but not *self* work.

I do not mean this in a disparaging way. I know personally how very useful and straightforward body work can be. I only wish to point out what makes this kind of work *psychotherapeutic* in focus and intent.

We worked to bring the client's awareness down the sides of her neck and through her shoulders to her arms, bypassing the core "bad" areas and going down her sides to her hips and then her legs, and eventually through her legs to her feet. This gradual process took many sessions and much practice by her at home, but she eventually began to feel that she took up more bodily space than the trauma did. She could now experience at least some aspects of her bodily experience as a source of grounding, comfort, and self-support. Eventually, this became the basis of her being able to explore the bodily areas that were more centrally associated with the trauma.

Grounding

The experience of being grounded typically brings with it feelings of being settled, present, in touch with the external world, solid, connected inside, and less vulnerable to emotions and contact with others. Therefore, the experience of being grounded is a direct antidote to survivors' common experience as being disconnected, out of touch, insubstantial, unsettled, and highly vulnerable to their own feelings, as well as to the impact of other people.

Lack of grounding may be characteristic of survivors, but it is really only an extension of our general cultural tendency to live "in our heads"—that is, to locate our predominant experience of self and identity in the upper body and head (Kepner, 1987). Survivors merely take this tendency a step or two farther, often locating their primary awareness and sense of self in the eyes, or even inside the skull.

The typical survivor in the support or presupport phase of healing has often vacated his body and lives predominantly within a small space in his head. His "self" is therefore smaller and less substantial than the trauma—that is, the *bodily areas* associated with trauma—and is certainly less substantial than the other people he encounters. Since most feelings and emotions are experienced as emerging from "below" (the torso) and traveling upward, the survivor must *retreat* upward from any evoked emotion. This retreat does not give the survivor the opportunity to live through and learn how to weather the feeling, since the cycle of emotion is truncated.

Most of the classic bodily therapy techniques directed at improving grounding are derived from the Reichian tradition. But the vigorous movement and breathing of Reichian therapies are problematic here because they are commonly experienced (as intended by their originators) as overstimulating and as promoting dearmoring, or loss of control. This is useful for the overcontrolled neurotic, who needs to learn how to "let go," but it is merely retraumatizing for the survivor, who must learn that it is possible to have *choice* and *grading* in experiences.

The grounding strategy for a survivor should start with some assessment of what is possible or useful for her at the time. Some survivors cannot tolerate any attention to the body without having difficult feelings or memories. For them, grounding must use methods that allow them to experience some contact with the world, but without going through the medium of inner bodily life: feeling the seat under them, touching the arms of the chair they are sitting in, using their eyes actively to look around the room and become more oriented. Other survivors can tolerate awareness of some bodily areas but not others, or perhaps they can tolerate awareness of their skin's surface but not of their internal bodily experience. Work with grounding must be creative, collaborative, and experimental. It will change over time as the survivor gradually reclaims her bodily life from the trauma and becomes a larger self.

One client quickly became ungrounded whenever we tried to talk about memories of abuse or about anything else that generated anxiety or uncomfortable feelings. She would draw all her energy and attention into her upper chest and head, lift her heels off the floor so that only her toes touched, stop her breathing by holding her diaphragm, and pull in her shoulders. This had the effect of actually making her more anxious, since energy and tension were now concentrated around her chest and heart. Initially, when I had her experiment with bringing her attention down from her chest, she would feel more overwhelmed as sensations from her lower torso and pelvis came into her awareness (her history included sexual abuse).

I worked with her instead to "find her feet" by putting them flat on the floor, concentrating her attention there, and imagining her feet sinking into the floor. This had the effect of bringing her energy down and relieving the tension in her chest, getting her more settled and in better contact with the environment while bypassing areas that carried traumatic experience.[34] Eventually, I also worked with her to use breathing and imagery for connecting her awareness and sense of self to her legs and bringing her energy downward by inhaling into her chest and imagining, as she exhaled, that her breath was traveling down her sides, into her legs, and downward into the floor, through her feet. This also allowed her to bypass her abdomen and pelvis while connecting with areas less associated with trauma and benefiting from the grounding she could acquire.

We practiced using these processes as ways for her to modulate and manage memories, feelings, and other aspects of her healing. As she moved through the support phase and became more interested in and able to learn new tools, I taught her leg stretches derived from hatha yoga and martial arts, as well as runner's stretches, to help her become more connected to her legs as a source of grounding. She could do these stretches on her own, and she found them as useful as relaxation procedures in managing her anxiety. Toward the end of the support phase, she was able to utilize hands-on work (when carefully contracted for, so that she had full control over what was being done and could tell me to stop or start) to help generate a feeling of energy flow down her legs, further opening up her contact with her legs as support and grounding. We also worked on her posture and alignment, exploring and experimenting with changes that increased her grounding and her sense of strength and self-support.

Another survivor could barely make any contact with her body without feeling overwhelmed by fear and terror. Both emotions were significant components of the kind of abuse she had been subjected to. The kind of work just described was not yet tolerable to her. Nevertheless, she was responsive to being asked to look at me and focus, and she could ask me to hold her hand. When she became overwhelmed or disoriented, I would bring her back into focus by telling her to look at me and asking her to feel my hand holding hers. These simple procedures eventually became anchors for her and the platform from which she could progress to other ways of connecting with her bodily ground. The resulting contact with her present environment depended less on my presence than on her developing her own independent resources for grounding.

Self-Care and Nurturance of the Body

In addition to the specific skills and techniques already described, survivors in the support phase of healing can benefit from developing ways to care for and nurture the bodily self. They often do well with methods that allow them to maintain some experiential distance from the body: exercise programs, attention to a healthy diet, seeing to adequate medical attention, and so on. They can learn to take care of "the" body as an object worthy of care, even when they are not yet ready to experience the body as the *self,* which could evoke too much awareness of how the bodily self was traumatized.

Because physical or sexual abuse often takes place in a larger context of neglect by caretakers, survivors often have had little direct experience of being cared for appropriately, even where the most basic of physical needs are concerned: being fed healthful food in a timely and appropriate fashion, receiving timely and adequate medical care, being helped to calm themselves when overwrought, getting adequate sleep, and so on. In adult survivors, we often see the same patterns of neglect in self-neglect. Therapists, because of psychoanalytic attitudes derived from Freud's outmoded "death instinct" theory, have interpreted such behavior as self-destructive. There certainly may be self-destructive elements in some of this behavior, but my observation is that it is more often due to *simple ignorance,* caused by the lack of modeling for appropriate self-care.

I have seen this profound inability to care for one's own simple needs among survivors who were welfare mothers and those who were professionals. Not knowing when to rest, having a poor or inadequate diet, minimizing signs of illness, not seeking medical care when it is needed, having few means of self-comfort, self-soothing, or managing stress, overworking and being unable to read the signs of their own exhaustion—these are not a socioeconomic thing. They are a measure of lack of attention by caretakers in the course of development. Children are *taught* that their bodily signals are important—or unimportant.

Contributions of Body Process to Self Functions

As the focus shifts from support to development of the self functions, our therapeutic concern becomes developing the capacities and competencies for managing experience. The major self functions involved here are boundary functions, feeling functions, reality-perception functions, experiencing functions, and self-support functions.

In one way or another, body process is intrinsic to all these self-functions. For example, much of how we manage our interpersonal boundaries with others has to do with how we manage our physical space, our distance from others, our posture, and the gestures by which we tell another person to come into our space or stay away. Similarly, emotions and feelings are bodily events. Joy includes a lifting of the chest, an increase in the rate of breathing, and so on. In anger, we set our jaw and clench our fists. To increase our tolerance for a wider range of emotion, we must gain access to the body that feels.

Reclaiming the Bodily Self

Abuse fundamentally takes the body away from the victim. The child no longer controls his bodily space, sensations, the level and pace of stimulation, and so on. In managing this unbearable dilemma, what the child intrinsically experiences as *self* must be rendered *not-self*, that is, cut off from by dissociation, desensitization, diminished liveliness, massive body tension, and so on.

To get back a sense of one's body as self, to live again in one's bodily self, to find strength, pleasure, substance, presence, boundaries and feelings, means that what has been claimed by abuse must be reclaimed for the self. But this may also mean that buried memories will emerge. As we have been seeing, when awareness develops in areas associated with episodes of abuse, the bodily sensations that were divorced from perception become available. To reclaim the bodily self is also to reclaim memory.

We begin to reclaim the bodily self by making basic bodily awareness a part of the data we attend to in the course of therapy. I may observe how, as a client is talking about something, she limits her breathing or tightens her shoulders in a certain way. I may ask her to notice what she is feeling in her body as we explore a particular topic or subject. I may report my own bodily reactions to what she is telling me, in order to model the importance of embodied life: "As you talked about how scared you were, I felt myself tighten in my own chest."

In beginning to explore and tolerate feelings, we use the fact that feelings are literally felt *somewhere* in the body. If a client reports feeling sad, I am interested in *where* in his body he feels his sadness, and in the nature of that sadness. Is it a heavy-hearted sadness? Strangled off in his throat? Does it feel like a kick in his belly? A melting in his eyes? What does happiness feel like in the body? Does it feel like a rising sensation in his chest? A lightness in his torso?

From a bodily perspective, what does it mean to have a boundary? It means to have awareness of one's physical limits (the skin boundary), to have a sense of ownership over what is contained within those limits, and to have choices about the entry of others into the proximal space of one's body. As we work with making the survivor's feelings available and tolerable through grounding, the survivor begins to articulate and differentiate an array of sensations in what was an amorphous or numbed bodily ground.

Rebuilding the Bodily Self

Rebuilding the bodily self means taking responsibility for owning the realities of having a physical existence. Of foremost importance for the survivor is physical exercise and movement. Usually a regular class is required, at least initially, to provide an external framework of consistency. Valuable programs range from traditional forms of exercise, such as swimming and aerobics, to martial arts and yoga. Exercise of this kind does more than aid physical health. It provides self-definition through the development of clearer sensations of the superficial musculature. It also builds a sense of mastery and capacity in an area that has been alien to the survivor. Different forms of exercise or physical work can be useful in addressing particular developmental issues for different survivors.

Hatha Yoga	Relaxation, gradual release of tension, poise, meditative orientation to the body
Aerobic exercise	Stress tolerance, increased physical capacity (and thus self capacity), definition of bodily self
Dance, dance therapy	Grace, flow of movement, self-expression
Weight training	Strength, power
Feldenkrais and Alexander methods	Alignment, poise, relaxation
Martial arts	Managing aggression, managing boundaries
Chi-kung	Building more energy, grounding, strengthening
Physical-release methods (massage, deep-tissue work, acupressure, energy work)	Opening the body, releasing deep tensions, finding more comfort in the body

It is possible to fine-tune a particular method to the needs of a particular client, but something must be done, even if it is not the ideal. A gentle start is most helpful. More vigorous activities can be experimented with as this phase progresses.

Contributions of Body Process
to Undoing, Redoing, and Mourning

As we reach this phase, the survivor finally has the resources to undo tensions and bodily patterns. There is a place here for direct work with the bodily self, which promotes the direct release of tension, realignment of posture, the acquisition of fluid movement, and strong physical expression of emotion. Several of the activities just listed can be very useful here. A psychotherapist trained in body-oriented methods can also be quite important at this point, so that as physical release and realignment are experimented with, emotions and underlying introjects and retroflections can be worked through in an integrated way (Kepner, 1987). Expressive work in therapy, using vigorous and aggressive body movements (kicking, hitting, punching, vocalizing) can also be helpful, since they allow the survivor to fully own the capacity for a range of expression that was previously denied.

Reclaiming of one's sexuality plays an important part during this phase. This is most crucial for survivors of sexual abuse, or of emotional abuse in which sexual ridicule and humiliation figured prominently. Maltz (1992) offers an excellent guide to this process, appropriate to all phases of healing. For many survivors, the most significant steps in reclaiming sexuality often cannot occur until this phase. Only at this point do core memories of abuse emerge. If the survivor had tried to reclaim her sexual functioning earlier, the memories would have been evoked prematurely.

Body Process in the Reconsolidation Phase

Bodily life and bodily experience are now much more intrinsic aspects of one's life and one's experience in general. Responsibility for one's continuing integration of self, through exercise, diet, meditation, and movement, now seems to be established. Growth and development are never "done," of course, but now they no longer have abuse as their central concern. Healing is about becoming whole in the broken places, but wholeness itself is beyond brokenness. It is something which is constantly being redefined, reformulated, and reorganized, at ever more encompassing levels, throughout life. Otherwise, we have stagnation and fixity, a kind of death before dying.

Body-Oriented Work in Context

The case that follows expands on body-oriented work already described with a woman survivor. It illustrates possibilities and directions that a body-oriented therapy can take, but it is not a prescription. This case is somewhat idealized, for a number of reasons. The client, whom we will call Jean, had a number of preexisting supports (stable work and a steady income, a network of friends and professional relationships) and self functions. She was familiar with dance, yoga, and health-oriented practices, and she had a deep commitment to reclaiming her bodily space. Her pattern of work was quite progressive. Other survivors might follow a more chaotic and less progressive course, and many would not tolerate the kinds of hands-on work that Jean could manage for her own benefit. Nevertheless, Jean's work, like that of all survivors, still had its fits and starts, its periods of stuckness. There were times when she felt flooded and overwhelmed, when we probed too much and worked too hard. I made errors and received correction from her. She tried to do too much at times and went through periods of letting her supports lapse. With these realities in mind, however, I hope that this case will be useful in furthering understanding of the value of body-oriented work in the healing process.

Beginning

Jean had been in psychotherapy for anxiety, depression, and somatic symptoms (vague pains, chronic tension) for a number of years when she spontaneously began to have flashbacks of abuse. She began recalling incidents of sexual abuse and sadistic punishment by her mother. Her therapist, whose expertise lay elsewhere, discussed her concerns with Jean, and they agreed that a referral was appropriate.

When she first came in to see me, Jean appeared physically quite stiff. She moved as if her body were a solid block, with a mechanical and almost robotic stiffness, entirely without flow or grace. Her face was particularly stiff and masklike in expression. She was somewhat overweight, but this left me with an impression of padding or insulation over a solid block, rather than with an impression of softening of angularity.

After some work together, during which we established a measure of supportive contact, we were able to explore and develop some understanding of her internal experience of her body. (See Figure 9.2.) Jean normally had little awareness of anything below her neck, represented by the dotted outline of her body in the figures. Her experience was that "she" (her identified and experienced "I") *was* her head; anything below was unknown,

Figure 9.2. Initial Presentation.

foreign territory. Most of her felt bodily experience consisted of symptoms (tension, pain, discomfort, anxiety, and so on) "down there," represented by dark areas in the figure, to which she was subject. (See Figure 9.3.) The rest of her experience of her bodily self was that it was absent. Her body below her head was a kind of solid object to which she had no entry. Nor did she want any, for even as we began directing her attention to her body, she began to feel anxious and scared, as if something bad were going to happen. At this point, almost any awareness of her torso—for instance, when I might try to direct her to attend to her breathing, or to inner sensations—would evoke anxiety. There appeared to be no part of her bodily self that could be attended to without some discomfort: fear, sadness, or pain.

Whenever Jean became anxious about anything as we worked in therapy, she did something that I have seen other women survivors do. She sat in her chair and lifted her heels so that only her toes touched the floor, holding her breath and stiffly poised as if

Figure 9.3. Bodily Experience as Symptoms.

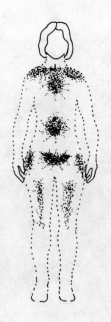

for flight. Her internal experience was of trying to get away from her anxiety and fear, which she experienced as rising from "below" and threatening to overwhelm her. (See Figure 9.4). She often felt as if her legs were literally "gone." She had no feeling of them under her. If the anxiety continued, Jean felt literally "pushed out" by the emerging feeling. At this point, she would feel even more disconnected from her body, as if her head, where "she" lived, were detached and floating. (See Figure 9.5.) With even more anxiety, "she" would even feel disembodied altogether.

Reclaiming the Legs

Over the course of our initial work together, my observations of Jean's body process, coupled with her own curiosity and self-awareness, made it apparent to both of us how ungrounded she was, and how this made for easy dissociation. Jean became aware of having no base from which to deal with the difficult memories

Figure 9.4. "Rising" Anxiety.

and feelings that were emerging. We needed some way of helping her connect more to her legs. But how? If she tried to direct her awareness downward from her head, she had to go through her torso, where she could become trapped, flooded with explosive feelings, and overwhelmed. Yet our hope was that she could use grounding work to help manage her mounting anxiety and counter her "leaving the body" and becoming dissociated.

As we experimented, I thought that if we could make her legs more available to her awareness and senses, without going through her torso, we might be able to increase the sensation in her legs enough so that they could stand out against the fear or anxiety, and she might then have a touchstone for grounding herself.

We agreed to try some simple hands-on work. Jean remained sitting in her chair. I would ask her permission to sit on the floor in front of her and place my hands on her feet. Jean could direct me to stop, back away, continue, and so on, as she felt she had to, so that she had complete control over the process.

Figure 9.5. Dissociation from the Body.

I used an "energy technique" to promote sensations of warmth and flow downward from her knees to her feet, and to support her having more of a sense of her feet on the floor. (See Figure 9.6.) We discovered that any feeling of energy or sensation moving upward through her legs increased her sense of being overwhelmed by "things emerging from below," and I encouraged her to tell me to stop or redirect what I was doing whenever this happened. This became a wonderful opportunity for Jean to experience setting boundaries with me and practice self-determination over her own bodily states.

As Jean began to have a sense of her feet, she could tolerate experimenting with my placing one hand lightly on one knee, with the other on her foot, so that I could encourage her to begin establishing contact with her lower legs, from her knee to her foot. We used the downward direction because this seemed to take the pressure off the emerging feeling that was overwhelming her. We supplemented this more direct work with gentle stretches and

Figure 9.6. Grounding Through the Feet.

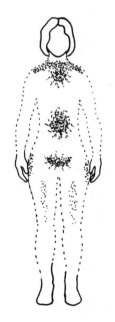

self-massage, as well as imagery work, which she could practice at home to support her connection with her legs.

Over time, and with other support-phase therapeutic work, Jean began to have the sense that her legs were "under" her, and that she could have some impact on her own grounding and on managing the rush of feelings and memories with less dissociation. She felt that she was beginning to reclaim herself from her trauma. She was less helpless in the face of flashbacks, panic reactions, and unfamiliar emotions. Although she could now feel her legs, they still did not feel completely hers. She had to work around the rest of the bodily space between her legs and her head in order to find her ground. The region associated with the trauma—the whole of her torso—was still bigger than "her" (her head). Her legs were "there" now but not yet experienced as "I." We joked that her legs were no longer aliens, but they were still new immigrants; she began to long for their full citizenship. (See Figure 9.7.)

Figure 9.7. Connecting the Legs.

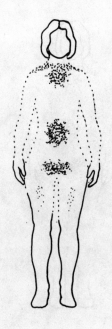

Finding a Route Downward

As Jean progressed through the work of the support phase, she became interested in finding a way to connect to more of her body, since she could experience how the work we had done so far was increasing her stability and self-management. Because she was trusting me more, and trusting that she could control and manage the process of our work as she needed to, and that I would respect this, she felt she could now tolerate a bit more body-focused work. She had experienced the energy work as gentle, nonintrusive, and easily controlled through feedback to me, and we agreed that this might be a modality to continue with. The problem, however, was that as she felt any sensation of energy in her torso, she would also begin to feel uncomfortable and potentially overwhelming sensations. We had to find a safe enough pathway through her torso to her legs, one that did not involve body areas involved in much trauma or emotion. It seemed, in the phrase of the old joke, we could not get there from here.

Eventually, we came up with the notion of directing awareness, energy, and sensation into her sides, creating contact from her head downward through the lateral lines of the body at the edge of the torso. We started this slowly. We used imagery of light and warmth flowing from my hands, as well as her active breathing into the parts of her body we were working with, to affirm her own activity and will in this process. I would help generate a flow of sensation from one hand placed on her head to the other placed lightly on one shoulder, helping her find a sense of connection between these points. Over time, as she found more connection to her shoulders, she was able to try a similar process, with one of my hands placed on one shoulder and the other on the side of her rib cage and then, eventually, on her hip. She came to feel that she could "travel" with her awareness through her sides and even down the sides of her hips.

After this development, we would often spend the first fifteen or twenty minutes of a session doing this kind of connecting work, until Jean felt well established in herself from her head down her sides and into her legs, before resuming our seats and dealing with the life issues common to the later support and early self-functions phases. This meant that Jean was increasingly more rooted in her own person as she faced her therapeutic work and sorted through the difficult issues and emerging memories. She had ready access to grounding if the issues we were discussing evoked difficult emotions or recollections.

Now Jean began to feel that she might be able to *contain* the abuse. She felt this quite literally, since "she" now existed in a space *around* the areas that had been traumatized, and which still seemed to evoke memories and feelings related to the trauma. The abuse still claimed the space within her torso and neck, but she now felt herself to be present in the lateral areas of her body, extending from her head down her neck, through her shoulders and sides, and, increasingly, into her legs, all the way to the ground.

We also were working on extending more of her connection and contact into her arms. This was a bit more difficult for her, since she had been tied by her wrists during various episodes of abuse. Connecting with her arms began to bring back these memories and the fearful emotions associated with this helpless position. Still, since she now had *someplace else* to be in herself, she could now better afford to bring these memories back. She did not need to dissociate and leave her body entirely as long as the pacing and grading of what she was remembering allowed her to stay in the parts of her that she was reclaiming.

Reclaiming the Upper Body

This work was enough for quite a long period as Jean and I worked with issues of boundaries, pacing and grading, tolerating feelings, and so on. The body-oriented therapeutic work now moved into the background, where its result—increased grounding and self-support—helped Jean focus on other figural issues. Jean was graced with a number of preexisting strengths in the self-functions area, and these allowed her to tolerate and utilize the body-oriented work early in the healing process.

Jean's involvement in hatha yoga helped her continue developing her bodily ground in a gentle, systematic, self-directed way. She was still aware of the forbidden territory of her torso, and of the numbness and discomfort this area held for her. She was also aware of how her panic attacks and flashbacks seemed to emerge from this area and disrupt her ability to hold her ground in the outer edges of her bodily self. But she was more concerned with establishing her ability to manage her life, her marriage, her work, her friendships, and so on, by developing her self functions. When crises occurred, as they do in life, Jean proved more resilient than she had been before. She fell apart less in the face of stress. She was more able to mobilize herself, instead of becoming depressed and immobile, and she could manage her anxiety in a way that allowed her to face crises more directly than before.

Jean eventually found her attention turning back to reclaiming the bodily territory occupied by the trauma. She now had more resources for facing this challenge, and she realized that it was going to be difficult for her to reclaim certain feelings and capacities (such as her anger, or the capacity to feel her insides) without also reclaiming more of her bodily core, the medial and central region of her torso. With these recognitions, we began to explore reclaiming her core body space.

First, making sure that Jean's connection to her legs was well established, we began to guide her awareness down into her neck and throat. As she began to feel more sensation here, she began to have the first sensations of choking and constriction, and then recollections of being held by the back of her head and forced to perform oral sex on her mother. The memories were stunning, quite vivid, and felt initially with the full terror and revulsion she had felt when the acts occurred, when she was four or five years old.

Now, however, she had other skills and capacities available for managing these feelings and memories. When the recollections associated with recovering the sensation in her neck became too much for her, we would shuttle her attention back to her sense of groundedness in her legs and her sides, and we fostered this connection by shifting the hands-on work to these places. When she felt grounded and calm again, we would return to her neck. Her "larger" bodily self, which she had already reclaimed, became the base to which these memories and experiences could be assimilated. She no longer had to feel pulled into and absorbed by the emerging traumatic memories. In between the body-focused work, we spent a number of sessions processing, mourning, and integrating the memories and their impact on her. Eventually, Jean was able to contact her neck, and the memories and feelings associated there, without being flooded or overwhelmed.

Over time, with body-oriented work and the more usual kind of therapy focused on life issues and self-functions tasks, we were able to move farther down, into her chest. As we moved into this area, a number of feelings became apparent. Jean began to experience a deep sense of sadness, hurt, and grief—what she began to refer to as "heartfelt" emotions, which she had had to deny, since no one had believed her as a child when she had tried to make the abuse known. She also became aware of her chest, upper torso, and breasts. Having been abused by her mother, the source of her sexual identity, Jean had been left with a terrible quandary as she faced her own budding femininity, in puberty. To become a woman was to become more like her abuser, and to blur the already confused boundary between Jean and her mother. Jean's solution, as a budding adolescent, was to ignore and deny her emerging secondary sex characteristics and desensitize her sensations in this area. Now, as she was undoing the physical numbing and tension that had served her denial, she had to sort out the whole issue of femininity and sexual identity, to pull apart her enmeshment with her mother so that she could begin to define for herself what being a woman meant. The work here was related to recovering her connection to her breasts, and it was the beginning of a theme that we visited and revisited over time. It also applied to her reclaiming of other aspects of her "female body" from the abuse and was part of the longer-term work of undoing the introjects and confluences (enmeshment) that had confused her own identity.

Connecting Upper and Lower Body

The work we had done so far brought us to a very different position from our original starting place. Jean now felt herself to be "in" much more of her body. She could find the ground underneath her and feel her legs and feet. She had a sense of connection to her legs (through her sides), and she was beginning to live in her chest and breasts, taking up residence in her heart and femininity, so to speak. She was not just a head sitting on a body. She was connected to the rest of herself, through her neck, and was reowning her arms and hands, as well as the capacity to reach out, push away (set limits with others), and experience the pleasure and comfort of touch. Much of this work she was doing on her own, through taking classes in hatha yoga, doing massage for friends, and starting to do more aerobic exercise (walking). She found a dance therapist to work with for a time, to help her find more grace and inner expression and to experience what a woman of healthy sexual identity was like in her body by experiencing the therapist's embodied femininity as she worked with Jean.

At about this time, Jean was also working on tolerating the feeling of anger and on integrating more capacity for forthrightness and useful aggression into her repertoire. We experimented in a graded way with martial arts movements (striking, kicking) and processed her feelings as they emerged, using grounding as support. She began to enjoy more vigorous use of her body, and she used this experience as a paradigm of self-support when she had to stand her ground at work or argue with her husband. In both places, she had tended to give in and avoid conflict, and this had often left her feeling weak and helpless.

Jean held the ground that she had gained through her continued work and self-development. She still could dissociate under stress or stimuli that triggered reenactments of the abuse, and could lose ground if she became lazy and avoided her exercises or otherwise did not maintain her connection to her bodily self. In other words, she worked to hold her gains. But she now had both tools, and enough of the trauma worked through, to reclaim her bodily ground and work her way out of restimulation and dissociation. She could experience herself as bigger than the trauma, which now seemed most focused in the unclaimed area of her abdomen and pelvis, although we did not know specifically what it was about. But, as we looked toward connecting her to her abdominal and pelvic space, all she could feel was terror.

Assimilating the Trauma to the Self

Current life issues moved us away, for a time, from Jean's bodily issues and the attention to her childhood trauma. This break gave her an opportunity to work on current self functions, which would help her when we returned to the work on the trauma, and helped us both to pace the work in a more assimilable way. When we turned our attention back to her body, Jean felt more able to face what might be stirred up by her reclaiming of her inner space.

Jean's experience of working on memories of abuse was of a "diving in," becoming so immersed and flooded by feelings and sensations and their intensity that she often felt lost in the past. Now, because the work of reclaiming her body was bringing her into contact with previously unknown memories, she felt that she might once again get lost in the past, after struggling so hard to become grounded in the present. This step backward felt wrong to her, and to me as well. We puzzled over how else we might approach this work.

Eventually, we came up with a process by which to approach these bodily areas and the trauma memories associated with them. We used the notion we had developed previously, of keeping her "bigger" than the trauma, even as a flood of feeling threatened to overwhelm her. We worked first to firmly root her in her body as a whole, all *around* the space of her abdomen and pelvis, so that she felt well connected and grounded in her legs, her sides, her arms, her chest, her neck, and her head. All this felt like "her," of a piece. (See Figure 9.8.)

Then Jean determined which area she wanted to make contact with. My instructions were that her job was to hold her awareness in the rest of her bodily self and stay grounded there. My job was to use hands-on techniques to make contact with the chosen area and support the possibility of sensation and aliveness there. Rather than Jean's becoming absorbed by this bodily area, and by the remembrance of whatever trauma was connected with it, through her direct attention to it, our idea was that she would stay rooted in herself and *absorb the trauma to her.* She was to tell me to stop the enlivening work *before* she became overwhelmed, so that we could pace and grade the work in a way that kept it assimilable.

Jean selected her diaphragm as the first area. She knew that this was a place where she clutched and tightened with fear. She

Figure 9.8. Clearing Memories of Trauma.

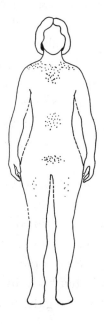

did not know whether there was a specific memory connected with this fear, or whether it came from her fearful stance toward life in general.

We began to work, bringing more energy and sensitivity to this area and slowly building up tolerance of her fearful feeling there by shuttling back and forth between work on her diaphragm and work on supporting her staying grounded in the rest of her bodily self. Gradually, as the feeling of fear in her diaphragm became less overwhelming and intolerable and could therefore be more in the background of her awareness, she could hold her own and pay attention to other impressions associated with the fear, including kinesthetic impressions of lying on something, certain smells, the sound of a door opening, and so on. These impressions eventually came together into a vivid scene of her grandfather coming upstairs into the room where she stayed when sleeping over at her grandparents' house. She could feel how she lay waiting in fear, and how frightened she was of his overwhelming physical power as he molested and raped her. She could feel how she clutched in her diaphragm and throat, to keep from calling out for help, as he had told her not to, and she feared his ability to hurt her.

Jean now recalled the family stories about how, as a young child, she had always kicked up a fuss about going to her grandparents' house, a fuss that was attributed to her stubbornness and willfulness, rather than to the real circumstances. She also began to put together a wider web of understanding: how much her mother was under the authoritarian control of Jean's grandfather, comments cousins had made about his inappropriate and sexualized behavior toward them, the relief Jean had felt but could not understand (and had therefore felt ashamed of) when he had died, and other facets associated with the intergenerational pattern of sexual abuse. Having held her ground in her reclaimed body, Jean had tapped into her diaphragm and discovered what emotions and events this area was connected to. It was not easy or pleasant, but it was not impossible. She was able to stay in her body, instead of dissociating, and have the experience of assimilating the trauma to *herself*, instead of feeling immersed in the trauma. She was able to feel larger as she reclaimed the trauma, rather than smaller and disorganized.

Maintaining this standpoint proved more challenging, however, as we moved her awareness into her abdomen and pelvis. As we faced the anger, grief, and sexuality that she discovered in these areas, Jean also had to face remembering that her father had ignored her mother's abuse, her own rage at her helplessness, her sense of abandonment and desperation, the ways in which she had been overstimulated and hypersensitized to sexual stimuli by the abuse, and her sense that her body had betrayed her by responding with pleasure to abuse that she abhorred.

These recognitions and their therapeutic working through did not come all at once. The work took place over perhaps a year and a half, embedded in the continued work on present-day interactions and problems and careful and graded body-oriented work. There was time to shuttle her attention away from the more intense work and allow for the integration and assimilation of the material and the feelings that she had discovered. We paid attention to indications that she needed to attend to support, grading, pacing, and so on, so that we could minimize any retraumatizing effect of the emerging memories.

Jean was also highly motivated to use follow-up strategies for self-care and self-development outside our work. She continued her practice of hatha yoga and stretching. She began to pursue martial arts training on her own, to learn how to tolerate and handle physical aggression. She was willing to commit resources to a trusted massage therapist, who would help her experience comfort and soothing to counter the pain and discomfort that she was recalling and ground her in the reality that the present was different from the past. Her commitment to pursuing her growth and healing outside therapy helped her assimilate the memories and feelings that she was contacting deep in her bodily core and maintain the ground she had regained.

Becoming a more fully embodied person supported Jean in having a fuller life in the present. She felt more substantial because now she could live in most of her body. Her increased sense of substantiality allowed her to feel more real, more able to withstand contact with other people (both pleasurable and conflictual), and more significant as a person. We joked that she was finally becoming "a person of substance." She felt that she was more than the abuse, even though there were pockets of feeling and areas of numbness still to be reclaimed. This was no longer work "on her body" or work "on *it*" but work on her *self*.

Undoing and Release

Jean's increased ownership of her bodily experience and her increased presence in her bodily self became apparent in one session, when she said that it was time for her to "unravel the knots" she had tied herself into. She meant that she felt ready to do direct work on the significant tensions and patterns of holding that she could now feel in her body. The shift in her tone was remarkable to me. There was no trepidation in her voice, no sense of "I hate to have to do this, but know I must." Instead, she clearly looked forward to facing and grappling with what was before her. It was *herself* she was reclaiming, and she felt that she could face and support herself through anything.

We explored this possibility by exaggerating and heightening a pattern of tension and strain in her body that she had felt for years but had avoided approaching. It began as tension in her arms, shoulders, and neck. As we explored these sensations and worked to find ways of emphasizing them by consciously exaggerating the tensions and postural compensations, a whole stance emerged. Jean's hands were crossed behind her back. Her head was turned to the side, her legs and pelvis were held stiffly and rigidly, and her breath was minimal. I encouraged her to breathe fully, despite the tension, to support her sensation and awareness. As she did so, recollections began to come to her of having been tied by her wrists and pinched and probed, digitally and with kitchen utensils, by her mother as "punishment" for some minor infraction.

We stopped our experiment for a moment as these memories washed through her. It was clear that Jean was remaining grounded, solidly in herself, despite the trauma she was remembering. I asked her how she felt, expecting to hear her say, "Afraid." Instead, she looked me in the eye, smiled with some self-satisfaction, and said, "Angry!" She was clearly ready to undo the trauma that this posture encapsulated and represented.

Together, we formulated the next step of our experiment. Jean returned to her exaggeration of this frozen stance. This time, with her permission, I held her wrists together behind her, so that she could experiment with activating what had been frozen tensions and rigidities by pulling against me and consciously mobilizing herself into movement. By doing this, Jean could also experience what it would be like to use her building anger on her own behalf, as the fuel for undoing the passivity and helplessness that she had experienced in this and other traumatic situations.

Jean began to struggle with increasing force against my holding of her wrists behind her back. I coached her to use her breathing, her legs, and her back, and to get her musculature mobilized and useful to her in this struggle. Jean could hear words in her head that she wanted to say, and I encouraged her to voice them.

"I'm not going to let you do this to me any more!" she yelled. With that, she broke free of my grasp and stood there breathing strongly, glowing with power. I immediately suggested that she imagine her mother in a chair across from her and continue her expression. Jean let loose a tirade against her mother, shaking her fists and striding about the room, calling down all her wrath at the abuse, pain, and humiliation that her mother had heaped on her. Jean was literally shaking with fury, but whereas before she would have dissociated in the face of such intense, forbidden feeling (since any expression of rebellion at her abuse had been met in childhood by a doubling of her punishment), she could now experience her anger as a self function that served her to throw off the yoke of her oppression by her mother and by the way in which she herself had limited her own nature to adapt to the trauma. (See Figure 9.9.)

Figure 9.9. Clear Body, Clear Self.

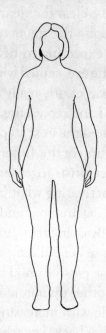

This work allowed Jean a sense of freedom and power that she had never had before. We followed this session up with some hands-on work that focused on supporting more physical release of these bodily tensions and increasing her flexibility and range of motion. This in turn increased her capacity for movement and self-expression. In further empty-chair work, she continued to "unload" much that she had to say to her mother. We used martial arts movements to support her need to mobilize her body into a physical expression of aggression. Jean chose this way of expression, rather than hitting an object imagined as her mother (as I might have encouraged with other survivors), so that she could experience owning this quality in herself without feeling that she was directing abuse at her mother as her mother had done to her. With another survivor, the symbolic act of hitting back against the abuser directly might have been perfectly appropriate, but for Jean to feel whole it was not. Each expressive experiment is precisely that: an experiment, not a prescription. It must be shaped to fit the needs of the person rather than reshaping the person to fit the rigidities of the experiment.

Letting Go

During this period, we worked through a number of tension patterns related to other episodes of abuse. Increasingly, Jean entered our sessions knowing what she wanted to focus on and how she wished to go about it. She accepted collaboration from me on formulating experiments, but she clearly took charge. This was not the passive, compliant mode that she had operated from since childhood.

Jean had maintained contact with her mother, despite her mother's failure to acknowledge her abusiveness. Having owned her anger about the abuse and experienced herself as able to express what she had held in for so long, Jean now felt a contrast between herself and her mother that she had never felt before. On a holiday visit, Jean, who even as an adult, had always felt afraid and cautious around her mother, recognized how small and pathetic her mother really was. Because she herself now felt powerful and strong, had a clear sense of her own depth and inner richness as a person, and had deep and rich relationships with other people in her life, Jean finally saw her mother as narrow, restricted, and damaged. No longer afraid of her mother, Jean could observe her mother's behavior more carefully. She saw her mother's manipulativeness as a way of bolstering her weak self-esteem. She saw her mother's lack of real relationships with others, the desperation her mother had to make contact while defensively alienating others because she could not tolerate any real closeness or intimacy. These insights came about as much because Jean was experiencing herself and her relationship to others from a different bodily ground as because she had new intellectual understanding.

From this work, Jean found herself letting go of her resentment toward her mother. Jean described this less as "forgiveness" than as a simple recognition of who her mother really was. She no longer seemed the powerful figure that Jean had known as a child. She was not the manipulative, vicious figure Jean had known as an adult. From this new perspective, Jean said: "She's really nothing but a shell. She has so little that is really warm and human. She has no richness, no depth. All of her life is cordoned off into a narrow range of feeling and behavior. I still hold her responsible for what she did to me. Her own limitations don't let her off the hook. But I see now that actually owning her responsibility for her behavior is clearly beyond her. She is far more damaged than I am."

Jean now found a kind of reconciliation and could let go of her need to have more from her mother than her mother could give. She could pity her mother, even pray that mercy be given to what she believed was the tortured soul beneath the shell her mother showed the world and herself. Jean's self and Jean's world were no longer determined by her mother. These things were now Jean's own.

Epilogue

I hope that readers now have a perspective on the Healing Tasks approach that will allow them to integrate their own findings and techniques into a wider framework. Much remains to be done: application of the Healing Tasks Model to group therapy for survivors, an examination of how this perspective can shape treatment of Multiple Personality Disorder, research on how temperament and character affect survivors' modes of adaptation to abuse, and other kinds of research. For now, let us review the main conclusions of this volume.

Healing Is Possible

Healing from childhood abuse, as devastating to one's life functioning as abuse can be, is possible. Given sufficient support, a safe environment in which to experiment with learning the self functions, and a challenging but caring environment in which to face undoing, redoing, and mourning, the survivors can formulate and claim a new self, transcending the helplessness and humiliations of childhood.

Healing Is Development and Growth

Survivors feel wounded, flawed, and damaged by their experience, and by the sense of inadequacy and difference from others that it engenders. But healing is less a process of treating wounds than of growth and development. Healing is the restoration and completion of developmental processes that were directed along less fruitful and less rewarding paths, as a creative adjustment to trauma. The same capacity for creative adjustment can be turned toward developing new adaptations and responses in the present, so that the course of growth is reestablished for a rich and satisfying life.

Healing Is Contextual

Healing is not the curing of pathology. It is the creation of a healing context, where changes can occur that could not occur before. This context is not limited to the therapeutic relationship. It must involve the survivor's support, interpersonal relationships, and human environment. Healing is not just a change within the individual survivor. It is a challenge to and reformulation of the whole field. It is a series of incremental developments that, taken as a whole, result in a truly transformational process.

Healing Is Wholeness

Healing is not just the patching up of tears in the fabric. It is the formulation of wholeness. And wholeness is not about trying to restore the lost innocence of childhood. Even if it could be found again, it would not encompass everything the survivor needs to become a mature, adult self. Healing is the reaching for ever larger and more encompassing contexts involving oneself, one's history, and one's future. It includes a sense of transcendence, which imbues life with meaning that reaches into and beyond the particulars, the tragedies and joys that make up existence.

With these things in mind and heart, we can face the tasks of our own healing, and of helping others heal and discover wholeness, with light, hope, and groundedness. We cannot deny the darkness that we see around us, but we can learn not to feed it with the darkness of hopelessness, and we can learn to hold to the light of hope.

Notes

1. The notion of the Organism/Environment Field, or O/E field, is derived from Kurt Lewin (1951) and is a basic concept in the theory of Gestalt therapy (Perls, Hefferline, and Goodman, 1953). The field is the fundamental "unit of study" in the Gestalt approach and resolves the apparent dichotomy of person and environment by asserting that these are essentially aspects of the same whole and must always be spoken of together. We may refer to one side or the other of an identified boundary for the sake of description, such as to the person or to the environment with which they are in contact, but these are always in relation to one another. In this view, the "self" is the experience at the boundary of one's organism (one's person) and one's environment. One's "self" is the intermediary between organismic process and experience, as well as engagement with the environment so as to achieve a balance between one's internal needs and what is available or coming from that environment. In this volume, I will use the term *person* interchangeably with the term *organism*, which I find too impersonal in the context of healing and therapy, and I will always be implying both the human *and* the physical by the term *environment*. It is abstract but, in my view, far better than the use of the term *object* to refer to other human beings (as in "object relations," by which is really meant relations with others who are indeed *not* objects but fellow subjects).

2. I wish to express my appreciation to Mark McConville (private conversation), who first pointed out to me the holographic model for understanding the healing process.

3. *Support*, in Gestalt therapy, refers to the concept of *support for contacting*, as developed by Laura Perls. Perls was particularly interested in what kinds of support had to be developed in order for contacting to become more possible, fuller, and more viable. Her thinking had considerable influence on the orientation toward Gestalt process at the Gestalt Institute of Cleveland, where I was trained, and where it was extended not only into physical support for contacting (breathing, posture, and so on) but also into interpersonal and systemic support for contacting. In my opinion, theory about support for contacting has been the neglected developmental and "feminine" voice in Gestalt therapy, as it has been in most other forms of traditional psychotherapy, whose theory has shown a persistently male bent for interpretation, experiment, risk taking, cognitive understanding, and confrontation. The notion of support provides the ground on which experimentation and risk taking can occur *without* the need for the rigid character adaptations that are called for when one extends oneself beyond one's true means of support.

4. I put this phrase in quotation marks because, despite concerns on the part of Loftus (1993), Yapko (1994), and others, there is no research whatsoever—apart from that based on children's reports in the context of divorce and custody hearings—corroborating such "false memory" as a syndrome or anything else within the population of adult survivors of childhood sexual abuse. Legitimate questions about suggestibility have been used to cast doubt on all cases of recovered memory. All the reports of this "syndrome" come from accused perpetrators who have their own reasons for denying the accusations. There is ample

clinical evidence that perpetrators of childhood sexual abuse deny their behavior even when there can be no reasonable doubt that it occurred. This is not to say that the "syndrome" does not exist, but only that there is no direct *evidence* to support this claim. By contrast, there is much direct evidence to support the existence of childhood sexual abuse, its denial by the perpetrators, and its repression by their victims.

5. Therapists, as part of our Freudian inheritance, have a predilection for seeing such behaviors as "unconscious defenses," which therefore need to be undone. From the perspective of Gestalt therapy, which sees contact processes as creative solutions to particular configurations between organism and environment, the point is not so much to undo a defense as to bring it into conscious and lively interplay, so that it becomes one of the available self functions, and so that the possibilities for interaction and contact can be *expanded.* As for mistrust, when the survivor can explore the full range of the trust-mistrust continuum, he or she can learn to listen to otherwise ignored signals, drawing on both sides of this polarity as the field requires.

6. Note that, in offering these statements for experiment, I try to stay close to the phenomenological descriptions we have developed. The aim here is not interpretation; rather, it is to take the actual processes and experiences seriously, as expressions of the self in action.

7. I might behave differently with another client in the support phase. For example, a client with fewer available resources for contacting might hear my self-disclosure as an implied shaming of her: as a statement that she was not progressing fast enough, or that she should take responsibility for keeping me company when I feel lonely or disconnected from her. With this client, I would be much more selective in what I disclosed about myself. My

intention would be similar—to clarify and own my part in our interaction, so that the therapy could be a truly relational process between two human beings, and productive of healing—but my action would have to be keyed to the developmental resources available to the client in the moment. Like any other relational process, self-disclosure must be considered in context.

8. The recent controversy over "false memory syndrome" has highlighted concerns about whether therapists lead or pressure clients into fabricating or inventing memories. This controversy has created a dilemma in clinical judgment: In the absence of proof or some objective evidence, to what extent should the therapist validate adult clients' reports of sexual abuse in childhood? There probably are a few cases in which false reports have been used as bids for attention or have been manipulated for other purposes. Nevertheless, unless there is some reason *not* to believe the client, I think that we as psychotherapists are required to take an attitude that is more than simply neutral. Our role is not that of courtroom expert. We are there *for the client.* In the support phase, a survivor's early memories or impressions are often vague and unclear, which is all the more reason why the client needs support from the outside, someone to say, "I trust that something did happen to you, even if it's not clear yet what it was." Over the course of therapy, I believe, the truth will come out. See Chapter Seven for a complete discussion.

9. This can take various forms: the survivor's unwitting reenactment of having been threatened with death or physical harm; a way out of the internal pressure experienced as a result of coming too close to an "unknowable" secret; a hypnotic implant used by a cult to ward off the possibility of the child's telling about the abuse as an adult.

10. This is why the investigatory stance suggested by Yapko (1994) is so inappropriate in the support phase. It mimics

the doubt, denial, and minimization in the original field conditions surrounding the abuse.

11. A term used by Gordon Wheeler, in a private conversation with me, to describe the experience of shame.

12. This is true even when the child is in the process of individuating through motor behavior, willfulness, or rebellion. Disagreeable behavior *requires* another person for its success, whether we are talking about a two-year-old's "no" or an adolescent's minute specification of her parents' hypocrisy (McConville, 1995). Individuation always occurs within the holding of the interpersonal field.

13. This is easy to demonstrate. After a minute or two of vigorous breathing (hyperventilation), there will be a noticeable increase in various bodily sensations of tingling and streaming. If some exercise immediately follows (jumping jacks, for example), the flood of sensation quickly recedes. This is why the preparation for flight, as represented by the increased respiration of the panic reaction, is so problematic: if there is no *opportunity* for flight, then there is no opportunity for useful discharge of the accumulated energy.

14. The sense of continuity of the self over time comes from the combination of temperament (tendencies and predilections "hardwired in" by nature), our tendency to develop patterns of organization in our perceptions and behavior, and our tendency to develop a description of the self, which we call *personality* or *identity*, as if it were highly consistent. These things become the patterns or "structures of ground" (Wheeler) that influence our contacting in the present, in particular ways.

15. The self functions discussed here are not those discussed by Perls, Hefferline, and Goodman (1951), nor are they the "contact functions" discussed by Polster and Polster (1973).

In my view, the first are too constrained by reifying terminology derived from psychoanalysis (*ego, id, personality*) and are therefore limited in their ability to describe specific or differently configured self processes. The second have more the nature of "faculties of contact" and leave out the role of the self. I have chosen to specify the apparent self functions (processes) that become obvious (often by their absence) in work with survivors; my teachers and colleagues at the Gestalt Institute of Cleveland, especially Joseph Zinker and Sonia Nevis, have influenced this orientation on my part. Clearly, these self functions are also relevant to people who have not been abused, and they have implications for a developmental psychology based on the contact process. There certainly must be other self functions that could be catalogued in a fuller developmental Gestalt psychology.

16. There are other self functions, no doubt, than the ones discussed here. Indeed, as we begin to understand more about the developmental process from this perspective, we may be able to outline many others, and to see how their absence or the course of their development may have contributed to problems in creative adjustment.

17. The "normal" male mode of contacting, in and of itself, is indicative of the shaming and abuse considered customary in bringing up boys. Therefore, to use the male mode of contacting as a way of managing more severe or more extensive abuse is simply to extend the adaptation that one has made to "normal" abuse. I am indebted to Gordon Wheeler for this insight.

18. We see such fixation in many adults' sexual preferences and paraphilias (for example, sadomasochism, promiscuity, and various pedophilias).

19. Called *ego* or *personality* by Perls, Hefferline, and Goodman (1951).

20. Here, *aggression* means active, direct engagement, which may involve anger and other such "negative" feelings but may also be simply firmness or persistence.

21. In Gestalt therapy, the classical meaning of retroflection is the turning of a self-originated impulse or want against the self. Here, I also mean the reenactment on oneself of things originally done to one by the environment. In this phase of healing, the emphasis is on experiencing one's capacity to *act* and *express*, and so I am emphasizing the retroflective side of that capacity. I believe that this broadening of the term *retroflection* is in keeping with the spirit of Gestalt therapy in that the boundary between organism and environment is not as sharp as it seems; see discussions in the second half of Perls, Hefferline, and Goodman (1951).

22. To be conducted safely and in a controlled manner, experiments using this kind of physical expression require special training on the part of the therapist.

23. There are a number of dissertation possibilities here, having to do with the validity and reliability of the checklist items in terms of the Healing Tasks Model. Interested students are invited to contact me for permission.

24. Licensed clinicians may direct inquiries to me at 20600 Chagrin Boulevard, #750, Shaker Heights, Ohio 44122.

25. Note the term *events*. There is still no proof that any false memories of sexual abuse *specifically* exist in the adult population; all the research on creation of false memories comes from laboratory research concerning *nontraumatic* memories (Loftus, 1993).

26. My appreciation to Lynne Jacobs, Ph.D., for calling my attention to those psychoanalytic thinkers who stayed true to the phenomenology of their patients, despite the reigning Oedipal dogma.

27. The term *not remembering* is probably the most clearly

phenomenological one we can use, since it does not imply any mechanism or carry the burden of theory as do the terms *repression, dissociation,* and *forgetting.*

28. For the survivors with whom I have worked, full-blown flashbacks are not the common experience. Survivors more often report disconnected feelings, "triggers" found in otherwise benign situations or objects, partial images, unusual bodily sensations, fears, phobias, and other fragmentary experiences.

29. Some survivors have protected themselves from the full devastation of their helplessness by fantasizing that they controlled or influenced their abusers in some way.

30. The enactment of abuse in behavior and symptoms is a form of retroflection: in this case, doing to oneself what others in the environment have done to one. It involves elements of introjection, but in the sphere of motor activity.

31. The term *good gestalt* is derived from Gestalt perceptual psychology and refers to something that has good form, stands out clearly and brightly from its background, and is meaningfully organized in relation to its background.

32. Elsewhere (Kepner, 1987), I have outlined a body-oriented therapy from the Gestalt perspective. Readers who wish to expand their understanding of this approach are encouraged to consult that volume.

33. In Reichian analysis of the body and character pathology, this has been called schizoid, but I believe it is more accurately viewed as dissociative than as psychotic. The nomenclature of Reich's era did not discriminate clearly between dissociative and psychotic processes in the way that we, having begun to come to grips with the realities of trauma, are now doing. By implication, the Reichian notion of the "schizoid" character should be reexamined in light of what we now know about trauma and dissociation. Reich's observation

that the "schizoid" (read "dissociative") character is disconnected from bodily life is certainly correct, but his understanding of the reasons why this is so was limited by the psychoanalytic dogma of his times.

34. This experiment may not work for a survivor whose experience of abuse has entailed being tied or held by the ankles. Attention to the feet could stir up intolerable associations to the abuse.

References

American Psychological Association (1994, December). Interim report issued on memories of abuse. *APA Monitor*, pp. 8–9.

Bass, E., and Davis, L. (1988). *The courage to heal*. New York: HarperCollins.

Bloom, P. B. (1994). Clinical guidelines in using hypnosis in uncovering memories of sexual abuse: A master class commentary. *International Journal of Clinical and Experimental Hypnosis, 42*(3), 173–178.

Bloom, S. (1995). When good people do bad things: Meditations on the "backlash." *Journal of Psychohistory, 22*(3), 273–304.

Bowlby, J. (1969). *Attachment and loss*. New York: Basic Books.

Braun, B. G. (ed.). (1986). *The treatment of multiple personality disorder*. Washington D.C.: American Psychiatric Press.

Briere, J. (1989). *Therapy for adults molested as children: Beyond survival*. New York: Springer.

Briere, J. (1992). *Child abuse trauma: Theory and treatment of the lasting effects*. New York: Sage.

British Psychological Society. (1995). Recovered memories. London, England: author.

Burgess, A., and Hartman, C. (1987). Psychological damage associated with extreme eroticism in young children. *Psychiatric Annals, 17(4)*, 257–260.

Butler, S. (1985). *Conspiracy of silence*. San Francisco: Volcano Press.

Courtois, C. (1988). *Healing the incest wound*. New York: W.W. Norton.

Cronin, J. (1994, April). False memory. *Z Magazine*, pp. 31–37.

Dolan, Y. (1991). *Resolving sexual abuse*. New York: W.W. Norton.

Dupont, J. (ed.). (1988). *The clinical diary of sandor ferenczi*. Cambridge, Mass.: Harvard University Press.

Erikson, E. (1968). *Identity, youth, and crisis*. New York: W.W. Norton.

Feldman, G. C. (1995). Satanic ritual abuse: A chapter in the history of human cruelty. *Journal of Psychohistory, 22*(3), 340–357.

Finklehor, D. (1984). *Child sexual abuse*. New York: Free Press.

Forward, S., and Buck, C. (1978). *Betrayal of innocence*. New York: Penguin Books.

Freyd, J. J. (1993, August). *Theoretical and personal perspectives on the delayed* memory syndrome. Paper presented at the continuing education conference on controversies around recovered memories of incest and ritualistic abuse, Center for Mental Health, Foote Hospital, Ann Arbor, Mich.

Gendlin, E. (1978). *Focusing*. New York: Everest House.

Gil, E. (1988). *Treatment of adult survivors of childhood abuse*. Walnut Creek, Calif.: Lauch Press.

Herman, D. (1992). *Recovery and trauma*. New York: Basic Books.

Herman, D. (1993, March–April). The abuses of memory. *Mother Jones*, March/April, 3–4.

Herman, D. (1994). Presuming to know the truth. *Moving Forward, 3*(1), pp. 12–13.

Herman, D., and Schatzow, E. (1987). Recovery and verification of memories of childhood sexual trauma. *Psychoanalytic Psychology, 4*(1), 1–14.

Janet, P. (1890). *The major symptoms of hysteria*. New York: Macmillan.

Kaufman, G. (1992). *Shame: The power of caring*. Rochester, Vt.: Schenkman Books.

Kepner, J. I. (1987). *Body process*. San Francisco: Jossey-Bass.

Kluft, R. P. (1990, February). "Sitting duck" incest victims vulnerable to repeat abuse. *Psychiatric Times*, pp. 15–17.

Kolb, L. C. (1987). A neuropsychological hypothesis explaining posttraumatic stress disorder. *American Journal of Psychiatry, 144*(8), 989–995.

Kramer, P. D. (1993). *Listening to prozac*. New York: Viking.

Kuhn, T. E. (1970). *The structure of scientific revolutions*. Chicago: University of Chicago Press.

Kuyen, W., and Brewin, C. (1994). Intrusive memories of childhood abuse during depressive episodes. *Behavior Research and Therapy, 32*(5), 525–528.

Lawrence, L. R. (1994). Backlash: A look at the abuse-related amnesia and delayed memory controversy. *Moving Forward, 2*(4), 1–13.

Lew, M. (1988). *Victims no longer*. New York: HarperCollins.

Lewin, K. (1951). *Field theory in social science*. New York: HarperCollins.

Loftus, E. (1993). The reality of repressed memories. *American Psychologist, 48*, 518–537.

Loftus, E., Plonsky, S., and Fullilove, M. (1994). Memories of childhood sexual abuse: Remembering and repressing. *Psychology of Women Quarterly, 18*(1), 67–84.

McConville, M. (1995). Adolescence: Psychotherapy and the emergent self. San Francisco: Jossey-Bass.

Maltz, W. (1992). *The sexual healing journey: A guide for survivors of sexual abuse*. New York: HarperCollins.

Miller, A. (1983a). *The drama of the gifted child*. New York: Farrar, Straus & Giroux.

Miller, A. (1983b). *For your own good*. New York: Farrar, Straus & Giroux.

Miller, A. (1984). *Thou shalt not be aware*. New York: Farrar, Straus & Giroux.

Perls, F. S., Hefferline, R., and Goodman, P. (1951). *Gestalt therapy*. New York: Julian Press.

Piaget, J. (1962). *Play, dreams, and imitation in childhood*. New York: W.W. Norton.

Polster, E., and Polster, M. (1973). *Gestalt therapy integrated*. New York: Vintage Books.

Putnam, F. (1989). *Multiple personality disorder*. New York: Guilford Press.

Robbins, A. (1995). False memories or hidden agendas? *Journal of Psychohistory*, 22(3), 305–311.

Rockwell, R. (1995). Insidious deception. *Journal of Psychohistory*, 22(3), 312–329.

Rush, F. (1980). *The best-kept secret*. New York: McGraw-Hill.

Russell, D. (1986). *The secret trauma*. New York: Basic Books.

Sgroi, S. (1982). *Handbook of clinical intervention in child sexual abuse*. Lexington, Mass.: Lexington Books.

Stern, D. N. (1985). *The interpersonal world of the infant: A view from psychoanalysis and developmental psychology*. New York: Basic Books.

Sugar, M. (1992). Toddlers' traumatic memories. *Infant Mental Health Journal*, 13(3), 245–251.

Summit, R. (1983). The child sexual abuse accommodation syndrome. *Child Abuse and Neglect*, 7, 177-193.

Tomkins, S. S. (1962). *Affect, imagery, and consciousness: Vol. 1. The positive affects*. New York: Springer.

Tomkins, S. S. (1987). Shame. In D. Nathanson (Ed.), *The many faces of shame* (pp. 133–161). New York: Guilford Press.

van der Kolk, B. (1987). *Psychological trauma*. Washington DC: American Psychiatric Press.

van der Kolk, B., and Fisler, R. (1994). Child abuse and neglect and the loss of self-regulation. *Bulletin of the Menninger Clinic*, 58(2), 145–148.

van der Kolk, B., and van der Hart, O. (1991). The intrusive past: The flexibility of memory and the engraving of trauma. *American Image*, 48(4), 425–454.

Ventura M. (1995). Queen of cups. *New Age Journal*, March/April, 55–58.

Wheeler, G. (1991). *Gestalt reconsidered*. New York: Gardner Press.

Whitfield, C. (1994). *Memory and abuse*. Deerfield Beach, Fla.: Health Communications.

Williams, L. M. (1994). Recall of childhood trauma: A prospective study of women's memories of child sexual abuse. *Journal of Consulting and Clinical Psychology*, 62 (6), 1167–1176.

Wilson, J. P. (1989). *Trauma, transformation, and healing*. New York: Brunner/Mazel.

Winnicott, D. W. (1960). The theory of the parent-infant relationship. *International Journal of Psychoanalysis*, 41, 585-595.

Winnicott, D. W. (1988). *Human nature*. New York: Schocken Books.

Wyatt, G. E., and Powell, G. J. (Eds.) (1988). *The lasting effects of child sexual abuse*. Newbury Park, Calif.: Sage.

Yapko, M. D. (1994). *Suggestions of abuse: True and false memories of childhood sexual trauma*. New York: Simon & Schuster.

Zinker, J. (1977). *Creative process in gestalt therapy*. New York: Brunner/Mazel.

Assessment Instrument

Part A: Identifying the Phase of Healing

Client _____

✔ Check any items that apply for this client.

Category	Beginning of Support Phase	Beginning of Self-Functions Phase	Beginning of Undoing, Redoing, and Mourning Phase	Beginning of Reconsolidation Phase
General functioning	❑ Serious impairment of relationships: family, work, school	❑ Effort focused on developing more stable functioning in one or two areas of impairment	❑ Good general functioning in most areas ❑ Ability to address directly those areas where difficulties exist	❑ Good functioning in relationships: family, work, school
Posttraumatic Stress Disorder (PTSD) symptomatology (numbing, restricted affect, flooding, depression, anxiety, hypersensitivity to cues recalling abuse, avoidance of cues recalling abuse, intrusive recollections, flashbacks)	❑ Predominance of PTSD symptoms ❑ Little ability to cope with PTSD symptoms ❑ Feeling of helplessness predominates	❑ Frequent presence but not predominance of PTSD symptoms ❑ Continued periods of feeling flooded and overwhelmed by memories and waves of feeling accompanied by somatic sensations and anxiety ❑ Emphasis on learning to manage PTSD symptoms	❑ Occasional PTSD symptoms, but with significantly diminished intensity ❑ Application of coping strategies to management of PTSD symptoms when they occur	❑ Rarity or absence of PTSD symptoms

Systemic support	• Little or no interpersonal or community support • Tendency to shift between rigid self-support and dependence on others for support • Some awareness of need for more support, but fear of reaching out, with consequent immobilization	• Basic sense of support felt from therapist • Some support with abuse issues found from friends or significant others • Contact with basic social service systems, as appropriate	• Increased ability to manage differences and conflict in relationships • Willingness to renegotiate and/or terminate unhealthy relationships • Seeking out of a broader, more nurturing network of support • Working through of therapeutic transference	• Mutual support and interdependence in relationships • Little needed from therapist, but contact welcomed and appreciated
Management of affect, stress, and restimulation	• Poor stress tolerance • Unpredictable feelings of being overwhelmed that occur often • Often experiences disruption, disorganization, when under stress • Lack of coping skills • Frequent restimulation of trauma	• Poor stress tolerance but some coping skills • Tentative stability when dealing with difficult feelings and memories • Difficulty clearly discriminating between overreactions and appropriate reactions to stressors • Understanding that overreactions are restimulations	• General sense of mastery and ability to cope with stress reactions • Awareness of overreactions to stressors, ability to sort through overreactions or seek help • Ability to constructively use and assimilate strong reactions to memories	• Trauma rarely restimulated • Emotional response produced by remembering trauma, but not associated with disruption or disorganization of functioning • Ability to experience and tolerate broad range of feelings

Part A: Identifying the Phase of Healing (cont'd.)

Category	Beginning of Support Phase	Beginning of Self-Functions Phase	Beginning of Undoing, Redoing, and Mourning Phase	Beginning of Reconsolidation Phase
Self perceptions and self-care	❑ Feeling of shame, self-critical or self-diminishing thoughts predominant ❑ Comfort, soothing derived from addictive or compulsive behaviors in response to difficult feelings or thoughts	❑ Acceptance of the idea that the sense of "badness" and lack of worth is related to something that happened to them rather than their "nature" ❑ Acceptance of responsibility for dealing with addictive and compulsive patterns	❑ Recognition of shame and self-criticism as habitual processes rather than as "truths" about self ❑ Working through and referring back to abusive context (shame and self-critical and self-diminishing thoughts) ❑ Availability of healthy self-care, self-soothing, and self-comforting as "antidotes" to abusive context	❑ Ability to accept shame as an appropriate feeling in response to violations of personal values rather than as a definition of self ❑ Ability to respect, nurture, and celebrate self
Acknowledgment of abuse	❑ Shifts between denial and belief in possible history of abuse	❑ Acceptance of reality and possibility of abuse but hesitation in moving toward addressing it directly	❑ Acceptance of reality of abuse and willingness to move toward difficult issues associated with trauma	❑ Acceptance and working through most aspects of abuse ❑ Integration of abuse experience into wider view of self

Stance toward survivorship	☐ Denied, limited, highly tentative, or intellectualized acceptance of survivorship, with little or no evidence of its emotional impact	☐ Identification of self as possibly a survivor (or recognition that more information is necessary before survivorship can be affirmed) ☐ Acquisition of basic understanding of relationship between abuse and current experience and behavior ☐ Acknowledgment that past abuse influences current feelings	☐ Acceptance of not knowing everything about abuse, and recognition that it is not necessary to work through absolutely everything in order to have a good life ☐ Power of discrimination, as evidenced by recognition that not everything difficult in life was caused by the abuse	☐ Abuse seen as part of history that influences but does not define self ☐ Sense of opening to new possibilities beyond abuse-related issues
Reality testing (ability to distinguish between past and current experiences)	☐ Inability to distinguish reactions to current circumstances from reactions conditioned or influenced by past experiences ☐ Feeling that present and past are blurred together and poorly bounded	☐ Tendency to be defensive or denying about suggestions that perceptions of current situations may be distorted by abusive past experiences ☐ Frequent appearance of projecting past abusive context onto current interactions, with no awareness of doing so	☐ Ability to recognize when reactions to current circumstances reflect responses or perceptions related to past traumatic context ☐ Ability to begin recognizing, confronting, and understanding ways of having a negative impact on others	☐ Ability to own and take responsibility for negative impact on others without feeling overwhelmed by shame or self-blame ☐ Ability to recognize own human failings and flaws without feeling overwhelmed by shame or self-blame

Part A: Identifying the Phase of Healing (cont'd.)

Category	Beginning of Support Phase	Beginning of Self-Functions Phase	Beginning of Undoing, Redoing, and Mourning Phase	Beginning of Reconsolidation Phase
Orientation to past, present, and future	☐ Sensation of being gripped or flooded by the past ☐ Belief that there is "no future"	☐ Sensation of being less gripped by the past, but still with no strong anchoring in the present	☐ Interest in grappling with and finishing with the past ☐ Sense of "possible future" emerging ☐ Good anchoring in a sense of the present	☐ Realistic and optimistic orientation toward present and future ☐ Integration of past issues
Spiritual perspective	☐ Tendency of traumatic symptoms to overwhelm any preexisting spiritual or philosophical perspective	☐ Movement toward looking to the spiritual or the philosophical for support and understanding in facing the reality of trauma ☐ Beginning of ability to consider abuse in a larger context of spiritual or other encompassing meaning	☐ Heightened interest in spiritual perspective, with possible return to previous spiritual and philosophical involvements or exploration of new areas	☐ Integration of spiritual perspective into viewpoint and life ☐ Understanding of abuse within larger spiritual perspective
Percentage of items checked	(checked items) / 21 (total items) ×100 = ___ %	(checked items) / 22 (total items) ×100 = ___ %	(checked items) / 23 (total items) ×100 = ___ %	(checked items) / 19 (total items) ×100 = ___ %

Part B: Healing Tasks

✔ Check any items that are *true now* for this client.

I. Support Tasks
   A. Trust/Mistrust
   ❑ 1. Aware of having concerns about trust, boundaries (for example, ethical issues or issues of sexual boundaries) and/or your attitude toward working with issues related to abuse and survivors of abuse?
   ❑ 2. Able to express to you concerns related to trust?
   ❑ 3. Able to express to you concerns about boundary violations?
   ❑ 4. Able to express to you concerns, as they arise, about your attitude toward abuse and working with survivors of abuse?
   B. Safety and Containment Boundaries
   ❑ 1. Able to understand and be responsive to the boundaries and limits of the therapy environment and the therapeutic relationship?
   ❑ 2. Able to manage self in basic ways to ensure personal safety (that is, absence of suicidal ideation and doing of harm to self and others; presence of ability and willingness to channel emotions into safe forms of expression)?
   C. Validation of History of Abuse (the clinician using this checklist should be familiar with the stance taken in the Healing Tasks Model toward the validity of memories and the proper role of the therapist in validating memories; before beginning or assessing this aspect of the work, the clinician should also be aware of the potential for biasing the client's beliefs)
   ❑ 1. Able to accept support and validation from you regarding importance of his or her feelings, impressions, or memories?

❑ 2. Able to entertain the possibility of a history of abuse, and of his or her own survivorship?

❑ 3. Able to entertain this possibility with relatively little denial, disbelief, disconfirmation, or self-doubt (this ability expected only toward the end of the support phase)?

D. Systemic Social Support (a "healthy" relationship is characterized as having good boundaries and as being nonabusive)

❑ 1. Able to turn to others outside therapy for support?

	Available?	Healthy?	Unhealthy?
Intimate relationship	❑	❑	❑
Friends	❑	❑	❑
Co-workers	❑	❑	❑
Family of origin	❑	❑	❑
Family of choice	❑	❑	❑
Support groups	❑	❑	❑

❑ 2. Medical resources available, if needed?

❑ 3. Social service resources available, if needed?

❑ 4. Able to use these kinds of support in appropriate and timely ways?

E. Basic Self-Functions as Self-Support

1. Able to manage stimulation and intensity of feelings and responses with any of the following basic tools?

❑ Relaxation methods

❑ Grounding methods (for example, sensory awareness of body and environment)

❑ Breathing

❑ Self-comforting (for example, attending to and appropriately responding to own needs for food, rest, relaxation, exercise)

❑ Others (for example, psychotropic medication, internal "safe space," journal writing)

❑ 2. Able to use these basic tools with your coaching?

❏ 3. Able to use these basic tools without your coaching (on own initiative)?

❏ 4. Able to use contact with you for self-grounding in the present (through eye contact, verbal expression, and so on)?

F. Reconsolidation Task

❏ Sense of self redefined to include possibility of abuse in childhood?

II. Self-Functions Tasks

A. Boundary Functions

❏ 1. Able to manage *interpersonal* boundaries competently?

❏ Able to say yes or no as the need arises?

❏ Able to withdraw from potentially dangerous or problematic situations?

❏ Able to refuse, modify, or question your interventions in accordance with own feelings and needs?

❏ Able to have some flexibility in interpersonal boundaries instead of maintaining a fixed stance (consistently guarded and rigid, or uniformly compliant)?

❏ 2. Able to manage *bodily* boundaries competently (for example, by making and expressing choices about whether he or she wishes to be touched, and how)?

❏ 3. Able to manage *sexual* boundaries?

❏ Consents or refuses according to own wishes?

❏ Makes realistic assessment of a situation's safety and appropriateness?

B. Experiencing Functions

❏ 1. Able to make useful choices for managing the *grading* (intensity) of any experience (including therapy, work, school)?

❏ Usually does not overstimulate self with activity, entertainment (TV, movies), or reading that leads to feeling stirred up, anxious, out of control?

❑ Knows when a particular memory of topic is too much to deal with, given current support, and takes appropriate action to reduce intensity?

❑ Knows when a particular topic, experiment, or level of work in therapy is too difficult or over-stimulating and is able to express this?

❑ Tends not to take on too much work on the job and is able to express workload needs to super-visor or employer?

❑ 2. Able to make self-respectful choices for managing the *pacing* (frequency) of any experience (including therapy, work, school)?

❑ Knows when to take a break from focusing on issues related to abuse and when to focus instead on other things in therapy?

❑ Knows when it is time to move back toward dif-ficult subjects, so that these are not avoided?

❑ At work, makes appropriate use of breaks to relax?

❑ Makes appropriate use of sick days, vacation time, and so on, to meet health-related needs, spend time with family, or take time for self?

C. Self-Support Functions

❑ 1. Knows how to self-soothe (for example, by eating when hungry, resting when tired, refraining from self-criticism for perceived mistakes)?

❑ 2. Able to act toward self in loving, caring ways (for example, by praising self for a job well done, pre-paring a tasty meal for self, "being lazy")?

❑ 3. Seeks adequate medical care in a timely fashion?

D. Feeling Functions (an "integrated" feeling is experienced as appropriate to the situation, and as originating in the self)

❑ 1. Experiences a variety of feelings over a range of *tolerable* intensity?

	Integrated	Tolerated	Disruptive	Absent
Sadness	❑	❑	❑	❑
Anger	❑	❑	❑	❑
Vulnerability	❑	❑	❑	❑
Joy	❑	❑	❑	❑
Disgust	❑	❑	❑	❑
Pride	❑	❑	❑	❑
Happiness	❑	❑	❑	❑
Shame	❑	❑	❑	❑
Excitement	❑	❑	❑	❑
Love	❑	❑	❑	❑

❑ 2. Able to work actively with strong feelings as they emerge, so as to tolerate and assimilate them?

❑ 3. Able to tell when emotional reactions are stronger than the current stimulus warrants and are more related to events in the past?

❑ 4. Able to use this awareness to modulate strong feelings reactions?

E. Reality-Perception Functions

❑ 1. Able to have some sense of distorting or projecting onto others or external circumstances?

❑ 2. Generally aware when some response may be over-determined (that is, influenced by some background factor related to the history of abuse)?

❑ 3. Generally able to perceive situations and others in graded ways (that is, able to avoid extreme polarizing, categorizing, and labeling), so that people who are angry are not necessarily labeled "abusive" or "abusers," and so that people are not seen as either "trustworthy" or "untrustworthy" but are seen as possibly displaying both qualities at different times?

❑ 4. Able to sort out personal sensitivities from external circumstances (for example, by understanding that *feeling* attacked does not necessarily mean *being* attacked, and so on)?

F. Reconsolidation Tasks

❏ 1. Beginning to see the larger question of how history of abuse fits into life as a whole (that is, beginning to see how he or she has grown and developed with respect to the abuse, and how he or she may have developed personal strengths from the experience of having been abused)?

❏ 2. Beginning to use a spiritual or philosophical framework to encompass the abuse in some larger context of meaning (that is, beginning to understand how the experience of abuse and healing has guided his or her transcendent development)?

III. Undoing, Redoing, and Mourning

A. Reality Perception

❏ 1. Able to tolerate considering both sides of an issue?

❏ 2. Able to tolerate looking at own "shadow aspects" (own negative or self-alienated qualities), as encountered in projections, without becoming overwhelmed by shame or self-blame?

B. Undoing and Mourning

❏ 1. Able to manage and *usefully assimilate* higher-intensity undoing and redoing (experimental reenactments and reworkings of scenes of abuse, symbolic or actual confrontations with the abuser, use of new skills and capacities with memories and reenactments of the original abusive environment)?

❏ 2. Working to bring back from the past those parts of the self and those capacities that have been left there (child-self left behind, possibility of saying words that were left unsaid, possibility of taking actions that were not taken, possibility of now offering recognitions—for example, that abuser was weak and stupid, rather than powerful and cunning—to abused child-self)?

❏ 3. Able to mourn the losses caused by the abuse and

its effects in a way that brings some sense of closure (as opposed to a way that is overwhelming)?

❑ 4. In process of returning internalized or self-destructive attitudes and behavior to original abusive environment (self-criticism as introjected words of abuser, self-punishment as acting out what abuser did, dissociated behavior revealed as replication of abuse, self-cutting as abuser's threat, promiscuity as reenactment of gang rape, and so on)?

❑ 5. Allowing core memories (those that are most traumatic and most difficult to face) to emerge, and working them through?

❑ 6. Facing and reowning sexual life?

IV. Reconsolidation

❑ 1. Integrating abuse into context of larger meaning?

❑ 2. Affirming meaning of abuse to life purpose?

❑ 3. Redefining self as larger than survivorship?

❑ 4. Celebrating healing (for example, by taking pride in resolution of abuse-related issues, feeling excited about moving on in life, and so on)?

❑ 5. Attending to completion and closure of the healing process (for example, by moving toward assimilation and integration of work in therapy, setting new goals, and/or terminating therapy)?

❑ 6. Continuing to develop the bodily self (for example, by showing more interest and involvement in physical movement, exercise, martial arts, and so on)?

Index

A

Abuse survivors: aspects of healing tasks for, 1–13; assessing, 149–177; body process for, 235–276; conclusions on, 277–278; developmental issues for, 2; fragility of, 20; memories of, 179–221; as over- and underbounded, 74–75; reconsolidation for, 131–147; recontextualization for, 223–233; relationships for, 63–64; self-functions phase for, 59–105; stimulation and arousal for, 42–50; support phase for, 15–58; truth behind symptoms of, 20–42, 282; undoing phase for, 107–129

Affect. *See* Feeling

Affirmation: barrier to, 36–42, 283; and memories, 202

Aggression: concept of, 285; and fixed gestalt, 107–108

American Psychological Association, 151, 180–181, 190

Anger, in healing phases, 10

Anxiety: and reconsolidation, 55; and recontextualization, 228–229

Arousal, for abuse survivors, 42–50

Artwork, for memories, 217–218

Assessment: of abuse survivors, 149–177; background on, 149–151; checklist for, 153–175; of reconsolidation tasks, 174–175; of self-function tasks, 167–172; of support tasks, 155–160, 161–167; understanding results of, 175–177; of undoing tasks, 172–174

B

Bass, E., 76, 122

Beliefs. *See* Introjection

Bloom, P. B., 219

Bloom, S., 182

Bob, 209–210

Body: awareness of, for grounding, 45; boundaries for, 71–75; reclaiming upper, 264–267; reconnecting upper and lower, 267–268; symptoms of, for memories, 218

Body process: aspects of, 235–276; background on, 235–236; beginning, 256–259; continuum for, 244; holistic view of, 236–238; letting go in, 275–276; in reconsolidation phase, 255–256; and self, 238–241; and self-care, 251–252, 271; and self functions, 244, 252–254; and support, 244–252; techniques for, 242–243; and therapy, 241–244, 256–276, 286; and undoing phase, 244, 255, 272–275

Boundaries: and abusive trauma, 65–66; aspects of functioning for, 65–78; assessing, 161–162, 167; in body process, 71–75, 266–267; containment, in therapeutic environment, 28–29; continuum of statements on, 70; experiment with, 69–70, 71–75; by healing phase, 66–67; and memories, 212–213; negotiation of, 67–70; and perpetrator, 75–78

Bowlby, J., 2, 3

Breathing: and boundaries, 72; for grounding, 46, 283

M

McConville, M., 135, 280, 283

Maltz, W., 255

Marion, 210

Meanings, preset, and reality perceptions, 96–97

Medications, psychotropic, 13, 47–50

Memories: approaches to traumatic, 191–194; aspects of, 179–221; background on, 179–180; in body process, 265–266, 268–269; conclusions on, 181–183; core, and expressive work, 113–119; core, in undoing phase, 112–123; corroboration for, 182–183, 185, 219; cycle for, 198–203; delayed, 183–184, 196–198; and experiencing, 79; experiments for, 114–122, 208–211, 212–213, 285; false, 19, 179, 185, 280–281, 282, 285; and feelings, 85–86; and field, 32–34, 282–283; and forgetting, 31–32, 182–184; fragmentary, 198–201, 286; good enough, 207–208; in healing phases, 11–12, 205–221; as impressions, 34; inclusion of traumatic, 54; in intrusion phase, 19; and metaphor, 82; narrative, 183; and not remembering, 194–196, 204, 285–286; purpose of, 203–221; and reconsolidation, 103–104; as reconstruction, 240–241; and redoing, 119–122; and suggestibility, 187–191; techniques for recovering, 189, 215–219; and trauma, 180–191; validity and accuracy of, 184–187

Miller, A., 193, 224

Mourning: aspects of, 123–129; assessing, 172–174; fullness of, 108, 128–129; in reconsolidation, 142–143; and self functions, 126–128; and support, 124–126. *See also* Undoing, redoing, and mourning

Multiple Personality Disorder (MPD): and checklist, 154–155, 162; and self functions, 66, 75; and support issues, 47, 57–58

N

Nevis, S., 284

O

Organism/environment (O/E) field. *See* Field

P

Pacing: of experiences, 79–82; for feelings, 93

Panic, and breathing, 46–47, 283

Perception. *See* Reality perception

Perls, F. D., 59, 79, 194, 279, 283, 284, 285

Perls, L., 280

Perpetrator, confronting, 75–78, 115, 122–123

Personality, and self functions, 59, 283

Phases. *See* Healing phases

Philosophy. *See* Spiritual and philosophical integration

Physical expression, for core memories, 114, 118–119

Piaget, J., 2, 6

Plonsky, S., 183

Polarities, disowned, and reality perceptions, 97–98, 284

Polster, E., 96, 283

Polster, M., 96, 283

Posttraumatic stress disorder (PTSD): and bodily self, 238; and memories, 184–185, 189; and support phase, 43

Posture, and boundaries, 72, 73–74

Present, differentiated from past, 89–92, 95

Projection: and feelings, 91–92; as perspective taking, 135

Psychotropic medications: in healing phases, 13; in support phase, 47–50; therapeutic issues of, 48–49

Purpose, sense of, and reconsolidation 102–103

Putnam, F., 57

R

Reality perception: assessing, 170–171, 172; and bodily self, 245–247; and disowned polarities, 97–98, 284; of figure and ground, 94–95; and healing phases, 98–100; and present differentiated from past, 95; and preset meanings, 96–97; reorganizing, 53–55; self functions for, 93–100; and sense making, 98; and sensory contact, 96

Reconsolidation: aspects of, 131–147; assessing, 155–160, 166–167, 171–172, 174–175; background on, 131–132; body process in, 255–256; concept of, 7, 131; and forgiveness, 143–145; by healing phases, 136–147; issues in, 11–13; and memories, 183, 206–207; in self-functions phase, 100–105, 139–141; and sense of self, 183; summary of, 147; in support phase, 53–55, 137–139; and transcendence, 132–136; in undoing phase, 141–143

Recontextualization: aspects of, 223–233; background on, 223–224; experiments for, 230–232; figure and ground for, 224–225, 286; in healing phases, 232–233; statements for, 225–226, 229–230, 231–232; from symptoms and experiences, 226–230. *See also* Enactments

Redoing. *See* Undoing, redoing, and mourning

Reich, W., 248, 286–287

Relaxation processes, for grounding, 47

Remembering. *See* Memories

Repression, and reality perception, 94–95

Resistance, and pacing, 81–82

Retroflection: in abusive context, 20; and bodily self, 239; concept of, 5; and mourning, 127; and self functions, 69, 73, 84; and shame, 38, 40–41; in undoing phase, 109–112

Robbins, A., 182

Rockwell, R., 182

S

Safe space, for grounding, 47

Safety, in therapeutic environment, 28

Schatzow, E., 184

Schizoid character, and dissociation, 286–287

Secrecy: in abusive context, 18; and truth discovery, 30, 282

Self: assimilating trauma to, 268–272; concept of, 6, 59, 279; as embodied, 237; and inclusion of traumatic memory, 54; polarized, 97; rebuilding, 253–254; reclaiming, 214, 252–253; reorganizing sense of, 53–55; therapist's use of, 12–13

Self-care, and body process, 251–252, 271

Self-contact, in body process, 247

Self-disclosure, in context, 281–282

Self-enactments. *See* Enactments; Recontextualization

Self-esteem: and boundaries, 69–70; and retroflection, 110

Self functions: aspects of developing, 59–105; assessing, 155–160, 165–166, 167–172; background on, 59–65; and body process, 244, 252–254; and boundary, 65–78; celebration of accomplishments in, 104–105; concept of, 4–5, 59–60, 283–284; and development, 60–64; early phase of, 99; for experiencing, 78–82; for feeling, 84–93; grounding skills for, 43–47; issues in, 11–13; later phase of, 100; learning, 60; and memories, 196–197, 205–206, 211–219; and mourning, 126–128; for reality perception, 93–100; reconsolidation in, 100–105, 139–141; and recontextualization, 232–233; for self support, 83–84; and shame, 38–39; of shifting perspectives, 135; summary of, 145–146; for support phase, 42–50; truncated, 62–63; and trust, 25, 281

Self-management, and shame, 38, 39

Self-regulation, and bodily self, 240

Self-support: assessing, 169; functioning for, 83–84

Sense making, and reality perception, 98

Sensory contact: for grounding, 44; and reality perception, 96

Sexuality, reclaiming, 255

Shame: aspects of, 37–38; awareness of, 42; as barrier to affirmation, 36–42, 283; and bodily self, 241; concept of, 36; and medication, 49; as psychic death, 40, 283; and retroflection, 110

Shock, and memories, 198–201, 286

Spiritual and philosophical integration: in field, 136; and mourning, 129; for self functions, 101–103; in support phase, 138–139

Splitting, and meaning of abuse, 32

Stern, D. N., 3, 40

Stimulation: for abuse survivors, 42–50; and experiencing functions, 78–82; modulation of, 46–47, 283

Stress, and memories, 197–198